GULLIVERIANA VI

Critiques of *Gulliver's Travels* and Allusions Thereto

BOOK TWO

FACSIMILE REPRODUCTIONS
WITH AN INTRODUCTION
BY JEANNE K. WELCHER
AND
GEORGE E. BUSH, JR.

SCHOLARS' FACSIMILES & REPRINTS
DELMAR, NEW YORK, 1976

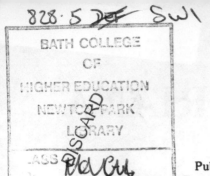
Published by
Scholars' Facsimiles & Reprints, Inc.
Delmar, New York 12054

Library of Congress Cataloging in Publication Data

Main entry under title:

Gulliveriana.

"Facsimile reproductions."
Vols. 4-6 published in New York.
CONTENTS: 1. McDermot, M. A trip to the moon (1728).
Gentleman, F. A trip to the moon (1764-5)—
2. Desfontaines, P. F. G.
The travels of Mr. John Gulliver, son to Capt. Lemuel Gulliver (1731).
Gulliver, L. Modern Gulliver's travels: Lilliput (1796). [etc.]
1. English fiction—18th century.
2. Voyages, Imaginary. 3. Satire, English.
4. Swift, Jonathan, 1667-1745. Gulliver's travels.
I. Welcher, Jeanne K., ed.
II. Bush, George E., 1938-   ed.
III. Swift, Jonathan, 1667-1745. Gulliver's travels.
PR1134.G8   823'.5'08   70-18975
SBN 0-8201-1168-6 (v. 6)

GULLIVERIANA VI

PART II.
WORKS ATTRIBUTED
TO LEMUEL GULLIVER

The Anatomist Dissected:

OR THE

Man-Midwife finely brought to Bed.

BEING AN

EXAMINATION

OF THE

CONDUCT

OF

Mr. St. ANDRE.

Touching the late pretended Rab-
bit-bearer; as it appears from
his own Narrative.

By *LEMUEL GULLIVER*,
Surgeon and Anatomist to the Kings of
Lilliput and *Blefuscu*, and Fellow of
the Academy of Sciences in *Balnibarbi*.

---

*Asses and Owls, unseen, themselves betray,
When these attempt to hoot, or those to bray.*
Garth.

WESTMINSTER:
Printed by and for A. CAMPBELI, and
sold by the Booksellers of *London* and
Westminster. 1727.   (Price 6 *d.*)

The Anatomist Diſſected :

OR THE

Man-Midwife finely brought to Bed.

BEING AN

EXAMINATION

OF THE

CONDUCT

OF

Mr. *St. ANDRE,* &c.

FTER that long and particular Detail of my ſelf, and of my various Adventures in ſo many different and remote parts of the Globe, as I have lately entertain'd

B   the

the Public with, I little thought
any private Occurrence, in fo fmall
a Spot as the Ifland of *Great Britain*,
could have rous'd my Attention, and
broke in upon that Repofe, in which
I hop'd to have fpent the Remains of
a declining Life. But fmall and inconfiderable as it is, I confider it is
my own Country; the Thought of
which, together with that inextin-
guifhable Thirft after Truth and
Knowledge, in regard to myfelf, and
an ardent Inclination of communi-
cating it to others, have prevail'd
upon me once more to be expos'd in
Print, in order to exprefs my Abhorrence of a late diabolical Impofture; propagated, not fo much by
the Knavery of fome, as by the Ignorance and Stupidity of others. I
need not fay I mean the Rabbit Affair;

fair; with which, for fome Weeks
paft, the Minds of the People of this
Ifland have been fo ferioufly and fo
furprizingly employ'd; fo as fcarce
to leave them any leifure for things
of a more fublime Nature, and of
vaftly greater Confequence and Importance.

And tho' I verily believe this to
be the real and only Caufe, why the
Perufal of my Travels has been fo
neglected of late, which, by the Decay of the Sale, has fenfibly affected
a worthy and honeft Bookfeller; yet
I declare to the World, that my Motives for entering the Lifts againft
Mr. *St. André* (a Perfon to me whol-
ly unknown, and unheard of till I
faw his Name in the News-Papers,
upon that unfortunate Accident,

which

which befel him, when he fancied
he was poyson'd) are, that little Skill
which, by my Education and Experience, I have attain'd in Surgery
and Anatomy, and that great Ignorance in both, which he has betray'd
upon this Occafion.

For tho' that Gentleman's Can-
dor is very great in fhewing fuch
a remarkable Alertnefs, at confefling
that he has been impos'd upon in
this Paltry Bufinefs; and tho' perhaps, by that he may flatter himfelf,
that he fhall efcape all further Cen-
fure, yet I fhall be at the Pains of
Convincing the World that he is
miftaken, even in this alfo; and that,
had he not been moft profoundly deficient in that difcerning Penetration, with which all true Surgeons
make

make Enquiries of this Sort, he
might have difcover'd this Impofture at the very firft Sight, and not
have drawn in fo many Perfons of
diftinguifh'd Senfe and Figure, to
be gull'd and deluded by fo coarfe
and palpable a Fraud.

For, to begin with his Narative; a
true Surgeon, one, I mean, orderly
and properly educated in that worthy
Profeffion, would never have fuffer'd
his Curiofity to be at all alarm'd by
feeing a Letter from *Guilford*, which
mention'd *a Woman's being deliver'd
of five Rabbits*: Suppofe one were
to fee a Letter from *Batterfea*, im-
porting that a Woman there had
been deliver'd of five Cucumbers, or
indeed a hundred Letters, would
that lead a Man of Senfe to believe
any

any Thing, but, either that the People who wrote thofe Letters had been grofsly impos'd upon themfelves, or intended to impofe upon him. Either of thefe two Things may, and do happen every Day; but it was never known, that ever any Creature brought forth any one Creature of a Species in all Refpects different from it felf, much lefs five or feventeen fuch Creatures; for which therefore, a Man of common Senfe, much more a penetrating and quickfighted Anatomift, fhould look upon all fuch Letters with the utmoft Contempt.

Yet it was the Sight of two or three fuch Letters (and thofe flagrant with moft confpicuous Tokens of Impofture) which induc'd

Mr.

Mr. *St. André*, at this Time of the Year, to take two Journeys to *Guildford*, in Order to enquire into the Truth of what, in Nature, it was impoffible fhould be true. However, to *Guildford* he came for the firft Time; where I fhall attend him a while, and watch his Motions, perhaps to a better Purpofe than he did thofe of the Rabbit-bearing Woman: For tho', with all his Skill he was not able to detect her Fraud, I hope with very little of mine to difplay his Ignorance.

In the firft Place, how ftupid muft he have been, not to fufpect a Trick, when *Howard*, upon being fent for, came and acquainted him, *that the Woman was actually in Labour of the fifteenth Rabbit.* This

puts

puts me in Mind of what, above fix
and Forty Years ago, I learn'd at School;
where the Sagacity of old *Simo* in
the *Andria* of *Terence* appears, to
the utter Shame of our modern
St. Andrians: The old Gentleman
had Reafon to fufpect Fraud from
the known Character of a crafty
Knave he had to deal with; and
whofe Bufinefs it was to make him
believe, that a certain Lady was juft
then in Labour : Accordingly as
they approach her Houfe, fhe con-
trives to be in one of her Labour
Pains, and cries out fo loud that the
old Man muft needs hear it; upon
which, I remember, be fays, with
much Humour and Judgment, *Hui
tam cito? ridiculum. Poftquam ante ofti-
um me audivit ftare, approperat. Non.
fat commode divifa funt temporibus
tibi*

tibi, Dave, &c. For thus, had he been credulous enough to go to *Guildford* to inquire into this Cheat, he would have said, in plain *English*, upon the like Occasion, *What a pox, is she so quick? this is the damn'dest Joke that ever was! the Moment she hears I am arrived, she falls into one of her Labour Pains: ah, Howard! this was not well tim'd of you by any means.*

But, to return from this Digression, if the Woman was *actually in Labour of the fifteenth Rabbit,* why should Mr. *Howard* leave her, and stay with Mr. *St. André* till they call'd him again, when she was said to be in one of her Labour Pains? Here a wife Man would have smelt a Rat instead of a Rab-

bit:

bit : And much more, when this Woman in Labour Pains, and who had been in Labour fome time then, nay fourteen times before, was *found dreſs'd in her Stays, and ſitting on the Bed-ſide*; and that not for want Help to put her to Bed ; for there were *ſeveral Women near her*. A Man muſt have a ſpritely Genius for ſwallowing Impoſture that was not ſtagger'd at ſuch an Appearance. This ſure it was that prompted Mr. *St. André* to wave all ſuch Reflections, and proceed *immediately to examine her* ; when, tho' by his own Confeſſion, he *did not find the Parts prepar'd for her Labour*, (which was another plain Indication of the Roguery) yet he was weak enough to *wait for the coming on of freſh Pains*, and *in three or four Minutes after to* *think*

think he deliver'd her of the intire Trunk, strip'd of its Skin, of a Rabbit about four Months Growth (he meant to have said, of an Animal of the Size and Figure of a Rabbit of four Months growth) in which the Heart and Lungs were contain'd, with the Diaphragm intire. Well, what does my Gentleman then? He instantly cut of a piece of them, and tried them in Water; in which they swam, and when they were press'd to the Bottom, rose again, Now, it being notoriously the Property of the Lungs of a Fœtus to sink, and of a Creature which has been some time brought forth alive to swim, in Water; what but an absolute Prepossession in favour of this filthy Miracle, or a consummate Ignorance in these Matters could have hinder'd any so-

ber

ber Inquirer from being determin'd
in relation to this Cheat, by the
foregoing Trial. Yet Mr. *St. André*
never boggles at this, nor at the
Impoffibility of the Trunk of fuch
a Creature's (fuppos'd but juft before to be alive) being ftript of its
Skin, by the contractive Faculty of
the Womb; nor at the Woman's
being *chearful and eafy, and walking
by her felf from the Bed-fide to the
Fire the Moment fhe was deliver'd:*
But goes on *conjecturing* in a yet more
abfurd manner, that thefe Creatures,
(as big as Rabbits of four Months
Growth, which muft be within a
Trifle as big as full-grown ones,)
were bred in the *Fallopian Tubes*;
and came into the *Uterus* one after
another, where they lay and kick'd;
till they were prefs'd to Death, and
flead,

flead, and all their Bones broken, in
fuch Manner, that they were *fenfibly heard to fnap,* by the violent
convulfive Motions of it.

I take the Liberty to inform my
Readers, upon this Occafion, that
the *Fallopian Tubes* are a Paffage of
Communication, of fcarce three In-
ches long, between the *Ovaria* and
the *Uterus*; thro' which the *Embryo,*
after Conception, is conveyed from
the one to the other. And tho', at
that End next the *Uterus* they o-
pen, fomewhat like the Mouth of
a Trumpet, yet, when ftretch'd to
the utmoft, the general Canal of
them fcarce exceeds the Thicknefs
of ones Finger: And therefore the
Impoffibility of any one fuch Creature being contain'd there, much
lefs

lefs of eighteen, as this Gentleman
fuppos'd, muft appear to every one
of a common Underftanding. He
tells us, no Blood nor Water iffued
from the *Vagina* after this Delivery,
and that her Pulfe was regular.
Monftrous! that none of thefe Indications fhould open Mr. *St. André's*
Eyes. If he thought at all, what
could he be thinking of? It is notorious, that in Births of dead Children, Women fuffer much more
Pain than in thofe of Living ones;
fo as to be, during the Operation, in
high Fevers, with irregular Pulfes,
and left in great Weaknefs afterwards. Yet this Woman is deliver'd of fifteen dead Rabbits, fuch as
of four Months Growth, without any
Alteration in her Pulfe, without the
leaft Inflammation or Laceration in
her

her *Vagina*, walking from the Bed-Side, fitting down in a Chair by the Fire, as well as if nothing had happen'd; and skilful Mr. *St. André* fwallowing this foul Impofture, without the leaft Squeamifhnefs or Reluctance.

In the *Rectum* of this Animal, which remain'd affix'd to the Body, Mr. *St. André* finds *five or fix Pellets, much of the fame Colour and Confiftence as the common Dung of a Rabbit.* Strange! that this fhould not alarm him! but this he fwallows likewife; as he does *the Skin roll'd and fqueez'd up like a Ball*, which he delivers her of fome Time after: And not long after that, of *the Head, with the Furr on, Part of one of the Ears, being torn off.* Upon

all

all which Occasions, I mean those of the Womb's having a Faculty of skinning a Rabbit all but the Head, of rolling this Skin up like a Ball, and tearing off a Piece of an Ear; this Gentleman speaks as familiarly as if they were common Cases, which wanted not in the least to be accounted for, or wonder'd at.

In the Intervals between these notable Deliveries, Mr. *St. André* diverted himself and his Company, *by examining the several Rabbits, which were kept separate, in distinct Pots, with Spirits of Wine, in the Order that they were brought away.* Here likewise, I will do my self the Honour to attend him. And now, methinks, I see him expatiating, in a very genteel adroit Manner, upon
the

the general Refemblance, but particular and fignificant Difference between them and natural Rabbits.
" *The firft, fays he, does not appear to*
" *be a perfect Rabbit, in all its Parts.*
(Here one would fuppofe, the Difference lay in fome one or two at
moft minute, not eafily obfervable
Circumftances, in which this Creature varied from a Rabbit: But, on
the Contrary, it feems 'twas a perfect Cat in all its Parts, one or two
only excepted.) " *Three of the Feet*
" *being like the Paws of a Cat ; the*
" *Stomach and Inteftines like thofe in*
" *the fame Animal ; as alfo the Shape*
" *and Figure of the* Thoracx. Ob-
" ferve, *the Lungs and Heart, how*
" *entirely they are out of their natu-*
" *ral Situation ; and fqueez'd out be-*
" *tween the upper Ribs, and* Verte-
D   bræ

" bræ *of the* Neck *(*doubtleſs by the
" convulſive Motion of the *Uterus)*
" *to which* Parts, obſerve how
" *ſtrongly they grow and adhere. The*
" *Lungs of this Creature, had they*
" *been plac'd in their natural Cavi-*
" *ty, would not have fill'd above a ſixth*
" Part *of it. The Bones of this Crea-*
" *ture are likewiſe all ſo different in*
" *Subſtance and Structure from thoſe*
" *of common Rabbits,* that o' my Con-
" ſcience, *the Head and one Paw*
" *only excepted,* I think it has not the
" leaſt Reſemblance of them. *All*
" *the other thirteen Animals* I pro-
" nounce *to be in every particular, like*
" *well-form'd, common, natural Rab-*
" *bits, from the ſize of two Months*
" Growth *to four. Theſe have been*
" *all broken to pieces much in the*
" *ſame manner ; but when theſe ſeve-*
ral

" ral parts are put together in their pro-
" per order, they manifeftly make up
" and appear to belong to the abovemen-
" tion'd Animals. I confefs the Vif-
" cera are wanting in four or five of
" them; but that is not very materi-
" al; that Defect is amply fupply'd
" by this one remarkable Circumftance,
" which is, that moft of thefe Animals
" (for Rabbits I will not call them)
" as far as I can judge, are Females.
" The Flefh of thefe Creatures, parti-
" cularly of that which I extracted, has
" the Smell of Rabbits juft kill'd; and
" the Subftance of their Bones are, in
" all refpects, like the Bones of Fœtus
" Rabbits. (How particular, how
" dilucid and exact is this part of
" his Lecture!) From all thefe Con-
" fiderations (and many more too te-
" dious and impertinent to be reci-

ted

" ted) with greater Affurance than
" Knowledge, *I am fully convinc'd,*
" *that, at the fame time that the ex-*
" *ternal Appearance of thefe Animals*
" *is exactly like fuch Creatures as muft*
" *inevitably undergo the Changes that*
" *happen to adult Animals, by Food*
" *and Air, they carry within them the*
" *ftrongeft Marks of* Fœtus's, *even in*
" *fuch Parts as cannot exift in an A-*
" *dult, and without which a* Fœtus
" *cannot poffibly be fuppos'd to live,*
" *This, I think, proves in the ftrongeft*
" *Terms poffible, that thefe Animals*
" *are of a particalar kind, and not bred*
" *in a natural way; nor will there be*
" *any Doubt remaining (even with the*
" *leaft knowing in thefe Matters)*
" when thefe things come to be
" clear'd up by *the Anatomy of thefe*
" *præternatual Rabbits* (a præterna-
                                    tural

" tural Anatomiſt Thou art without
" Diſpute) *which I ſhall publiſh with*
" *all convenient Speed, with their Fi-*
" *gures taken from the Life, and com-*
" *par'd with the Parts of Rabbits of*
" *the ſame Growth* (he would have
" ſaid *the ſame ſize*) *that the Diffe-*
" *rences before-mention'd may be fully*
" *underſtood.*

This therefore the publick has
ſtill juſt Reaſon to infiſt upon from
Mr. *St. André*; for, however he may
pretend to be impos'd upon by o-
thers in the Delivery of theſe Sup-
poſitious Rabbits, the learned anatomical Obſervations recited above,
are purely the Reſult of his own
Skill and Judgment; and cannot
with any Colour of Reaſon be
plac'd to the Account of Fraud and
Impoſture

impofture in others. Efpecially *thofe Facts* which he has the Affurance to fay *were verified before his Majefty on* Saturday, Nov. *the* 26*th, by the anatomical Demonftration of the firft, the third, fifth and ninth of thefe Animals.*

However, not content with havingly fufficiently plac'd his Reputation at ftake in this audacious manner (for fuch I muft call it) on the wretched Obfervations abovemention'd, *out he fets for* Guildford *again, being refolv'd to bring the Woman to Town if there was any Profpect of more Rabbits.* What could this Creature, this Animal have in his Head to hinder him from concluding that a Woman in fuch a Condition (were it poffible any Woman could be in fuch a Condition) fhould

ſhould not be mov'd out of her Bed ;
much leſs out of her Houſe, and
much leſs from *Guildford* to *London.* Yet ſince he is reſolv'd upon
another Expedition, I am reſolv'd
once more to attend him thither,
and obſerve his Motions.

And here he is again ſo keen upon this vile falſe Scent, that tho' he
finds Mr. *Howard* ſtanding at his
Door, who tells him that he hop'd
all was over, becauſe that he did
not perceive in the *Uterus* any Motion as uſual, yet he viſited her ſeveral Times that Day, proceeded in
every Reſpect, with the ſame Sagacity as before ; and towards eight
a Clock that Evening, deliver'd her
of a Piece of one of the Membranes
of a *Placenta* (admirable !) roll'd
up

up like Parchment. This shews how well he is acquainted with the Texture of those Membranes. And his Deficiency in that Point was further confirm'd by a second Delivery of (what he took to be) *another Piece of Membrane, in Structure Shape and Size, exactly like the former.*

Thus I have touch'd upon, and I hope abundantly expos'd the profound Observations contain'd in Mr. *St. Andrè's* short *Narative.* Whenever he appears in Print again, upon this Occasion, as I find he threatens to do, I shall again be ready to guard the Public against being deluded by his pretended Discoveries. And, tho' it is not my Nature to insult any Man upon Account of his Misfortunes, whether brought up-

on

on him by his own Folly, or the
Malice of others; yet give me
Leave to fay, it is, of the two, a
much more eligible Evil, that the
Prefumption of one ignorant Empi-
ric, fhould undergo a public Chafti-
fement, than the Underftandings of
fo many of his Majefty's Loyal Subjects, be corrupted by fuch fham De-
monftrations.

But, after all, as I am a no lefs
ftrict Lover of Juftice, than an indefatigable Searcher after Truth;
now my Refentment of Mr. *St André's* ill Conduct in this Affair, is
fomewhat cool'd by the Liberty I
have taken in cenfuring and ex-
pofing it, I fhall offer fomething, by
Way of Abatement of that fevere
Conftruction, the World will be apt

E   to

to pass upon his Judgment in this Affair.

In the *first* Place, I have the Charity to believe, he has been egregiously impos'd upon, in Relation to the Character he has publish'd of Mr. *Howard*, whom he stiles, *a Man of known Probity*; whereas that Name is as notorious at *Guildford*, and the Parts adjacent, for denoting a Whisker, as ever mine was at *Redriff*, for establishing a Truth. *Secondly*, it must be consider'd that the Pleasure of being talk'd of, and heard to talk, in all Companies public and private, as the very second Discoverer (Mr. *Howard* being indisputably the first) of this extraordinary and preternatural Production, must needs swell the Mind of

a

a raw Practitioner with Vanity, and make him run blindfold into a Series of Abfurdities; no one of which, at another Time, would have found any Admittance within the Bar of his Judgment. And *Thirdly*, The Nature of Climates, together with the feveral Makes, Capacities and Tempers of the Inhabitants of different Countries, are the Reafon why Things may appear puzzling and perplexing in one Place, which in another would be accounted for, with the greateft Eafe and Certainty imaginable; and why that, which is here a Caufe of the higheft Ridicule, in a contrary Part of the Globe, would be the Occafion of raifing a Man's Character to the moft exalted Pitch of Dignity and Reputation.

For

For Example, had a Native of the Kingdom of *Lilliput,* happen'd to be in this our Island, when the Story of the Rabbits was first vented at Court; and had such a one been dispatch'd to *Guildford,* in Order to enquire into the Truth of that Matter; upon the first View of those Pellets, against which Mr. *St. André* had no Objection, he with his fine Microscopic Eyes, would have instantly discover'd every particular Herb the Creature had fed on that Meal. And what Mr. *St. André* calls *a dirty-colour'd* Mucus, *such as is constantly found in the Bowels of all* Fœtus *Animals, and such as in those that void their Excrements in Pellets, is commonly hard and dry,* our *Lilliputian*

putian would have diftinguifh'd to
have been nothing but a Parcel of
mere Rabbit's Dung, which to him
would have appear'd as coarfe and
and large, as a Scavenger's Load
frefh taken from a Butcher's Lay-ftall
would do to us. And that which,
in the middle of the Gut Ilium *of the*
Cat, Mr. *St. André* thought was *like a*
very fmall Fifh Bones, the more quickfighted little Man would have de-
monftrated to have been nothing
more than the Bones of a Herring,
which that Creature had devoured
a few Hours before it was thruft into the *Vagina* of *Mary Toft*'s *Uterus.*
Tho, as Arts are very much im-
prov'd with us, I queftion whether
a very ordinary magnifying Glafs,
fuch as Children ufe to divert themfelves

felves with, might not have made the Difcovery as well.

But, if I am rightly inform'd as to the Nature of Mr. *St. André*'s Education, I am ftrangely furpriz'd that He, of all People, fhould appear fo unacquainted with the Materials of which the Strings of a Fiddle are compos'd.

Again, tho' in any of the *European* Nations, thofe that pretend to any Skill in Anatomy or Midwifery would be fcouted to Eternity for only queftioning, or going to make Inquiry, whether it was poffible for a Woman to be delivered of eighteen Rabbits, from two to four Months Growth ; or a *Fœtus* of that Size, but juft dead, and whofe *Flefh fmelt*
like

like that of a Rabbit newly kill'd,
fhould be voided in Fragments and
Bits ; or that the fame Woman, not-
withftanding all thefe Deliveries,
fhould be, during the whole time,
perfectly healthy and well, feeding
on nothing but Beef, Red-herring,
&c. or that a Piece of Hog's Bladder
could be part of the *Chorion,* or
Membrane of the *Placenta* ; yet give
me leave to fay, that in the Kingdom of *Balnibarbi,* thefe things
would appear in quite another Light.
There, tho' a *Virtuofo* fhould only
endeavour at a Demonftration of
this kind, fpend many Years in the
Attempt, and all his Labours prove
abortive at laft, yet would his Sup-
pofitions be fure to meet with fo kind
a Reception from the publick, as to
procure, at leaft, his being adopted

nemine

nemine contradicente, into the Academy of Sciences there; (of which I profeſs my ſelf an unworthy Member.) Nay, it is ten to one but he would be taken up into the floating Iſland, and appointed Anatomiſt extraordinary to the Court of *Laputa.*

Such is the Uſe I am always determin'd to make of this my Knowledge of the World and Mankind. As I will not ſuffer any upſtart Pretender of what Profeſſion ſoever, to monopolize and vend his Abſurdities within this my native Country, without ſuch Animadverſions as may ſerve to warn the publick againſt him: So, on the other ſide, if he happens to have any Merit which would ſhine and be diſtinguiſh'd in other Regions of the Earth, I
ſhall

ſhall be ready to do Juſtice in that
Point alſo, by letting him know in
what part of the World he may be
ſure to find a proper Reward.

But I can't conclude, without ſeriouſly lamenting the great Detri-
ment like to accrue to our Nation
by the Stir which has been made a-
bout this foul Impoſture, both by
the Actors and Examiners of it; and
that as well in regard to the War-
reners and Poulterers, (who complain that the Conſumption of Rabbits, within this Metropolis, is become, by two thirds, leſs than it
was formerly;) as in relation to
thoſe obſcene and indecent Images,
which for more than theſe nine Days
laſt paſt, beyond all Example, have
fill'd the Minds, and furniſh'd out

F   the

the Conversation of People of all
Ranks, Ages and Conditions. And
whether Ideas of this Nature are fit
to be put into the Heads of rude
Boys, Boarding-school Girls, and
Old Maids, I leave every discreet
and prudent Matron to judge.

F I N I S.

THE
TOTNESS
ADDRESS,
VERSIFIED.

To which is Annex'd,

The Original ADDRESS, as presented to
His MAJESTY.

" *Look not askew at what it faith;*
" *There's no* Petition *in it ---Faith!*

PRIOR.

LONDON:

Printed for H. WHITRIDGE, at the *Royal-*
Exchange. M.DCC.XXVII.

THE
TOTNESS
ADDRESS,
VERSIFIED.

Mong the many warm *Addreſſes*
Of *Mayors, Aldermen, Burgeſſes,*
And other People, truly Loyal,
(Who, now, their Zeal and Wits employ all,
To ſhew Your *Majeſty,* that They
Reſolve to *Do,* as well as *Say.*)
We, Men of TOTNESS, DEVON, beg
Our *Liege,* to let us make a *Leg,*
And eke a Speech to daunt our Foes,
Where-e'er the LONDON-GAZETTE goes.

Imprimis, Sir, in Strain moſt humble,
We'd have you know how much we grumble,

At

At GERMANY and SPAIN, who durst
Unite — before they warn'd us first !
And might have (had we not found out
Their *Machinations*) brought about
A World of Woe to *You* and *Your Hope*,
To TOTNESS, BRITAIN, and to EUROPE.

Their Schemes, too black to be reveal'd,
And yet too true to be conceal'd,
Must strike, with terrible Surprize,
All People, who have Ears and Eyes ;
When 'tis but known they were intended
By *Princes*, we, so late, defended !
Princes, in whose *divided* Cause,
All *Christendom* a Deluge was !
But, now *colleagu'd*, wou'd Matters jumble,
And Treaties topsy-turvy tumble !
Anticipate the Conflagration,
By setting Fire to every Nation !
Tho' we *(who made 'em)* go to Ruin ——
Did ever Mortals see such Doing ?

But vain are Menaces and Threats —
Forsooth, we know their former Feats ;

And

And value, like fo many Pofts,
Spanish ARMADA's, *German* HOSTS!
Such fcare-fcrow *Potentates* may vaunt,
But not your valiant *Britons* daunt:
Alas! their whimfical Chimeras
Can ne'er affright a *Land of Heroes!*
Efpecially, fince *You*, no doubt,
Have been at Pains to look fharp out,
And, timely, taken fuch wife Meafures,
As will *enfure* our Lives and Treafures.
Then, there's your *Parliament*, fo able!
And *Miniftry*, incomparable,
With Spirits, indefatigable!

But, moft of all —— now Blood is up —— behold
Your Men of DEVON, ever brave and bold!
Blefs us! what *Heroes* has our *County* bred?
And how your *Royal Anceftors* have fped,
In like Conjunctures, by their gallant Aid?
We furnifh'd DRAKE, a Man of mighty Fame!
The Sons of SPAIN ftill tremble at his Name!
A RALEIGH, too, from *Devonfhire* proceeded ——
But him we claim not — for he was *beheaded!*
And, tho' the *Dorfet* Gentry make a *Fufs*,
CHURCHILL firft breath'd the vital Air with *Us*——

We

We mean great MARLBOROUGH, of immortal Story,
(HOCHSTEDT's a Witness of this HERO's Glory)
To whose sole Arm the *Empire* Safety owes,
And its great *Head* his Victory o'er his Foes!
True; These are *Dust*——But some remain alive,
Who to the *Devil* Your Enemies will drive.
WAGER and HOSIER! There's a *Brace of Tars!*
Each more than NEPTUNE, and at least a MARS!
We warrant it, they'll make the *Spaniards* mind 'em,
And leave to Fishes many Feasts behind em!
Besides, our *Borough* to your *Senate* sends,
A WILLS, among the bravest of Your Friends!
He, Sir, ev'n He, who now *Presents our Speech,*
Your Foreign Foes Fidelity will teach.
Lord, how he scourg'd rebellious Rogues, at PRESTON!
Ay, that's a Proof he's one, whom you may rest on!
Take but our *Words*, and give him *Chief Command*,
OSTEND shall sink, and GIBRALTAR shall stand.

     But, lest you think, Sir, this is *Rant*,
     Nothing but *Bamm*, and empty *Cant*,
     We, honest, hearty Cocks are willing,
     Per Pound Land Tax to pay FOUR SHILLING;
     Nay, with such Cheerfulness allow it,
     We'll toss the other SIXTEEN to it;

                          Tho'

Tho' we fhould mortgage Lands and Houfes,
And eke our Children and our Spoufes.
Moreover, we'll moft frankly part
With all we have, with all our Heart,
Rather than let our *Faith's Defender*
Be bullied, by a bafe *Pretender* ——
A fpurious, *Popifh* Brat, abjur'd
By all of Loyalty affur'd!
If This we did in fober Sadnefs,
What mayn't we do, when rouz'd to Madnefs?
We vow and fwear, by Life's great Giver,
To fight him to our *longeft Liver*;
And, when our *longeft Liver's* dead,
Our *Ghofts* fhall haunt Him, in our ftead,
And fill his Coward-Soul with Dread!

This Refolution we have taken,
That, warn'd, He may preferve his Bacon;
Or fhou'd he ever chance to win
A bloody Battle, and come in;
(Which Heav'n forbid fhou'd ever be!)
Know, by thefe prefent Lines, that we
Affure him, he'll be *fairly bit*,
And, on your Throne, unkingly fit;

When

When none is left for such a TARTAR
To head, and hang, and draw, and quarter!

And now, Sir, to conclude our *Speech*,
And shew we *pray*, as well as *preach*,
We've clubb'd an *Hymn*, and cordial given
Our Cares, in humble *Staves*, to HEAVEN.

I.

" GOD prosper well our noble *King*,
 " Our *Lives* and *Fortunes* all!
" May Peace, and Truth, and Wit, and Wealth,
 " The BRITONS brave befall!

II.

" Late, very late, may our good *Liege*
 " A *Heavenly Crown* obtain!
" And eke his Royal House ne'er want
 " A *Prince*, so fit to reign!

III.

" O may our Happiness, so rare,
 " To future Times go down!
" Let all the People say, *Amen!*
 " *Amen*, says TOTNESS *Town!*

The

The Humble *ADDRESS* of the *Mayor,*
Aldermen, Burgeſſes, &c. of the Town and
Borough of *TOTNESS,* in the County of
Devon.

To the KING's Moſt Excellent MAJESTY.

Moſt GRACIOUS SOVEREIGN,

E, *Your Majeſty's moſt Dutiful and Loyal Sub-*
jeɛts, the Mayor, Aldermen, Burgeſſes, and
Principal Inhabitants of the Town and Borough
of TOTNESS, *in the County of* Devon, *humbly*
beg Leave to approach Your Royal Preſence, to teſtify,
on the preſent Junɛture of Affairs, our utmoſt De-
teſtation and Abhorrence of the clandeſtine Machina-
tions and Confederacies, form'd by the Emperor of Ger-
many and King of Spain, *againſt Your Majeſty's Royal*
Perſon and Government, the Trade and Privileges of
theſe Kingdoms, and the general Peace and Tranquil-
lity of all Europe.

Such deſtruɛtive Schemes, too black *to be publickly*
own'd, and yet too true *to be abſolutely deny'd, can-*
not but be Matter of the greateſt Surprize and Aſto-
niſhment to the preſent, *and all* future *Ages, that ſhall*
ſee or hear of them, and know, that the ſame were
contriv'd by two Princes, *in whoſe Quarrel all* Chriſten-

C   dom

dom *hath already been* Deluged *in* Blood, *and* Exhausted *of* Immense Treasures ; *and who,* in Return, *are now setting the World in* fresh Flames, *by an* Unnatural *joining of Hands, to raise an Exorbitant and Formidable Power in themselves, with Views to Oppress and Injure their* quondam Allies, *and chief Instruments of setting them on their respective Thrones.*

But, alas! their vain, vaunting Menaces, and Threats of Spanish *Armadoes, and* German *Hosts, are too* Chimerical *to* Affrighten *and* Terrify *your* Ever - Valiant *Britons : Especially when we consider the consummate Wisdom of Your M A J E S T Y, in contracting such powerful Alliances, and taking such early Precautions, for the Safety of Your People ; the true* British *Zeal of Your* Glorious P A R L I A M E N T, *and the indefatigable Pains and Industry of Your* most Incomparable M I N I S T R Y.

Or, when we call to Remembrance, how that our single County *hath heretofore, in like critical Times, furnished Your Royal Predecessors with a* Renowned D R A K E, *whose Name the Sons of* Spain *still Tremble to hear ; and of later Years, with a* C H U R C H I L L *(the Immortal* M A R L B O R O U G H,) *to whom* Hochstedt *witnesseth, that all* Germany *owes its Preservation, and the* Head *of it, his now Imperial Greatness ; which* Heroes, *tho now* Laid down in the Dust, *Your Majesty hath still a* W A G E R *and a* H O S I E R, *whose gallant Actions,* we promise our selves, *will give the* Spaniards *equal Cause to remember them. And our Borough now sends to Your Senate, a* W I L L S ; *who, as he has been the Scourge of* Perfidious Rebels *at* Home, *will,* we doubt not, *on Occasion, with like Courage and Success,* Vanquish *and* Confound *all Your Majesty's* Faith-breaking *Enemies* Abroad.

The

The FOUR SHILLINGS per *Pound Land-Tax, set on us by Your Parliament, is so far from making us any-wise* Uneasy, *that we shall not only pay it with the greatest Chearfulness imaginable, but also readily add the other* SIXTEEN, *and* every thing else *that is* Dear and Valuable *to us, as a* FREEWILL-OFFERING *for the Publick Service, rather than that such* Provoking Indignities, *and* Insulting Threats, *shall ever be offered to Your most Sacred Majesty, or the* British *Nation, on behalf of a* Spurious Popish Pretender, whom, *as We, and* All your Loyal Subjects, *have so frequently and deliberately abjured, we are resolutely determined to oppose, to the very last Breath of the longest Liver of us all, that so, if ever, which Heavens forbid! he should at last happen to succeed, there shall not then remain one Protestant Briton left for him to exercise his Tyrannical Usurpation over.*

THESE, *may it please Your Majesty, are our* Solemn Vows, *and* Unalterable Resolutions; *and our most earnest Prayers to the Almighty* KING *of Kings, are, and constantly shall be, That long, very long and prosperous, may be Your Majesty's Reign over us ; and that, whenever it shall please God to take Your most Sacred Majesty from this Your Earthly Crown to a Heavenly Diadem, Your Royal House may never want a Prince, equal in* Virtue, Piety, *and* Magnanimity, *to fit on the Throne of these Realms, by whom the many* Blessings *and* Unspeakable Happinesses *we now enjoy under Your Majesty's* Most Glorious *and* Auspicious Reign, *may be perpetuated to our Children and latest Posterities.*

FINIS.

THE
Totneſs ADDRESS
TRANSVERSED.

By Captain GULLIVER.

Hæc placuit ſemel, hæc decies repetita placebit.

Now God be with him, ſaid the King,
    Sith 'twill no better be;
I truſt I have, within my Realm,
    Five hundred as good as he.

                           Chevy Chaſe.

To which is added,
SOMEWHAT beſide.

LONDON:
Printed for H. CURLL in the *Strand.* 1727.

THE
Totneſs ADDRESS
TRANSVERSED.

WE loyal Subjects, may it pleaſe Ye,
The May'r and Aldermen, addreſs Ye.
And Burgeſſes ; and tho' not all
The Inhabitants, the principal,
As, by our Breeding, may appear,
From *Totneſs*, begging Favour here,
We the brave Boys of *Devonſhire* ;
And if we don't, before we've done,
Exceed them ev'ry Mother's Son,
That e'er addreſs'd you heretofore,
Never believe Us any more.
　Firſt, we expreſs our Deteſtation
Of each clandeſtine Machination,

And

And secret Leagues, whate'er they be,
Form'd betwixt *Spain* and *Germany*,
Against your self, and Throne you sit on,
The Trade, and Privilege, of *Britain*;
Which *Europe* will to pieces tear,
And break the Peace,————if there be War :
Such Schemes too black to place in View,
And yet to be conceal'd too true ;
For we acknowledge, by the bye,
That *Spain* and *Cæsar* cannot lye;
These Schemes will strike, with vast surprize,
P esent and future Ears and Eyes ;
Always provided let it be,
That they shall hear of them or see ;
Provided also Men shall know,
These self-same Kings, these very two,
Had drain'd all *Christendom* before
Of Gold, and delug'd it in Gore ;
Who now, to fire the World, agree,
With most unnatural Amity :
To raise their Pow'r, and gain their Ends,
They value not their quondam Friends ;
Now join'd, in spite of former War,
As close as *France* and *Britain* are ;

Or,

Or, if at private Folks you look,
As *P———y* is with *B———ke.*

   Alas! the menacing Bravadoes
Of *German* Hosts, and *Spain*'s Armadoes,
Must not pretend to touch with Fear
Your ever-valiant *Devonshire*;
Empty *Chimæras* cannot fright,
Especially since your Foresight,
Which makes our Valour much the stranger,
Has timely put Us out of Danger;
And since, with hearty *British* Zeal,
Your Ministry, for publick Weal,
And glorious Parliament, so strains
With indefatigable Pains
Of most incomparable Brains!
What makes Us braver still, of old,
As in our Chronicles is told,
Many a Hero has been given
From our own County, that of *Devon*:
There's *Drake*'s great Name, what Foe can bear it!
The Sons of *Spain* still shake to hear it!
And several more, as well as he,
In *Fuller*'s Worthys you may see,
Who fought for Glory — or for Pension;
Another we beg leave to mention,   *Churchill,*

Churchill, who liv'd not long ago,
Who sav'd the Empire at a Blow ;
Immortal, tho', as Heroes muſt
Be, he and *Drake* are laid in Duſt.
But then, our Courage to revive ho,
Wager and *Hoſier* are alive ho ;
Nay, more than they, as you may ſee,
Our Member *Wills* will make up three ;
One to your Int'reſt firm and hearty,
And *tam Mercurio*, Sir, *quam Marte*,
For matchleſs Talents he poſſeſſes,
At leading Armys, or——Addreſſes;
He *Preſton* Rebels put in fright,
And ſcourg'd, becauſe they would not fight ;
And ſhall abroad, with like ſucceſs,
Maul your Faith-breaking Enemys ;
Truſt but your Troops with ſuch Commanders,
And make him General in *Flanders*,
So ſhall *Don Spaniard*, gracious Liege,
We promiſe you, break up the Siege ;
And *Britiſh* Ships ſhall take, at Will-a,
The Galeons, and the Flotilla ;
Oſtend ſhall Merchandize give o'er,
Nor practiſe Smugling any more.
Monk might be nam'd on this Occaſion,
Had he not caus'd the *Reſtoration*.   While

While thefe, Sir, are abroad engaging,
With all the Glee you can imagine,
We fhall at home your Foes confound,
By our Four Shillings in the Pound ;
Nor pay this only, but we truft
With equal Gladnefs, when needs muft,
The other Sixteen we fhall bring,
By way of Free-will Offering.
Tho' *Jacks* impertinently fay
We Nothing have, and Nothing pay,
Nay even that our Landed few
When tax'd four Shillings pay but two,
Proving by Computation then
Sixteen and Four will make but Ten.
When feiz'd of all our other Matters,
We beg you'd take our Wives and Daughters ;
Twenty per Pound we wou'd endure,
To make our Property fecure ;
So with our Dears we'll part with Eafe,
Might we preferve our Libertys ;
Our Sons too in your Caufe fhall fight,
By meer hereditary Right,
And boldly cry, *King George* for ever !
To the laft Breath of the laft Liver.

Let

Let the Pretender then, tho' furious,
A Popish Wight, abjur'd, and spurious,
When *Totness* has not left a Man,
Come, and be King on't, if he can :
If after all, tho' Heavens forbid it,
When *Totness* is extinct, he did it,
Would all *Great Britain* serve him so,
He needs must reign like *Trincalo*.

These are our solemn Vows most stable,
And full Resolves inutterable ;
And most absurd were his Desire,
Who any farther should require :
That you, in spite of *Pope* and *Spain*,
May rule at least as long again,
Before a safer Crown be given,
For no *Pretenders* are in Heaven ;
Then that his Royal Highness too
May scatter round, as well as you,
The Blessings which we shall not tell,
Because they are unspeakable,
That Heirs may to your Throne be gotten,
When we, and ours, are dead and rotten ;
Make him but General whom we say,
Thus your Petitioners shall pray, &c.

LETTER
To the
THOLSEL,
Concerning the present ELECTION.

WHAT Strife and Noife is this we have thro' the whole
City, and about the promotion of two Perfons, and when
all comes to pafs, God knows whether you are right or wrong,
be that as it will, it is nothing to me, but bleam no Man to beftow his Favours on whom he pleafes, for (if I be not miftaken)
when the Corpor;tion of Shoe-Makers went the other Day to
give their Votes, the Books were immediately fhut up: Pray
what Reafon had you for fo doing, is it becaufe they were for
Counfellor *Howard*; bleam them not for fo doing, for *Howard* is
no proud Man, he is Content to wear the pioduct of his Country, and the other is for the product of his, for nothing that is
Irifh will he wear, then how can you bleam them to ftand up for
the Man that ftands by them, for in my Opinion all Men ought
to be for the good and Intereft of his Country.

In the next place let us confider that *Howard* is a Native of this
Country, and S----e an *Englifh Man*, and fo great a lover of his
Country, that what ever he wants he fends there for it, but the
Native of your Country is content with the Product thereof.
Now Gentlemen S----s that are Natives of the Kingdome, be
not fo Reverft againft your Countryman, for in fo doing, you
fullfil the Old faying, that is, *Put an Irifhman on a Spit, and you
fhall get Twenty to turne him*: Oh! confider what fhame this is to
your Country, put an end to that faying, andftand by your Countryman, for why he is a Man of Sence, a Man (if Occafion be)
that can fpeak in the behalf of his Country and People, a Man
that willbe no way Biafed, a Man that will take neither Bribe nor Fee,
to hurt his Country. For fuch as are Carelefs in their own Caufes,
hardly can be Carefull about other Men's Affairs, nor that City
is of no value which is not of Ability enough to Punifh wrong
doers: Neither is that Commonweal any thing worth at all, where
Pardon and Interceffion prevail againft Laws. It is beter to
fight with an Enemy at his own home, than for him to fight with
us in our Country. Carelefs Men are ever moft nigh unto their
own harm. Where flatterers bear Rule, things come to Ruin.
By diligence and pains-taking all may be amended that is amifs.

Therefore dear Countrymen confider what you are about,
let Reafon be your Guide, and Plunge not your felves into a
Gulf of Sorrow, but take a Man of Learning, a Man that can
fpeak in the behalf of you and your Country, and you will o-
blidg your felves, your Country, and me who am your humble
Servant, *Guliver*.

The POLE laft Week is as follows. *Allerman Stoyte* 711. *Samuel Burt* Efq; 8:0.
William Howard Efq; 787.

To the Gentlemen Freeholders, and Freemen of the City, a few Words concerning the Alderman and Squire.

GENTLEMEN,

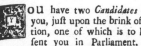

YOU have two *Candidates* before you, juſt upon the brink of Election, one of which is to Repreſent you in Parliament. The Queſtion is, Whether you are to chuſe the Perſon, who is beſt qualify'd for you, or him who is not —— I fancy you will all naturally think a good Citizen, one of your own Body, a Lover of his Country, a Loyal Subject to his Majeſty King *George*, a Perſon out of all Road of *Civil Preferment*, and conſequently of *Corruption*, and a favourer of tender Conſciences, muſt be the Man, and ſuch I take the *Alderman* to be. As for the SQUIRE, I ſhall make no Perſonal Reflections, but ſay that he is no more fit to Repreſent you, than the *Pageant* which is carryed before the *Corporation* of *Smiths*.

IN the firſt place, How can he be a Member for you, who is not of your Body? or he is no more a Citizen, than the *Wooden-man* in *Eſſex-ſtreet* ; Whereas Mr. *Alderman* is a Piece of your ſelves, a part of your very Vitals, and therefore muſt love you and your Intereſts more at heart, than a Man who comes from *Terra Incognito*; that is, *From the Devil's Arſe a Peak.*

CONSIDER too that Mr. *Alderman* is not gone from Door to Door, begging Votes, but has like an honeſt Man, as he is, left it to your own Conſciences to judge, which of the two is moſt Zealous for the Preſervation of your Rights, and Privileges, the Advancement of Trade, the good of your City, and the good of the Kingdom in General. Whereas the Squire does not at all apply to your Conſciences, but your Stomachs ; and thinks by filling them with *Cold Beef* and SOUR WINE, that you ſhall haſtily give away your *Votes*, and believe him to be the only Friend to you, to your City, and to your Country, who fills your Bellies for a ſeaſon, and turns your Heads, in Order to ſerve his TURN.

PRAY, Gentlemen, conſider ſeriouſly with your ſelves, whether you are to be led by the Guts, like ſo many Dogs in Strings? If you think ſo, and reſolve to be deluded, there is a *Dutch* Painter in Town, who ſays he will draw ye with Pack-threads, faſtened to your Guts, and the *Squire* leading you as Captain *Gulliver* drew the Ships.

IT will be a fine jeſt in the Mouths of your Adverſaries, on the Day of Election, *Make room, clear the Way, here come the* GUT-VOTERS.

SUPPOSE the *Squire*, when he demanded your Votes firſt, had ſaid in plain *Engliſh* to each of you, *Jack*, or *Tom*, or *Will*, prithy give me your Vote, and I will give you your Belly full of Meat and Drink, would not the Perſon thus ſpoken to think himſelf very much Affronted, and yet the Fact of treating you, amounts to the very ſame thing.

GENTLEMEN, let me once more deſire you to think better of the matter, your Treats are now all over, *Eaten Bread is forgotten*, is a good old Proverb. If the 'Squire hits you in the Teeth, with what you have eaten and drank, hit him in the Teeth again with it. Refund him his Reckonings, it will be but a Trifle to each of you ; For, to my Knowledge, the *Wine* which the 'Squire bought at the *Merchants*, ſtood him only in Three-pence a Bottle, which you may all recollect, if you have not forgotten your *Cholicks* and *Head-Achs*. I was told by a Gentleman of Veracity, that he was preſent, when the *Merchant* ſaid, theſe *Hogſheads*, Sir, are too Sour for Drinking, I intend them for *Vinegar*. Upon which the *Squire* replyed, *It is good Election Claret, the Raſcals I am to throw it away upon have no more Palates than my Shoe-ſoal. A parcel of Scoundrels, who are glad of a little ſour Small-beer at home.* If what I ſay be not true, may I Drink ſome of the ſame Wine for a Year to come.

BELIEVE

BELIEVE me, Gentlemen, he has no tender Regard for you in the least, or he wou'd never hazard your lives by giving you such *Poison*; for so I will call it. I wou'd rather take *Poison* my self, because I could get rid of it by the help of *Oyl* in half an Hour. But Seven Years *Phyfick* will not carry off th se Dregs, which your Veins have imbib'd upon this unfortunate Occasion.

TO Conclude all, I will tell you a Piece of History, and after that a Fable.

ONE *Corvinus Meffala*, a Lawyer at *Rome*, inveigled a vast Number of the Citizens, by Feasting and Junketting, to make him a Member of their *Senator*, which was the same thing as a *Parliament-Man* amongst us, and accordingly he was chosen in Opposition to a very worthy and good Citizen, a Nephew of *Cato* the Elder. When he had gai 'd his Point, it was Observ'd, that he never took the least Notice of one of his *Voters*. But what makes his Ingratitude very Monstrous, one *Ambustus Lanius*, Head of the Corporation of Butchers, a Man very Active in his Interest, happen'd to be most injuriously Treated by one of the Opposite Faction, and when he apply'd to *Meffala*, for Redress, the worthy *Senator* instead of taking the honest *Butcher* into his Protection, turns about to a Person he was Walking with, and said, This *Rafcal*, because I fill'd his Guts with Beef, which I bought of himself, imagins I must plead his Cause for

nothing. So turnd off the poor Fellow, without making the least *Apology*.

NOW, Gentlemen, for the *Fable*. Once upon a time, when other *Animals*, as well as *Men*, had their publick Affemblies and Meetings, a cunning *Fox*, by his Wheedling and Craft, had got so far into favour with the several wild Beasts of the Forrest to which he did not belong, that he set up for a *Member of Parliament*, against a good Old *Lyon*, who had been a Great Benefactor among them, and by his Dexterity and Art, had gained several of the *Lyon's Party* and *Species* from him, insomuch tha when the Day of Election came, it wa feared the *Fox* wou'd carry it from him Upon this a Horse of a good plain Understanding, stood up and said, *Here are two Candidates before us, the one has distinguish'd himself at all Times for the good of the Forrest, and is one of our felves. The other never did us any good, nor did I ever hear of see him before yesterday. My opinion is, i I have any Skill in Phyfiognomy, this fly Gentleman wou'd fet Fire to the Forrest, and de stroy us all for one fat Goofe. I shall say no more; for few Words are best.* He had no sooner done, but the Forrest Rung with Shouts of Approbation. The *Lyon* wa hoist upon Shoulders, and the *Fox* wa sent off with a few *Raggamuffin Currs* a his Tail, and so ended the Election.

F I N I S.

Seaforable *Reflections*

ADDRESS'D

To the Citizens of Dublin, by Captain Gulliver

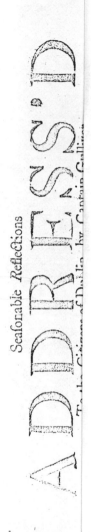

THE
GRUB-STREET
OPERA.

As it is Acted at the

THEATRE in the HAY-MARKET.

By SCRIBLERUS SECUNDUS.

Sing. Nom. *Hic, Hæc, Hoc.*
Gen. *Hujus.*
Dat. *Huic.*
Accuf. *Hunc, Hanc, Hoc.*
Voc. *Caret.*   Lil. Gram. quod vid.

By Henry Fielding

To which is added,

THE
MASQUERADE,
A
POEM.

Printed in MDCCXXVIII.

LONDON,
Printed, and fold by J. ROBERTS, in Warwick-lane.
MDCCXXXI.
[Price One Shilling and Six pence.]

THE
MASQUERADE,
A
POEM.

INSCRIBED TO

C - - - T   H - - D - - G - - R.

—— *Velut ægri fomnia, vanæ*
—— *Species* ——   Hor. Art. Poet.

By LEMUEL GULLIVER,
Poet Laureat to the King of LILLIPUT.

K with freedom

LONDON,
Printed, and fold by J. ROBERTS, in Warwick-lane;
and A. DODD, at the Peacock, without Temple-bar.
MDCCXXVIII.
[Price Six-pence.]

THE

DEDICATION.

SIR,

I Believe no one will difpute your right to this little poem, any more than your prefiding over that diverfion it celebrates ; therefore I fhall, without excufe, lay it at your feet.

The flattery of dedications has been often exploded : to avoid the moft diftant imputation of which, I fhall omit feveral things that (perhaps) might not be juftly fo called : and that the more readily, fince your merit is fo well known, it would be only publifhing what is in every one's mouth.

I cannot, however, help congratulating you on that gift of nature, by which you feem fo adapted to the poft you enjoy. I mean that natural mafque, which is too vifible a perfection to be infifted on here — and, I am fure, never fails of making an impreffion on the moft indifferent beholder.

Another gift of nature, which you feem to enjoy in no fmall degree, is that modeft confidence fupporting you in every act of your life. Certainly, a great bleffing ! for I always have obferved, that brafs in the forehead draws gold into the pocket.

As for what mankind call virtues, I fhall not compliment you on them : fince you are fo wife to keep them fecret from the world, far be it from me to publifh them ; efpecially fince they are things which lie out of the way of your calling.

Here I beg leave to contradict two fcandalous afperfions, which have been fpread againft you.

First,

DEDICATION.

First, That you are a b——d.

Secondly, A conjurer.

Whoever has seen you at a m-sq-r-de, cannot believe the first — and you have given several instances at White's, that you are not the other.

But what signifies attempting to confute what needs no confutation? — Besides, you have so great a soul, that you despise all scandal — and live in the world with the same indifference, that people have at a masquerade, where they are not known.

Smile then (if you can smile) on my endeavours, and this little poem, with candour — for which the author desires no more gratuity than a ticket for your next ball, and is,

SIR,

Your most obedient,

From my garret
in Grub-street.

Humble servant,

LEMUEL GULLIVER.

THE

MASQUERADE,

A

POEM.

 OME call Curiosity an evil,
And say 'twas that, by which the devil
With Eve succeeded in his suit,
To taste the dear forbidden fruit.
Others (allowing this) yet wou'd
Prove it has done less harm than good.
To this (say they) whate'er we know
In arts or sciences, we owe.
To this, how justly are attributed
What W—st—n, H—l—y, have exhibited!
From this we borrow hopes of greater
Discoveries of madam Nature.
Hence is our expectation gain'd,
To see the longitude explain'd.
'Tis this which sets the chemist on,
To seek that secret-natur'd stone,
Which the philosophers have told,
When found, turns all things into gold:
But being hunted, and not caught,
Oh! sad reverse! turns gold to nought.
Britain may hence her knowledge brag
Of Lilliput and Brobdingnag:

This

This paffion dictated that voyage,
Which will be parallel'd in no age.
'Twas this which furl'd my fwelling fails,
And bid me truft uncertain gales;
Gave me thro' unknown feas a lift,
And, fpight of dangers, made me Swift.
'Tis this which fends the Britifh fair
To fee Italians dance in air.
This crowds alike the repr'fentation
Of Lun's and Bullen's coronation.
By this embolden'd, tim'rous maids
Adventure to the mafquerades.
And, to confefs the truth, 'twas this
Which fent me there, as well as mifs.
Now for the benefit of thofe,
Whofe Curiofity oppofe,
Or parents ftrict, or jealous fpoufes,
(Rogues! who make prifons of their houfes)
The fequel all its joys unravels,
Plain as th' adventures in my travels.

The criticks wou'd be apt to bark,
Was I to leave them in the dark
As to my drefs — Faith! I appear'd
In the ftrange habit of a bard.
My fhabby coat you might have known
To have been black — tho' now 'twas brown:
My breeches (old tradition fays)
Were new in queen Eliza's days;
And to enforce our faith, we're told
They ne'er were worn with weighty gold:
My goat-fkin-aping wig (I've heard)
Was made of Hudibras's beard;
Its hairs, in quantity and hue,
Declare its ped'gree to be true.
The laurels did my temples grace,
As did a mafque my uglier face.
Thus when equipp'd, I call'd a chair,
Go, to th' Haymarket theatre.

O mufe, fome fimile indite,
To fhew the oddnefs of the fight.

A2

As in a madman's frantic skull,
When pale-fac'd Luna is at full,
In wild confusion huddled lies
A heap of incoherencies:
So here in one confusion hurl'd,
Seem all the nations of the world;
Cardinals, quakers, judges dance;
Grim Turks are coy, and nuns advance.
Grave churchmen here at hazard play;
Cinque-ace ten pound — done, quater-tray.
Known prudes there, libertines we find,
Who masque the face, t' unmasque the mind.
Here, running footmen guzzle tea;
There, milk-maids flasks of Burgundy.
I saw two shepherdesses dr-nk
And heard a friar call'd a p-nk.
Lost in amazement as I stood,
A lady in a velvet hood,
(Her mein St. James's seem'd t' explain,
But her assurance — Drury-lane,
Not Hercules was ever bolder)
Came up, and slapp'd me on the shoulder.
Why how now, poet! pray, how fare
Our friends, who feed on Grub-street air?
For, be assur'd, we all shall dub
Thy laureat-brow, with name of Scrub.
No man of any fashion wou'd
Appear a poet in a crowd.
A poet in this age we shun,
With as much terror as a dun:
Both are receiv'd with equal sorrow,
Who wou'd be paid, and who wou'd borrow.
And tho' you never speak — we spy
The craving beggar in your eye.
For poverty rules all your host,
The sin against the —— ——
Madam, to understand, we're giv'n
That poverty's the road to heav'n.
Why ay (says she) so churchmen say,
But still they chuse the other way.
Well, madam, (if it will allure you)
I am no poet, I assure you.

Tho'

Tho' in this garb — I'm in reality,
A young, smart, dapper man of quality.
No lawrels — but a smart toupée,
In drawing-rooms, distinguish me.
I often frisk it to the play,
To Norfolk's, Kemp's and Strafford's day.
An opera I never miss ;
To shew my teeth — I sometimes hiss.
I'm seen where-e'er the ladies flock ;
My conversation's — What's a clock ?
Then of the weather I complain ;
No matter whether wind or rain,
Or hot or cold; for in a breath,
I'm sometimes scorch'd, and froze to death.
Rain has been often the creation
Of a dry frozen conversation.
No wind e'er rages, but it blows
In sympathetic mouths of beaux.
Enough ! (the lady cry'd :) I see
You are, indeed, the man for me :
For all our wiser part despise
Those little apish butterflies ;
And if the breed been't quickly mended ;
Your empire shortly will be ended :
Breeches our brawny thighs shall grace,
(Another Amazonian race.)
For when men women turn — why then
May women not be chang'd to men ?

    But come, we'll take a turn, and try
What mysteries we can descry.

    Hold, madam, pray what hideous figure
Advances ? Sir, that's C——t H—d—g—r.
How could it come into his gizzard,
T' invent so horrible a vizzard ?
How could it, sir ? (says she) I'll tell you:
It came into his mother's belly ;
For you must know, that horrid phyz is
(*Puris naturalibus*) his visage.
Monstrous ! that human nature can
Have form'd so strange burlesque a man.

Why,

Why, fir, (fays fhe) there are who doubt
That nature's felf ne'er made it out:
For there's a little fcrip which refteth
Of an old regifter, attefteth,
That Amadis being convey'd,
By magic, to th' infernal fhade;
By magic, there begot upon
The fair Tyfiphone, a fon:
And that, as Mulciber was driv'n
Headlong, for's uglinefs, from heav'n;
So, for his uglinefs more fell,
Was H—d—g—r tofs'd out of hell,
And, in return, by Satan made
Firft minifter of 's mafquerade.
Now this his juft preferment bears,
'Mongft wits, the name of Kick-up-ftairs.
Madam (fays I) I am inclin'd,
(Tho' of no fuperftitious mind)
To think fome magic art is us'd,
By which our fenfes are abus'd:
For what can here this crowd purfue,
Where they all nothing have to do?
Nothing! why fee at yonder fide-board
What fweetmeats mifs does in her hide hoard.
A little farther take your eye,
And fee how faft the glaffes fly.
Again furvey the inner room,
There trembling gamefters wait their doom.
Here the gay dance the fair employs;
There, Damon fues forbidden joys,
Whilft Sylvia, liftening to his pray'r,
Gives him no reafon to defpair.
See, where poor Doris tries t' affwage
The haughty Laura's fiery rage;
Who caught him with a rival miftrefs,
(The fad occafion of her diftrefs.)
For drinking, gaming, dancing — and
Contriving to — you underftand —
(What well-bred fpoufes muft connive at)
Are the chief bus'neffes they drive at.
Some, indeed, hither fends good-nature,
To vent their o'er-grown wit in fatyr:

F   Some

Some spend their time in repartee;
Others, rare wits, in ribaldry:
Whilst others rally all they see,
With that smart phrase, " Do you know me?"
Below stairs hungry whores are picking
The bones of wild fowl, and of chicken;
And into pockets some convey
Provisions for another day;
Preparing thus for future wants,
They've both the sting and care of ants.
But see Loretta comes, that common —
Madam, how from another woman
Do you a strumpet masqu'd distinguish?
Because that thing, which we, in English,
Do virtue call, is always took
To hold its station in the look.
Poet, quoth she, (first having shaken
Her sides with laughter) you're mistaken.
Your brother bards have often sung,
That virtue's seated in the tongue:
With you, nor them can I agree;
For virtue's unconfin'd and free;
Is neither seated here nor there,
A perfect shadow, light as air,
It rambles loosely, every where.
In miss's heart, at ten it lies;
At twenty, mounts into her eyes;
Till forty, how it does dispose
Of its dear self, no mortal knows.
The tongue is then its certain station,
And thence it guards the reputation.
Again (says she) some others ask,
They'll tell you virtue is a masque:
But it wou'd look extremely queer
In any one, to wear it here.
Madam (says I) methinks you ramble;
What need we this your long preamble?
Well then, as in the different ages,
So virtue in the different stages
Of female life, its station alters:
It in the widow's jointure shelters;

In wives, 'tis not fo plain where laid ;
But in the virgin's maidenhead.
A maidenhead now never dies,
'Till, like true phœnix, it fupplies
Its lofs, by leaving us another :
For fhe's a maid, who is no mother.
And fhe may be — we fee in life,
A mother, who is not a wife.
Now 'tis this cafe, which in the trumpet
Of fame diftinguifhes a ftrumpet :
This, having been Loretta's fate,
Did to the world her lofs relate.
So, poor Califtho it befel,
With fecret injuries, to fwell ;
But had Diana thro' her clan,
(To try how far th'infection ran)
Forc'd all her followers to tryal
Of chaftity, by ordeal ;
Who knows (tho' it had rag'd no higher)
What pretty feet had fwell'd by fire ?

. But fee that knot of fhepherdeffes,
And fhepherds — well — they're pretty dreffes.
Such the Arcadian fhepherds were,
When love alone could charm the fair :
Such the Arcadian nymphs, when love
Beauty alone in men could move.
How happy did they fport away,
In fragrant bow'rs, the fcorching day ;
Or, to the Nightingale's foft tune,
Danc'd by the luftre of the moon !
Beauteous the nymphs, the fwains fincere,
They knew no jealoufy, no fear :
Together flock'd, like turtle-doves,
All conftant to their plighted loves.
How different is now their fate !
Both equally confpire to cheat.
Florus, with lying billet-doux
The charming Rofalind purfues ;
Follows her to the play — to court,
Where-ever the beau m nde refort.

Some

Some half a year he's made that tool,
The wise yclepe a woman's fool:
At last the pitying fair relents,
And to his utmost wish consents.
No sooner is the nymph enjoy'd,
Than Florus, fickle youth, is cloy'd.
He leaves her for another toast;
She laughs, and cries—pray—who has lost?

Madam, said I, a simile
Of mine will with your tale agree.
So have I seen two gamesters meet,
(Both ignorant that both wou'd cheat)
Throw half an hour of life away,
Cheating by turns in fruitless play.
At last each other's tricks discover,
And wisely give their throwing over:
At one another laugh, as fools,
And run away to seek new culls.

Poet, your simile is just.
But what comes here? quoth I—a ghost;
I hope the fantom does not scare you?
O no; says she: but see what's near you.
Oh hideous? what a dreadful face!
Worse than the master's of the place!
Has nature been so very sparing
Of ugliness, to th' age we are in;
That our deformity by nature
Art must contrive to render greater?
Quoth she, for different reasons here,
In different masques, we all appear,
Some ugly vizards are design'd
To raise ideas in the mind;
Which may, like foils, conspire to grace
The lesser horrors of the face.
Others in beauteous masques delight,
To be thought belles for half a night;
As proud of this short transformation,
As justice D——k at c--r--n--t--n.
For know, (tho' 'tis by few believ'd)
Most go away from hence deceiv'd:

Error,

Error, (ftrange goddefs !) ruleth here,
And from her caftle in the air,
Carefully watches o'er our motions,
Receives our off'rings and devotions.

Behold, aloft, the goddefs fit,
In her appearance a coquette ;
Six beaus, as many belles, are fhown,
On right, and left-hand of her throne.
See Venus, Bacchus, Fortune there ;
So, at this diftance, they appear :
But all are pictures, view them near.
The goddefs thefe, with fubtle art,
Has plac'd, to captivate each heart.
For whilft you with a vain entreaty,
Attack the favourite painted deity,
You fall into an unfeen net ;
(By Error on that purpofe fet.)
Thus caught, you are oblig'd to wander
Through a myfterious wild meander :
Wearied, at laft you find the door,
Then hey to wine, or wife or w——re.
Of thefe, no matter which, a dofe
Your fenfes does in fleep compofe ;
Waking, all your adventures feem
An idle, trifling, feverifh dream.
This fate, indeed, does not befal
(Tho' much the greater numbers) all :
For fome o'er-leap with nimble feet ;
Others, with ftronger, break the net :
Then kneeling at the favourite fhrine,
They make the deity benign.

Now that a g—d may be entreated,
By prayers to images related ;
'Twill not be credited by fome
In England, but by all at Rome.

Thus Fortune fends the gamefters luck,
Venus her votary a ———
— Miftrefs — Oh ! criticks, fpare the crime,
Of one who cou'd not find a rhyme.

Bacchus,

Bacchus, that jolly power divine,
To his petitioner sends wine.

    The lucky gamester, when repose
No longer will his eye-lids close,
With triumph feels his loaded breeches,
That bend beneath the weighty riches.
The happy lover, when he awakes,
And a survey of Celia takes,
As sleeping by his side she lies,
Kisses, in ecstasy, her eyes,
Her lips, her breast; devours her charms,
And dies in raptures, in her arms.
The honest sot, disdaining rest,
Finds joy-imperial in his breast;
As great an emperor as any
In Bedlam, Russia, or Germany.

    But tho' each godship kindly grants
To some petitioners their wants:
Each does refuse (I know not why)
With some petitions to comply;
And oft requites a hearty prayer,
(Instead of joys) with woes and care:
For view the young unseason'd drinker,
Oh L—d! methinks I smell him stink here;
Welt'ring, he in his pigsty lies,
And curses all debaucheries.
The undone gamester wakes, and tears,
From his ill-fated head, his hairs.
The lover, who has now possess'd,
From unknown Flora, his request;
(Who with a pretty, modest grace,
Discover'd all things but her face:)
Pulls off her masque in am'rous fury,
And finds a gentle nymph of Drury,
Curses his lust——laments his fate,
And kicks her out of bed too late.
From different springs, of equal pain,
The gamester and gallant complain;
The gamester mourns his losing lot,
The lover fears—that he has got.

These

These are the scenes—wherein engage
The numbers now upon this stage.
These are the different ends, which all
In different degrees befal.
Now I'll discover who I am:
A muse—Calliope my name.
I stood surpriz'd, whilst from my sight
She vanish'd, in a sudden flight.

F I N I S.

AN EXCELLENT NEW

BALLAD

ON

The *Wedding* of *Pritty Miss S--lly*
to *Jolly* Old *J---o.*

By Captain Gulliver.

YE *Gallants* of *Dublin*, come liſten a while,
A Story I'll tell you, will make you to Smile.
'Tis of Young Miſs *S——lly*, and Jolly old *J---o*,
Whoſe *Wedding* Pray Sing now where ever you go
     With Hy Dery Down, Down, Dery Down.

This Damſel who fair is, has been Sung often times,
By *Poets* of all ſorts, in all ſorts of Rhimes,
Then why ſhould not I to ſinging Incline,
Since the *Times* are ſo hard I can't tell where to Dine.
     Down dery down, dery down, down.

By this you may know my Head it is clear,
For not having Money, *I* could not get Beer,
And asking old *Jo*, are you Dry Saith he Rogue?
If ſo, I proteſt, it's a Diſeaſe in Vogue.
     Hey dery down, down, dery down.

But this is Digreſſion, my ſtory ſtands ſtill,
Then *Read* on my Friends, of *Words* take your fill
'Tis all you are like to get at this *Time*,
For to Tagg out this Verſe I muſt drag in Rhime.
     Down, dery down, down, dery down.

The Wedding's a Wedding I Vow and Proteſt,
Tho' by theſe *Strange-Verſes* you'd think it a Jeſt,
Miſs *S——lly* is Wedded and Bedded I ſay,
And ſhe and old *Jo*, do's continually Play.
     With Her down, down down, dery down.

When his Neighbours did ask him, how came it to Paſs?
He cry'd Fools hold your tongues and drink off your Glaſs,
Why is ſhe not Handſome, and Proper and Tall,
And can ſhe not Dance, and *Tall dex--lal-lal,*
     With Her down, dery down.

Oh now Crys the Mother ¡ my Heart is at reſt,
My Daughter is Married and I'm therein bleſt,
Old *Jo*, has got hold of her *Fair Maiden-Head,*
Which will hold him tugg, till We are both Dead,
     When with Her He lies Down, down, dery down.

LEZIONE

SU

D'un Vitello a due teste

DELL'

ACCADEMICO DELLE SCIENZE,

COLLE NOTE

DI LEMUEL GULLIVER.

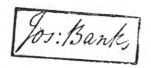

Jos: Banks

AVVISO.

E' uffizio d'un Calunniatore, e Malevolo, l'accufar d'un peccato colui, che conofce affatto immune da quello; del Satirico far palefe, e morder que' vizj, che sa, o fospetta negli Uomini ritrovarfi; ma l' uffizio del Critico fi è il notar folo quegli errori, da' quali penfa l'altrui mente ingannata, e portare contra i medefimi le proprie contrarie fentenze, guidato dal folo amore della Verità per pubblico bene. Di quefti tre così diverfi iftituti, il primo è certamente iniquo, ed ingiuriofo; il fecondo non è da condannarfi; il terzo da pienamente lodarfi (*).

(*) Vallisnier. delle vuov. delle Femin. Vivip. part. X. Cap. II.

L'ACCADEMICO
DELLE SCIENZE

A chi legge

Prendendo il RE nostro Signore grandissimo, e special diletto nell'osservazione di cose naturali più rare, di cui opportunamente sono questi suoi Regni feracissimi oltre ogni credere, e solendo assai volentieri trattenersi nell'esame delle cagioni, e de' rapporti che le cose anno infra loro, e di tutto ciò, che può servir di pabolo alle più composte menti di Filosofi assennati; quindi è che da tutte le parti, e dentro, e fuori de' suoi dominj, vengano alla giornata alla nostra Real Corte presenti speciosi di ogni genere di rarità, che in animali, e piante, che in altro. Nè solo ha questo Principe savissimo il gusto di vedere, ed osservare sì fatte cose; ma ne' casi più rilevanti ha ordinato pure, che se ne fosse scritto quanto la cosa comportava: ed ha voluto, che gli stranieri ancora, e gli assenti fossero stati in qualche modo a parte di quel giocondo spettacolo, di cui la Maestà Sua si era tanto compiaciuta. Tanto accadde nell'eruzione strepitosa del Vesuvio dell'anno 1737. tanto nel ricevere il dono di un grosso Elefante dal gran Signor de' Turchi. Di un Cignale parimente ucciso di colpo di archibuso da Lui, e che nello spararlo diede fuori del ventre una quantità di pallottole sciolte piene di acqua, qualche cosa pure ne fu scritto: ed ultimamente essendo morto un Leone nel suo Parco Reale, ordinò che ne fosse fatta

no.

notomia . Uniformemente a ciò essendo i mesi passati ca-
pitata alla sua Real Presenza una testa mostruosa di
Vitello, la quale esprimea due teste attaccate stretta-
mente insieme, ed appiccate ad un sol collo, e ad un
sol busto, comeche non fosse cotal mostruosità delle più
sorprendenti, poiche ne' Musei di cose naturali se ne
veggono di sì fatte assai frequentemente; si compiacque
nondimeno di vederne fatto il disegno: ed avendo man-
dato all'Accademia delle Scienze questa testa, perche vi
si facesse su qualche particolare osservazione, si è pen-
sato di accompagnare il disegno suddetto con alquante
riflessioni, ed illustrazioni sull'idea generale delle mostruosità solite a vedersi in ogni genere di animali, per
errore, come volgarmente suol dirsi, della loro primie-
ra formazione. Il che si è fatto in tal modo, che e gl'
intendenti di queste materie aver possano occasione di ri-
dursi a memoria le dottrine più celebrate nell'esame
di questi fenomeni: e coloro altresì i quali non anno
avuto luogo, e tempo di studiare ordinatamente queste cose, possano in qualche modo restarne istruiti, quanto si può
nell'oscurità somma, e da tutti confessata, di quelle
cose, che appartengono alla Generazione. Si spera che
il discreto Lettore, il quale si ricorderà dell'intendimento, che si è avuto in distendere questa Lezione, non
vorrà biasimarla per quella mezzana maniera in essa
tenuta, di spiegar le cose nè tanto sottilmente; ne all'
incontro con troppa materialità; maniera necessaria a
tenersi da chi volea riuscir bene del fine propossi.

L E fempliciſſime (1), ed ordinate leggi, delle quali nel-
A   la
  Parturient montes, nascetur ridiculus mus.

Finalmente il povero Sig. Accademico delle Scienze dopo sì lunga intumescenza di cervello ha, non so, se abortito, o partorito
un Moſtro! Poveretto, e che Moſtro! Un vitello con due teſte! Ognuna
che l'ha veduto girne sì gonfio, e pettoruto, cotanto allegro, e pien
di se ſteſſo, aspettava, che dalle profonde spaziose caverne del suo
cervello alla fine n'usciſſe un fiume di sapienza, un parto ben ordinato, e compoſto. Ma che! Ha per contrario versato un torrente d'ignoranza, un parto mal fatto, un Moſtro! Oh espettazion delusa! Egli
è, da quelche io veggio, pe' dolori sofferti, faticato, e ſtanco; perciò
non gli rincresca, ch'io il moſtro notomizzando, faccia sopra di
eſſo alcune oſſervazioni, per quanto le mie deboli forze permette-
ranno.

(1) Sempliciſſimi ſiam noi, Sig. Accademico, non la gran Madre,
e le di lei leggi. Hai tu forse letto della Natura le pandette? Aveſti tu
sì gran tesoro da quella Signora Nonna in dono, in retaggio, in
preſtanza? Dì finalmente per una sola volta la verità. Hai tu lette
quelle sempliciſſime, ed ordinate leggi; o parli, come il vulgo degli
uomini, che quelche non intende, semplice chiama? Tu che uccel-
lando alcuni Goccioloni dai loro ad intendere d'eſſere un gran
Meccanico, come in fatti lo sei, dì se la Natura, che è semplice, e per
vie semplici opera, e con leggi sempliciſſime, per qual ragione ha
fabbricato nel corpo degli animali una quantità numerosa di muscoli, i quali ſi riducono al vette di terzo genere, ſtrumento poco va-
levole a sollevare i peſi, perciocchè dee in qualunque caso la potenza eſſer sempre molto superiore alla reſiſtenza? Non era più semplice, che i muscoli opraſſero nel sollevare i peſi quai vetti di primo genere? Se Dio t'ajuti, Sig. Accademico, non sarebbe ſtato più semplice far dal ventricolo fin all'ano un inteſtino men lungo, men intri-
cato, e tortuoso? Senza dubbio. La conteſtura, la diramazione,
il consenso mirabile de' nervi, la fabbrica degli orecchi, degli occhi, del cervello, del cuore, e d'altri visceri, moſtrano non sempli-
cità, ma una compoſizione, un'artificio maraviglioso da confondere i più sublimi cervelli. Qualunque cibo, e bevanda, che giù per
l'esofago nel ventricolo ſi caccia, dee sù per l'epiglottide sdruc-
ciolare con pericolo di soffocazione, piccola porzione giù nella
                                                                    tra-

la formazione particolare delle foftanze (2) la gran Madre Natura fi avvale, e' fembra efser fin dalle fondamenta diftrutte dalla rara apparizione de' Moftri, refi di ogni tempo lo fcopo delle mareviglie degli uomini, fperimentandofi non folo nella vafta eftefa degli animali, ma eziandio nella innumerabile moltitudine degli alberi, e delle piante, ed in tutto quanto il genere de'vegetabili, come ne' fiori, nelle femenze, nelle foglie, ne' rami, e nelle frutta medefime; dove moftruofi attacchi, conneffioni, intrichi, e figure fogliono dì frequente ofservarfi.

Il perche ne'fecoli pregiudicati (3), e tenebrofi fono di
leg-

trachea cadendo; come avvenne al famoso Anacreonte (*) per un acino d'uva paffa; a Fabio Pretore (a) per un pelo nel bere il latte; ed a Druso (**) figliuol di Claudio per una pera. Maggior femplicità ftata non sarebbe porre prima il canal dell'esofago, e poi più in là la trachea, *ad fuffocationis periculum evitandum*. Ma *la gran Madre* mille comodi, da Noi non conosciuti, nè pensati, da una sola cosa ricava. L'intendimento umano è troppo corto, non può comprendere i mezzi del mirabil lavorio dalla Natura nelle di lei opere tenuto. Non dir più dunque *le fempliciffime, ed ordinate leggi*; poiche io ti risponderò, che tu non hai bene ftudiato la Notomia, nè sai punto della Storia Naturale.

Nè i moftri diftruggon, come tu dì, le leggi della Natura. Se tu conosciuto avefsi l' eftenfione dell' infinita potenza di lei nella produzione delle cose naturali, gli infiniti modi, e mezzi di operare, qualora ella tra'prescritti termini non fi mantenefse, e da quelli uscifse, avrefti allora motivo di dire, ch'ella non ofserva le leggi ftabilite; ma finche tu, *Sig. Accademico*, non dimoftri di aver veduto i termini'dell'infinita Potenza della *gran Madre*, tutte *le fempliciffime, ed ordinate leggi*, dir non puoi, che i moftri diftruggon le leggi della Natura.

(2) Non iftà ben detto, *Sig. Accademico mio, foftanza*; dovevi dire nella formazione de' Corpi; poiche foftanza è cosa generale, e comprende anche gli Angioli, i Demonj, gli Animi noftri, e Dio ftefso.

(3) Quali furon quei Secoli tenebrofi? Quando forse il Sole,
non

(*a) *Plin. lib. VII. cap. VII.* (**) *Sveton. in Claud. cap. XXVII.*

leggieri fufcitate tante , e sì varie ftravolte , ed incoerenti opinioni , fino a riputare i Moftri viventi ficuri effetti degl'incantefimi , o di altro diabolico artificio ; e perciò non mancavan le leggi di condannargli ad effer tofto affogati , e fommerfi nelle acque de'fiumi , e del mare . Altri gli ha riputati infaufti Nunzj, e Meffaggieri infelici di varie pubbliche calamità : a qual lentimento , dopo la superftiziofa Antichità , preftò tanta fede il credulo Pareo , che credette accefo quel gran fuoco di guerra tra' Pifani , e Fiorentini (per cui ne andò quafi in cenere l'Italia tutta), poiche poco tempo avanti era nato in Verona da una giumenta un puledro con la faccia di uomo: ficcome quel celebratiffimo Moftro nato in Ravenna l'anno 1512. precorfe di poco la rinomata battaglia feguita tra li due Efferciti di Giulio II., e Ludovico XII. Re di Francia .

  Molti han creduto effere (4) i Moftri pretti (5) errori della Natura , diventata talvolta smemorata , e fonnacchiofa. Altri gli ha riguardati , come macchine mifteriofe , ed a

A 2 qual-

non illuminava la terra di giorno , e la Luna di notte ? Que'poveri sventurati non ebbono la tua moftruosa lezione , che l'aveffe sgannati . Se foffi tu nato in quei tempi , avrefti loro senza dubbio aperti gli occhi , e la ftrada della verità moftrata

 (4) Queft'altra virtù tenevi nascofta? Tu sei un ottimo Copifta: aveffi almeno citato il Sig. Nigrisoli . Non iftà bene ad un uomo dotto , qual ti pretendi , trascrivere i periodi interi dagli Autori , e non far loro la dovuta civiltà di citarli . Sei tu dunque un Plagiario .

 (5) Chi sono ftati cotefti temerarj , empj , ed ignoranti ? Stimar la Natura capace di errare , chiamarla smemorata , e fonnacchiofa ? Che fien dati in tal empietà que' poveretti , che nacquero in que' Secoli pregiudicati , o tenebrofi , transeat; Ma tu che sei nato in un Secolo cotanto illuminato , tu che sai tanto di Mattematica , che puoi gloriarti di saper fare quadro il tonno , e tonno il quadro , sei caduto in tanta debolezza . Ma che fi vuol fare ; tu non hai ancora Logica ftudiato ; non sai perciò definire , dividere , e poi ragionare.

Tu

qualche intendimento dirette; ed altri infine affai più affen-
nato, ed accorto ha tenuto per vero effer i Moftri puri in-
nefti, ed accidentali accozzi, ed aggruppamenti di parti
nelle machine organizzate.

S'in-

Tu sei, *Sig. Accademico*, il terzo dopo Amafanio, e Rabirio, de' quali,
per bocca di Cicerone (*), così favella il dotto Varrone: *Didicisti
enim non posse Nos Amafanii, aut Rabirii similes esse, qui nulla arte adhibita, de rebus ante oculos positis, vulgari sermone disputant, nihil diffiniunt, nihil partiuntur, nihil apta interrogatione concludunt.*
La parola *Natura* è equivoca: ma lasciam da parte tutte le altre fign-
ficazioni, veniamo a quella, che i Fisici le danno. Natura, o dinota la
gran mole dell'Universo, o si prende pel di lui Fattore, e Conservatore.
Nel primo senso la Natura altro non è, che i Corpi: e poichè la materia, onde sono i corpi formati, è per sè stessa inerte; non è perciò di
operar bene, o male capace. Quella Sapienza, e Potenza infinita, che
l'Universo creò dal nulla, e con infinita Sapienza lo mantiene, essa è,
che nella materia operando, le cose tutte produce. La Natura dunque
operante è l'istesso che Dio: *Quoniam Deus ipsa Natura est*, scrisse (**)
Lattanzio; e più a proposito: (***) *Dum ego ipsam Naturam Deum esse
contendam; nec enim potest facere mirabilia, idest maxima, ratione
constantia, nisi qui habet mentem, providentiam, potestatem.* Vedi
dunque che tu bestemmi, quando dici la *Natura erra*. Chi riprende la
Natura d'aver errato, fassi a lei superiore, poiche ne conosce i difetti.
Dove tanta superbia *Sig. Accademico delle Scienze?* Torna in te stesso:
non vedi tu che dovunque fissiamo l'occhio troviamo cose, nella
contemplazion delle quali l'umano sapere si confonde, si perde. Noi
siam stati creati per ammirar le fattezze di questa bella macchina
del Mondo, non per saperne gli Arcani; per umiliarci nella con-
templazione di quelle, lodando, ed adorando il di lor Supremo
Fattore, non per gonfiarci, correggerlo, e censurarlo. Dopo tanti
secoli, dopo tante ricerche, tanti cimenti, tanti sudori, che sappiam
Noi, che siam venuti in questo secolo illuminato? O molto poco,
Sig. Accademico delle Scienze, o nulla.

Nè men siamo arrivati a comprendere la superficie de' Corpi:
ancora non sappiamo cosa sieno que' tanti, e sì varj colori, de' quali
i corpi, sopratutto i fiori, vanno con tanta vaghezza superbamente

ador-

(*) *Tuscul. quest. lib. I.*   (**) *Lib. de origin. error. pag. 210.*
(***) *Pag. 217.*

S'intende per Mostro qualunque Animale (6), che dalla
naturale organica conformazione si discosta gran fatto , in
guisa che può di ragione appellarsi più , o meno mostruoso
un animale, se di gran lunga, o per poco dall'ordine, e simmetria naturale allontanasi (7) . In tal senso , se si volesse
dar retta alla calda , e alterata fantasia de'Poeti , sarebbero
Mostri di grado sublime i Cerberi , le Sfingi , i Ciclopi , le
Idre , i Centauri ; nel qual ordine annoverar si potrebbono
i Mostri con più teste , con più braccia , e con numero, e
situazione sregolata , e non ordinaria di membra ; o pure
qualora nascon mancanti di molte parti . Tale per appunto
era il mostruoso Capro , che tempo fa ritrovavasi nel giar-
dino di Boboli, nato senz'alcun vestigio delle gambe ante-
riori ,

adornati . Siamo immersi in un abisso d'ignoranza ! Se dunque non
conosciamo i modi , i mezzi , de' quali la Natura nell'operar s'avvale , ed i fini , per cui tante cose produce , come vogliam credere
la Natura capace di errare , e chiamar errori que' prodotti , i quali,
come sian fatti , comprender non possiamo ?

(6) Io non so trovar la ragione , per cui tanto inimico della
Logica ti mostri. Ti metti a definire il mostro,e non sai quali,e quante cose debba avere una definizione , perche sia ben fatta . La prima
condizione necessaria è , che *debet constare ex genere , & differentia .*
Io mi vergogno, *Sig. Accademico mio*, di queste piccolezze ; ma come
tu non le sai, io sono in obbligo dirtele. Quella parola *animale, non
stai loco generis* ; poiche le pietre , le piante , le frutta non sono comprese in quella voce . Ma se m'opponi,
che hai voluto far del Mostro una definizione particolare , io non
ho , s'egli è così , che replicarti .

(7) Da questa definizione, *Sig. Accademico delle Scienze*,nasce,che tu
sei mostruoso , perciocchè hai così lunghi, e mal conformati i piedi,
ch'escon dall'ordinario , e *dalla simmetria naturale* . Ma tu non colpi
nulla in questo,poiche l'hai tu, ma la *gran Madre* formati . Tu
per certo non te l'averesti tanto in lungo tirati , perciocchè i piedi
lunghi sono Indicio d'un animo . . . . . . tel vò dire in latino , perche tu solo l'intenda *Oblongi pedes multa molientem , ac malorum ar-
tificem innuunt . Pedes plurimum prolixi , dolositatis , & perniciei
in-*

riori, il quale ingegnosamente 8) col petto callofo , e con le gambe deretane velocemente faltava , e fpeffo ritto a due piedi a guifa de' famofi Satiri (9) camminava. Moftruofi fog-getti eziandio appellar fi dovrebbono que', che confervano internamente un ordine contrario di parti;ficcome con pub-blica meraviglia,e ftupore nella fezione notomica d'un vec-chio foldato il Sig.Mery riconobbe vero quel, che da molti in diverfi cadaveri per offervato fpacciavafi; dove general-mente tutti gli organi,e le parti del baffo ventre,e del pet-to alla naturale , ed ordinaria fituazione fi divifarono inte-ramente contrarie .

I Moftri meno ammirabili , e più frequenti fono i ge-minati in tutto quanto l'ordine organico delle parti (10), e folamente in qualche regione del corpo attaccati , e , quafi diffi, inneftati, quali curiofi fpettacoli,non folo negli animali bru-

indicia præbent . Suum Pfeudolum Plautus , qui multa contra Leno-nem moliebatur , vafrumque hominem defcribens , ait , magnis pedibus effe; cui refpondens Leno: perii,inquit,quoniam dixti pedes. Quefto com-plimento te'l fa un gran letterato , il Signor Giambattifta Porta (*). Sappine profittare .

(8) Che domine dici : dai l'ingegno al capro : hoft eft fanctum da-re canibus . Grazie al Principe, che non ha il tremendo Tribunale del S. Ufficio ammeffo , poiche ora il rigido Inquifitore , Te , e'l Capro in ofcuro carcere metterebbe .

(9) Caro Signor Accademico delle Scienze , vuoi fin le favole adulterare. Fingevan gli Antichi il Satiro

    Mezzo uomo , mezzo capra , e tutto beftia .

Quel di Boboli piccolo , e tenerello effendo , s'alzava sopra le gambe pofteriori ; ma era tutto capro. Più moftruofo fu il porco,Sig. Accade-mico,di sei mefi,regalato al Sig.Vallisnieri (**) , nelle di cui opere fta Prima notato il porco, e poi il capro . Era il porco privo di tutte quattro le gambe , e fu creduto ermafrodita , ma non lo era .

(10) Che modo è mai cotefto di fpiegarti ? Confondi le parole, i fenfi in modo tale , che fembra , che parli Arabo . Sono

                                         i mo-

(*) De humana Phyfiognom.lib.II. cap.I. (**) Relaz.di varj moftri.

bruti,ma benanche negli uomini si ritrovano;così che spesse
fiate è accaduto essersi attaccati da prima : e poi venuti sù
crescendo soggetti di differentissima tempera , ridendo
l'uno,quando l'altro piagne,e giocolando l'altro quando dor-
me il compagno,siccome per tanti esempli nella storia naturale chiaro apparisce.

L'ultima differenza è di que'Mostri addoppiati in certe
determinate parti ; e singolari in tutto il restante del corpo;
ed a questa riduconsi i Mostri bicorporei , ma con un capo,
o pure quelli a due teste , o bicipiti , ma con un solo busto,
che sono invero maravigliosi , e più rari ; essendo piuttosto
favolosi , che veri que'Mostri dall'invenzione aggravati di
numero sorprendente di parti , non essendo confacenti alle
leggi inviolabili della gran Madre , che anche nelle mostruose stranezze , e negli errori (11) suoi suol mantenere
certi confini .

A quest'ultima differenza riducesi il mostruoso Vitello
con due teste presentato in questa Reale Accademia , dopo
essersene fatta altrove di tutto il tronco una grossolana se-
zione . Nacque adunque compiuto , e Perfetto in Piscopia
presso alla Città di Monteleone a dì 15. Marzo dell'anno
1744., riguardandosi unico , e singolare , oltre al capo,
in tutte le parti del corpo : uno era il collo , uno il fegato ,
il pancreas , il cuore : una spina , e tutto uniforme , e pro-
porzionato ad un solo compiuto animale. Tutta la mostuo-

sa

i mostri geminati più frequenti , e son prodotti , o dall'attacco scambievole in qualche parte de'loro corpi , o quando un membro , o più
nascono dal busto d'un solo corpo. Ma userai tu artificio in mala-
mente spiegarti , e non fart'intendere , perche rimanga in te solo ,
e non si diffonda il torrente della tua sapienza .

(11). Un'altra volta con questi complimenti.Credi tu forse trat
tar con tua Nonna , che sì spesso le ricordi gli errori ? E' vero che
non pochi Filosofi anno colla Natura le stesse inurbanità praticato ;
ma tu , che sei il piu garbato , il più gentil Letterato di Napoli ,

trat-

fa meccanica fi offerva nel capo, quivi effendo perfettamente addoppiato. Si attaccano amendue le tefte ne' lati interni delle offa temporali, e delle mafcelle sì fattamente, che la maggiore eftenfione delle medefime riman libera, e franca, e tanto fporta in fuori, che riguardandole dirimpetto, veggonfi le due tefte intiere, e perfette. Si offervano ricoperte di quel primo pelame proprio de' Vitelli, e in parecchi luoghi del comun cranio appajon certi rialti, ed imperfetti attacchi tra offo, ed offo. Compiuto era il numero de' denti per ciafcuna mafcella, e tutti bene incaftrati, ed allogati nelle proprie nicchie, o alveoli. Unico, e folo era altresì il gran forame dell'offo occipite (12), per dove comincia a diffonderfi la midolla fpinale; e fi vede fcolpito verfo la parte finiftra: Ma per quanto può dal decorfo degl'interni forami offervarfi, dal gran forame cominciava la doppia ramificazione de' nervi, e de' vafi (13); uno altresì effendo il canale dell'aria, ed uno quello degli alimenti, ma giunto nella parce deretana delle mafcelle, quivi con maraviglia s'ifcompartiva, reftando proporzionatamente le tefte del bifognevole provvedute.

Riefce intanto malagevole (14), e dura cofa a fpiegarfi, come un cuore baftato foffe a mantener libera, e franca la circolazione delle fluide foftanze in entrambe le tefte; e come

tratti così, come gli altri, rufticamente una veneranda Matrona!

(12) Non perder d'occhio cotefto *forame* : lì dentro fta il capo del gomitolo : ti prometto *taclo pectore* . . . . di fcioglierti tra poco, in luogo più a propofito, quel moftruofo nodo, di cui tu non fei affolutamente capace.

(13) Una è la verità, ma tu non la vedi, nè la conofci; uno è l'uovo, uno il tuorlo, uno il follicolo, da cui ti farò forgere il tuo moftro.

(14) Io non fo capire, *Sig. Accademico*, per qual ragione *ti riefca malagevole, e dura cofa* fpiegare, come un cuore baftaffe per la circolazione del fangue nelle due tefte. La tua difficoltà farebbe ragionevo-

le

me i doppj movimenti derivati da doppia forgiva avefsero
confervata quella fcambievole armonia con l'unico cuore
nel menzionato Vitello; ciò potendo verificarfi nell'utero, in
cui gran parte dell'impeto del fangue dalla Madre dipende.
Di quì è, che fomiglianti Moftri, o nafcono eftinti (ficcome
avvenne al noftro Vitello) o per poco tratto di tempo fogliono foppavivere .

Per ispiegare con la maggior chiarezza poffibile tali
moftruofe generazioni, che fono ftate fempre lo fcoglio, in
cui sfortunatamente fono urtati molti degli Antichi, e

B   de'

le, se avefli offervato i due cervelli, superar molto in grandezza là
mole d'un solo: se il cuore foffe ftato grande, quanto suol effere ordinariamente; ma poiche tu quefte cose del tuo moftro ignori, e degli altri addoppiati non hai letto le notomiche offervazioni; per
ciò la cosa ti sembra malagevole. A mantenere la circolazion del sangue nelle due tefte, altro neceffario non era, che le vene ripigliaffero
il sangue dal cuore, per le arterie nelle due tefte cacciato, e'l ri por-
taffero di nuovo nel cuore; il quale tanta potenza avendo di cacciar
il sangue nelle arterie, e di superar le refiftenze de' vafi, manterrà libera, e facile nelle due tefte la circolazione. Ma dì figliuolo, non
sono dal cuore più diftanti le due cosce, le due gambe, i due piedi, che
le due tefte? Il cuore non pertanto mantiene libera la circolazione per
quelle membra più lontane; e per qual ragione non la deve nelle più
vicine, comeche addoppiate? Tanto più che sogliono effere i cuori
ne' moftri addoppiati, molto più grandi dell'ordinario: e se ciò
vero non foffe, come pur troppo è vero, potrebbe il cuore la circolazion libera, e franca mantenere, e'l moftro vivo, ed intero
serbare. Il Principe de' Meccanici Giannalfonso Borelli dimoftra, che
la forza intera del cuore, colla quale spigne il sangue, ed ogni altra
salda parte del corpo muove, ha la ragione di 180000. ad 1.; e che'l
cuore di fatto poche forze adopera, ed impiega nel moto del corpo, non facendone di altre bisogno, che di quante baftano a vin-
cere l'intera refiftenza delle salde, e trascorrenti foftanze. Or se accade, che pe' membri addoppiati le refiftenze crescano, può il cuore
prenderne altra parte dalle sue forze morte, avanzar le vive, e così
promovere il giro de' liquori, il moto de' saldi, e la vita del moftro
conservare.

Pove-

de' novelli Scrittori (15) , ho riputata util cosa, ed al noſtro
propoſito confacente rapportare in accorcio le opinioni più
ventilate , e più celebri intorno a ciò ; ſicchè , o dalla loro
comparazione , e rapporto ; o dalla ſcelta , e diſamina particolare poteſſe rilevarſi la più vera , o la men contraſtata .

Suppongono alcuni , a'quali aggradiſce la Filoſofia mi-
ſterioſa , una forza ſpirituale penetrantiſſima , e priva di
qualunque intelligenza, od arbitrio , ch'entri, non per tanto
al gran lavorio della generazione, come formatrice particolare ; dirozzi, e ſtampi nell'uovo, o nell'utero l'embrione; ed
a ſomiglianza dell'idea archetipa di Platone (16) , ritenga la
ſua eſſenza anche , quando il compoſto è disfatto ; dal che
ha meritati varj famoſi titoli , di Forza Plaſtica , di Luce ſeminale , e di cento altre metafiſiche determinazioni affatto
affatto non inteſe dalla Natura. Or ſe queſta ſognata forza ſi
alteri , e ſi corrompa , l'impreſſione , e la ſtampa diverrà
moſtruoſa .

Nè vi ſon mancati di quelli , a'quali è piaciuto ricono-
ſcere l'origine immediata de'moſtri dalla varia fermentazio-
ne, e ribollimento delle particelle ſeminali dentro dell'uovo,
per cui prontamente più parti , e più membra nell'iſtante ſi
lavo-

(15) Poveri ſventurati ! La nave ſi è ſdrucita , e ſi ſono , per
ignoranza del Nocchiero , annegati . Dì , figliuol mio , un *De pro-*
fundis , in refrigerio di quell'anime miſeramente ſommerſe.

(16) *Quid Platoni cum monſtris ?* Che ha che fare il divin Platone co' moſtri ? Dov'entra l'*idea Archetipa* di Platone ? Per certo,
che tu ſei un uom d'Epicuro, d'atomi, a caſo, compoſto; poiche a caſo
non a ragion veduta, favelli. L'Idea archetipa dell'uomo è l'idea ori-
ginale , il modello , l'eſemplare , l'idea aſtratta dell'uomo , alla cui
ſomiglianza gli altri ſon formati . Ma tu coſa vuoi , che s'intenda ,
per quelle parole : *Ed a ſomiglianza dell'idea archetipa di Platone , ri-*
tenga la ſua eſenza , anche quando il compoſto è disfatto ? Platone non
diſſe mai, che l'idea archetipa formaſſe le coſe; ma che le coſe ſon fatte
a ſomiglianza di quell'eſemplare. Adunque nulla ha di comune la forza
Plaſtica ſpirituale, coll'idea Archetipa di Platone.   Co-

lavoraffero , e fi architettaffero, come per parecchi efempli
delle chimiche operazioni pretendono comprovare (17).
Qual fentenza , comeche appaja nell'efpreffioni ragionevole,
pure riguardandofi la maniera di operare , poco , o nulla di.
fcoftafi dalla forza plaftica accennata , ricercandofi un reale
principio , che formi , che architetti , e che fabrichi , ca-
pricciofamente fermentando due tefte, un cuore , e tutto il
maravigliofo concerto di tante macchine nel moftro archi-
tettate , e compiute.

(18) Maggior voga , e fpaccio ha incontrato l'opinione
di que'Filofofi, che la moftruofità de' bruti, o degli uomini
han ricavata dalla immaginativa , o fantafia de' Genitori.
E quì sì , che non pochi intrigatiffimi pregiudizj fi afcondo-
no ; poichè le graziofe novelle di tanti , e tanti, bene , ed a
fondo difaminate , non reggono punto al cimento della ragione , e della fperienza. Che l'immaginativa , alterando
i movimenti dell'utero, increfpando talvolta le fibre, e fpi-
gnendo con empito sregolato il fangue , produca nell'infen-
fibile macchinetta varie alterazioni nella grandezza, e *nella*
efterna divifa delle membra , con agevolezza s'intende :
che col movimento de' faldi impetuofo in vece di uno fi
ftacchino da' proprj picciuoli due uova gallate , donde pof-

B 2   fo-

sono sorgere, e nutricarsi i mostri addoppiati; o pure, che
per mezzo di quel turbato, e sconvolto empito de' fluidi
si stacchi di facile il feto appiccato al fondo della Matrice,
e ne succedan gli aborti, non involve alcuna difficoltà; ma
il voler poi credere, e tener per fermo, che immaginando
un Orso, o un Cavallo, o un Satiro, o vedendone la di-
pintura, abbiasi ad iscolpire nell'uovo quello, o quell'altro animale: nasca la ciriegia, la pera, o la prugna ne' luoghi, dove la Madre si è per caso, ed inavvedutamente toc-
cata in tempo, che quelle frutta ardentemente desidera-
va, questo è quello, che sembra pieno di fallacie, e di
pregiudizj. La donna è credula, e fantastica; le di lei fibre
sono sensitive, ed irritabili, accade una concrezione livi-
da, rubiconda, o giallognola, o ritondetta, *o pelosa* per
compressione, o strignimento, e depravata nutrizione di parte

per *false*, e *graziose novelle* ancora le voglie! Figliuol mio, se l'immaginazione, per te, può produrre alterazioni nel tenero germe, può
scomporre la simmetria delle parti (qual cosa, secondo la tua definì-
zione è mostruosa): e se l'alterazione può nella grandezza, e simmetria delle parti influire; per qual ragione non potrà produrre le voglie? L'argomento nasce dalle tue proposizioni. Quella tua *concrezione pelosa* mi fa insorgere un'altra difficoltà. I peli dell'uomo sono
in qualunque caso, nell'*esterna divisa* sempre differenti da que' del
Cinghiale, della Vacca, del Porco. Tutta volta osserviamo alcuni,
portar in qualche parte del corpo peli di Vacca, di Porco.

Il vulgo innocente, dice, che sien voglie. Tu se mi domandi,
che cosa io ne senta; ti rispondo, che fin'ora non ho argomenti
bastevoli, se negar le volessi, nè di francamente ammetterle.

Sono le donne, nella facoltà d'immaginare, all'uomo molto su-
periori, e per tali tutta la veneranda Antichità l'ha riconosciute,
e tu mal fai ad opporti, e negare una cosa, per consenso di tutte le
Nazioni, come vera tenuta, non che negli uomini, ma ne' bruti
ancora. Ricordati della storia delle pecore tra Laban, e Giacobbe.
Vedi quanto antica è la credenza! Se tu nieghi la gran facoltà d'immaginare alle donne; come *Domine* puoi dar conto di tanti strani
avvenimenti delle gravide?

Le

te , tofto fi prende quella marca innocente per prugna ,
per fragola , o per altra ftrana foftanza ; e già pare di ricor-
darfi quello talvolta , a cui non mai in tempo di gravidanza
la donna ha badato . Così , per far bianca , o nera la pelle,
io non so , fe bafta l'immaginare , e'l guardar fiffamente ad
un immagine efterna ; ma vi bifogna la ftruttura mecanica,
e l'orditura antecedente nell'uovo , nonche la particolare
azione del principio fecondatore . Adunque i Moftri nati
a cagion dell'alterata immaginativa per altre accidentali cagioni fogliono qualche fiata all'immagine premeditata fer-
bar fomiglianza ; ficcome con altre convincentiffime ragioni potrei dimoftrare .

Tralafcio a bella pofta moltiffime altre oppinioni , che
alla

Le voglie , o fieno que'ardenti appetiti , a' quali foggiaccion le
donne , fon cosa troppo chiara , e manifefta ; e fe una voglia è capace d'indurre uno sconvolgimento nel corpo tutto , specialmente nell'
utero , e di far abortire , che tanto vale , di aprire i vafi , spre-
merne il sangue , ftaccar la placenta , e cacciar fuora il feto immatu-
ro : per qual ragione non potrà l'imaginazione agire in un vifcere ,
qual'è il campo della generazione , in cui esercita tanta potenza ,
ed in un corpo tenero , qual'è l'embrione ? Io non oso negarlo . Le
ftorie di tanti Scrittori , il giudizio di tanti Maeftri , l'offervazioni
quotidiane , e finalmente il consenso di tutte le Nazioni mi eftor-
quono la credenza , comeche io non sappia nè 'l modo , nè i mezzi
com'ella operi l'immaginazione. Ma senta, figliuolo: Noi non poffiam
negare tutto quel che non comprendiamo , nè sò quante , e quali fien
quelle cose in Fifica , le quali poffon dalla mente umana effer chiaramente comprese . So che'l feto è un animal da se , altra comunicazione
colla Madre non avendo , che per l'attacco delle spoglie nell'utero ,
per mezzo delle quali paffan i sughi dalla Madre nel corpo del feto . Ciò non oftante non so , nè poffo negarla francamente , come tu
hai fatto . Annovero quefta cosa tra le altre , sopra delle quali niun
uomo , per dotto ch'egli fia , può dar un decifivo parere .

Io so che cotefto sentimento non è tuo , ma d'un dotto Medico
Inglese il Signor Giaccmo B'ondel . Ha quefti a bella pofta scritto un
libro sulla forza dell'Immaginazione . Tu se'l modo d'argomentar intendi , ben veder puoi , che i di lui argomenti fon la maggior parte
ne-

alla generazione de'Mostri appartengono, come quelle, che gran tratto si allontanan dal vero (19), bastandomi per ora mette-
negativi, e pieni di sofismi. A dichiarar falsa una cosa, non basta provare, ch'ella è stata detta, o scritta da un uomo, il quale altre volte ha mentito. Se questo argomento valesse, poiche tu sei a sbagliar così pronto, niuna cosa, da te detta, credenza meritarebbe. Altro non prova l'argomento, che la cosa è dubbia, e che ha bisogno d'esame, non già che sia falsa.

Nel nominar ch'io ho fatto la storia di Giacobbe, tu hai fatto il solito riso Sardonico. T'intendo. Il Signor Blondel nel Supplemento, alla Dissertazion Fisica, conoscendo, che tutti gli argomenti addotti contro l'Immaginazione, non avrebbono quell'approvazione avuta, ch'ei credeva, meritassero; s'impegna finalmente ad interpetrare altrimente la storia di Giacobbe, dandole altro senso, altra lezione. Confessa, che la versione Inglese è molto difficile a chiaramente comprendersi: ora vuol, che le verghe sieno state poste nell'acqua per fortificar gli uteri delle pecore: altra volta ricorre a miracoli; ma dica ciocch' e' vuole il Signor Blondel, dal testo della nostra vulgata è chiaro, che l'astuto Giacobbe scorticò parte delle verghe di Pioppo, di Platano, perchè le pecore concependo, partorissero gli agnelli di varj colori chiazzati: *Posuitque eas* (cioè le verghe) *in canalibus, ubi effundebatur aqua, ut cum venissent greges ad bibendum, ante oculos haberent virgas, & in earum conspectu conciperent: Factumque est, ut in ipso colore coitus oves intuerentur virgas, & parerent maculosa, & varia, & diverso colore respersa* (*). Ecco spiegato chiaramente il motivo, per cui usò l'astuzia Giacobbe: ma tu dirai dietro al Blondel: io non veggo sempre avvenire coteste cose, come dovrebbe essere, se ciò vero fosse. Adagio figliuolo, non giudicar sempre *more solito*. L'immaginazione non è in tutte le donne eguale: quindi avviene, che quando la potenza immaginativa è robusta, dirò così, straordinaria, può in certe occasioni, in alcuni punti, in certi stati di spirito, e di corpo, turbare, alterare, confondere la connessione, l'ordine, il sito delle parti dell'Embrione, ed altre cose, come noi giornalmente l'osserviamo. Non è dunque vano il ricorso de' Filosofi all'immaginazione, chiare ragioni, e sufficienti non avendo da cacciarla dal campo della generazione delle voglie, e de' mostri.

(19) Ma tu figliuolo, che tratti con tanta confidenza con cotesto Cavaliere *del Vero*, rimetti, per tua fè, nella strada della verità quei poveretti, che ne sono allontanati. Io ancora, così negli anni avanzato, come sono, vorrei il piacere, che tu quel vero conoscer mi

(*) *Gen. Cap.* XXX.

mettere in chiaro le due più plaufibili , e più celebrate fentenze ; la prima delle quali è quella di fare i vermi fperma-
tici fabri de'Moftri ; la feconda è quella delle uova.

Offervato il seme de'maschi con finiffimo microfcopio ,
ritrovafi pieno zeppo d'innumerabil turba d'infetti d'una
determinata figura,che tutta quella maffa ravvivano, fcon-
certandofi , e guizzando in varie guife nella maniera de'pe-
fci . Li partigiani di sì fatto fiftema fi vantano d'aver veduti , o han creduto di vedere cotali infetti effer veri , e reali
feti di quella medefima fpezie , nel feme di cui annidano ,
involti in una fottiliffima membrana , e quafi che immafche-
rati , e coperti nella figura de'vermi ; in modo che tengon
per fermo , che i vermi spermatici dell'uomo fono tanti
omaccini , que' de' Cavalli tanti puledri , que' de'Tori tanti vitelli . Or (20) , fe accada , che due de'menzionati meno-
                                                            miffi-

mi faceffi . Ne ti rincresca figliuolo , che se tu mi farai la carità di
farmi vedere la bella faccia della Verità , io te la renderò , moftran-
doti gli errori , ne' quali fei non volendo , caduto.

(20) Nel fistema de'Vermicelli spermatici , che fian vermifeti,
fi poffono chiaramente spiegare quei moftri congiunti , o in una
parte , o in parecchie ; ma que' che nascono con le membra raddop-
piate , non poffono in conto alcuno spiegarfi . Va , e leggi quel trattato *de ovo* (*) , *ovi aere* , *&c.* dell'incomparabil Bellini , e troverai,
ch'egli confidera l'animale in tre ftati molto tra loro differenti : *dum*
fit , cum jam factum eft , & ultimo , cum ex utero exclufum eft . I moftri veri s'ingenerano , quando l'animale fi fa , cioè quando le parti
integranti fono teneriffime , e fluide ; ma quando è formato , allora
fatta effendo la congiunzione, la giacitura, e l'attacco scambievole delle
parti , non poffono più confonderfi con altre : non può dunque gene-
rarfi il vero moftro , bensì una congiunzione , un'attacco efterno di
due corpi , li quali fono impropriamente moftro chiamato . E le co-
ftantiffime *preffioni di due vermi ?* Che preffioni figliuolo : cotefti viventi fono solamente vifibili coll'ajuto di finiffimi microscopj , come
quelli,che di ftrana picciolezza fono,e dovunque fi ficchino,faran mai
sempre tra loro lontani . Effi fono liberi nel seme , non fi congiungo-
                                                                    I. D,

(*) *Digreff. de ovo , &c. Prepoft. X.*

miſſimi viventi ſi avanzino inerpicandoſi, e ſi caccino dentro
dell'uovo, o, come altri vuole dentro della Matrice : e
quivi giunti, e ſtivati l'un l'altro ſcambievolmente premen-
doſi, giungano a tal grado le compreſſioni, che un buſto
più forte prevalga al meno forte, ed impediſca in queſto
l'ulteriore diſpiegamento di parti; fintanto che s'invinci-
diſca, privo del neceſſario nutrimento, e ſi logori, e ſi diſtrugga, reſtando libero, ed aggrandito il buſto predomi-
nante : mentre tali coſtantiſſime preſſioni ſeguano nella maniera deſcritta, e reſti libero, e franco il diſpiegarſi delle
teſte ſuppoſte dell'uovo in tal ſituazione, ne avverrà il Moſtro bicipite, doppio ſolo nel capo; ma unico, e ſingolare
nel buſto. Se poi per altre cagioni ſi deſſe luogo a tre,
quattro, o più vermi di farſi ſtrada, ed allogarſi entro dell'
uovo, naſceranno Moſtri di ſtraniſsima differenza. Tal forſe riconobbe l'origne, e 'l naſcimento il ſerpentello a due
teſte notomizzato dall'oculatiſſimo Redi (21).

Speſſe fiate la compreſſione (22), e 'l diſtruggimento dello Sviluppo accade nelle teſte, coſì che una più vigoroſa,
e meno premuta ſi diſpieghi, e quaſi ſoffoghi la più premuta, e più debole, e la diſſecchi, e diſtrugga; ed in tal modo
naſce il vivente con una teſta perfetta, ma raddoppiato in
tutto

no, non ſi attaccano, non ſi premono, non s'inneſtano, non oſtante
che in poca porzion di ſeme ne ſtiano, e guizzino francamente millioni di millioni, e poi due in un uovo per eſſi vaſtiſſimo Paeſe,
ſi vogliono ſtivati, e compreſſi ? Eh via, che tu parli a caſo, e quelche dici, non intendi.

(21) Che linguaggio è mai coteſto ? Spiegati più chiaramente:
ho ſquinternati i Leſſici tutti, e non ho potuto trovare di quella
voce *tal forſe* il valore.

(22) Un'altra volta colla compreſſione. Che credi figliuolo,
che ſtiano ſotto al torchio ? Sono que' vermifeti in luogo capaciſſi-
mo, vaſtiſſimo : aveſſi tu tanto un Feudo, che ſareſti il più ricco
de' Baroni del Cilento.

Sarà

tutto il reſtante del corpo ; e tale doppia diviſa , oltre tanti altri eſempli , moſtrò la talpa del Signor Capello , che avea una teſta ſola , e un collo ſolo con l'ordinaria proporzione formati con due corpi diſtintiſſimi dotati delle quattro ſue gambe.

Ed ecco , che il più luminoſo (23) , e'l più accettato Siſtema dello Sviluppo arreca qualche ſembianza di vero al più ſpiritoſo , e bizzarro ritrovato , in credendo quegl'inſetti cotanti reali viventi di quella preciſa razza , in cui annidano.

Ma la baſe , sù di cui ſta fondato il ſiſtema de' vermi è vana , e fallace ; conciofiachè la diloro figura (24) niente ſi adatta a quel , che pretendono rappreſentare ; la di loro moltitudine innumerabile, in guiſa che in uno impercettibile ſpazio migliaja , e migliaja ritrovanſi, dimoſtra chiaramente eſſer contrario al buon ſenſo, ed alla buona ragione il ſupporre , che uno , o due di quegl'inſetti eſſer debba fortunato abitatore dell'uovo ; e che tutta la reſtante numeroſiſſima moltitudine debba miſeramente perire. Inoltre tutti quanti i licori del corpo umano ſono pieniſſimi di vermi particolari , li quali , come in amichevol terreno ſi nudriſcono , e muovonſi ; onde la linfa ammette i ſuoi niente meno , che il ſangue , la bile , ed il ſeme : altri vivono nel ſegato , altri nelle budella ; e così di mano in mano ciaſcuna ragione del corpo conſerva i ſuoi particolari viventi ; perloche può ,

C

(23) Sarà mai qualche ſiſtema Celeſte , s'egli è cotanto luminoſo ? Se la generazion degli animali foſſe da que' vermicelli , non ſi farebbe concetto , il quale non ſarebbe moſtruoſo ; poiche in ogni schizzata di ſeme, ſi caccian nella femina millioni di millioni di vermicelli .

(24) Che ragione è mai coteſta figliuolo ? Credi tu , che l'embrione dell'Animale , allorche ſi fa , quella figura ſerbi , che dopo fatto , ed è fuor dell'utero ? T'inganni .

Il Se-

può, come per conseguenza dedurſi, eſſer tutt'altro l'uſo
de'vermicelli spermatici, ſiccome con maravigliosa avvedutezza, e ſoprafino diſcernimento ha dimoſtrato il famoſiſ-
ſimo Vallisnieri .

Di quì è che il Levennoechio, comeche provveduto
di mirabili , e ſorprendentiſſimi microſcopj non potè mai,
ricercando, oſſervare alcuno (25) inſettto nella cicatrice dell'
uovo d'una gallina teſtè fecondato dal gallo , quantunque
aveſſe più, e più volte iſtituita la ſteſſa sperienza, per raſſo-
dare il ſuo specioſo ſiſtema (26). Piuttoſto riuſcitebbe all'
ope-

(25) Il Segretario della Regia ſocietà d'Inghilterra (*) ſcriſſe
al Signor Levenoechio, che aveſſe ricercato il vermicello nell'uovo fecondato, e ſe mai l'aveſſe trovato, ſi ſarebbe la ſocietà perſua-
ſa della verità del ſiſtema : cioè, che i vermicelli spermatici foſſer
i feti naſcituri , ma non avendolo veduto, non ſiegue che non vi ſia;
poiche ſe in una mole di ſeme , che ſta in una punta d'ago appiccica-
ta , ſe ne veggono molte migliaja; un ſolo non ſi potrà mai vedere:
direbbe un partegiano de' vermicelli , ſta confuſo , ed imboſcato il
verme tra le linfe .

(26) Per qual Teatro Sig. Roberti, per quello di S. Carlo, del
Teatro nuovo , de'Fiorentini , o pel Teatro della Lava *riuſcirebbe
coteſt'opera ? Se'l nuovo ſtupendo ritrovato riuſciſſe all'opera , tu* ſareſti cotto; perciocchè ſareſti obbligato ammettere il germe moſtruoſo;
cioè, che i moſtri naſcono per vizio d'uno, e non per la congiunzione di più uova . *Il nuovo ſtupendo ritrovato di quell'inſetti , che tagliati in pezzi ,* quaſi novelle Idre metton fuora e capo, e coda,
ſenza dubbio è maraviglioſo - E qual coſa di queſto Mondo non
è mirabile ? S. Agoſtino qualche coſa di ſimile nella ſcolopendra
oſſervato avea , allorche in pezzi tagliata, ſeguiva caminare .
La proprietà di quell'inſetti la troviamo ancora nelle piante : tu
forſe non l'avrai notata . In ogni punto della pianta, ſien le bar-
be, ſia il tronco, ſien ovvero i rami, evvi un principio, una potenza di produrre germi, fiori, frutta, e ſemi, e da quei ſemi
altre piante . Volli un giorno calcolare quanti ſemi contenea in
que' baccelli una pianta di Joſquiamo, ne contenea intorno a ſedici
mila . Quella pianta nacque da un ſolo ſeme ; ſicchè in un picciolis-
ſi-

(*) *Valliſn. de Vermicelli spermatici part.1. cap. 9. pag. 127.*

opera de' Moſtri il nuovo ſtupendo ritrovato di quella razza d'inſetti , che tagliati in più parti , a capo di tempo
ciaſcuna diventa un inſetto organico intiero ſomigliantiſſi-
mo nelle fattezze , e nell'ordine di parti al di loro tut-

C 2   to

ſimo granello ſtava tutta la pianta , e que' ſedici mila ſemi , ciaſ-
cun de' quali contenea i ſtami della pianta futura con un numero ſtravagante di ſemi , ed in que' ſemi altre piante . Che imbro-
gli , che confuſioni ! Figliuol mio , queſto è 'l vero moſtro ; queſta
è coſa veramente ſtupenda , non già la tua bicipite vacca . L'intendimento umano non può queſti arcani della natura capire , ne'l ſenſo della viſta ſa ritrovare nella corteccia degli alberi ombra
veruna d'occhi : con tutto ciò dove il ſenſo non trova principio
alcuno apparente di germi , da quel punto fa l'infinita potenza faſci
di rampolli pullulare . Tanto può a' menzionati inſetti avvenire : e ſe non è moſtruoſo nelle piante reputato ; per qual ragione lo dev'eſſer negl'inſetti?
    Se foſſi , figliuol mio , un po più pratico nella Zootomia , tan-
te meraviglie non fareſti . Sappi dunque , che la Natura ha molti
inſetti aquatici , e terreſtri ſenza cervello formati ; ma ſe non gli ha
dato il cervello , ha dati loro più cuori . Va , e leggi un po la notomia de' Lumaconi fatta dal Redi , ed in eſſa troverai ancora la catena de'cuori , che ſta lungo il corpo de' Lumaconi diſteſa , potrebb'
eſſere lo ſteſſo di quell'inſetti , che in pezzi tagliati , rimangon vivi ,
e non periſcono;perciocchè in ciaſcuna di quelle ſezioni rimane uno,
o più cuori . E poiche i liquori de' medeſimi ſono tenaci , e molto
viſcoſi ; perciò non eſcon fuori da vaſi reciſi , reſtan chiuſi , ed
a loro pigri motori , quali ſono i cuori , ſubordinati . E fuor di
dubbio , che la diviſata viſcoſità de'liquori far poſſa luſſureggiare ,
e creſcere l'inciſe parti , come alcune volte avviene alle piaghe :
quindi è che mentiſcono intanto il capo , ma vero capo non è :
Queſto non è luoco, nè tempo di ragionare di queſta ſtupenda apparenza ; puoi però da ciò comprendere quanto ſia più maraviglioſa
la propoſta germinazion delle piante ; intanto niſſun Filoſofo , ch'io
ſappia , l'ha moſtruoſa chiamata , come nè men tale può quella degl'
inſetti chiamarſi : e quando queſto *ſtupendo ritrovato ſi verificaſ-
ſe; come piuttoſto riuſcirebbe all'opera de' moſtri ? Per te il moſtro è qualunque animale , che dalla naturale organica conformazione ſi diſcoſta
gran fatto: di queſti inſetti diviſi in pezzi , ogni parte diventa un inſet-*
                                                                      to

to (27). Cofa , che fe mai fi verificaffe negli altri viventi ,
indicibile , e ftrano fconvolgimento, nella Natura s'ifcorge-
rebbe.

Cheche ne fia di tali fentenze, uopo è rifletter fonda-
tamente fulla bafe più certa , ed appoggiata fopra ftabili
offervazioni , e fperienze di moltiffimi Scrittori dalla fa-
ma , e daltempo celebratiffimi . Quefta è per appunto il
determinare , che tutto nafce dall'uovo , nella cui men o-
miffima cicatrice fta delineata , e fcolpita con tutta la diftinzione (28) la macchinetta del futuro vivente quale , per
mantenere , e confervare l' intiera ftruttura , e pofcia
a tempo manifeftarla , d' altro non ha di bifogno, che
d'un movimento intimo delle parti , che vien communi-
cato dal mafchio : quindi comincia lo sviluppo, l'ingrandi-
mento , e la calata dell'uovo, nella Matrice , dopo efferfi
ftaccato , a guifa di maturo frutto pe'l picciuolo dall'ova-
ja ,

to organico intiero , fomigliantiffimo nelle fattezze , e nell'ordine di
parti al di loro tutto : dunque non moftro , ma vero infetto farebbe.
Come domine piuttefto riufcirebbe all'opera de'moftri?

(27) Non si fconvolgerebbe , figliuol mio , la natura, no ; ma
il tuo , il mio cervello , ed i fiftemi tutti . Dì , s'è sconvolta, perche
tanto fuccede nelle piante ?

(28) Come hai tu sì belle cose veduto, coll'occhio nudo,
o da microfcopj ajutato ? Nè men nella cicatricola del pollo fi veggono con diftinzione quelle cose, che tu dì : bifogna, che ti
prendi un po di faftidio . Va, leggi Aiveo, e'l famofo Malpighi (*) :
penfa , e poi fcrivi ; fon certo , che allora non ifcriverai : nella cui
menomiffima cicatrice fia delineata , e fcolpita con tutta la diftinzione
la macchinetta del futuro vivente . Dove domine l'hai letto ? Il Sig.
Vallisnieri , da cui hai la tua lezione copiata , tanto dir non ardi-
sce;poiche non ebbe mai la fortuna di veder l'uovo . Ma fe'l fegreto
trovato avefti d'aver tralle mani l'uova delle donne,e fopra di quelle
già fatto avefli le tue distinte offervazioni , io mi rimetto , e chieg-
goti di questa nota , perdono .

Non

(*) De ovo incubato.

ja, a cui appiccato trovavaſi. Fa duopo por mente alla
picciolezza dell'uova, eſſendo quaſi inviſibili, e per con-
ſeguenza alle di lor cicatrici di gran lunga minori ; nè ſia
meraviglia, ſecondo riflette un dotto Scrittore, ſe i vola-
tili fanno le uova loro viſibili, e palpabili con la croſta,
o boccia duretta a proporzione del peſo delle Madri, perche debbono tenerle a covare, e debbono naſcere i loro
figliuoli perfetti da quelle : ma li vivipari fanno le uova
loro, o fecondate, o non fecondate così ſtranamente pic.
cole, così diafane, e d'una membrana teneriſſima veſtite,
che è affatto impoſſibile di diviſarle, eſſendo floſcie, ce-
devoli, ed acquoſe.

Giunto dunque il menomiſſimo uovo nella Matrice,
come in proprio adattato terreno ſi apprende, e ſi attac-
ca al fondo di quella, eſſendo inumidita, e ſpongioſa ;
onde comincia una nuova meravigliosa circolazione tra la
madre, e'l feto, e nell'interno de'vaſi dell'uovo vieppiù
energetico, e vigoroſo diventa il moto progreſſivo de'liquidi ; ſicchè tratto tratto ſi diſpiegano i canali, e ſi
ſvolgono, e ſi ſviluppano in guiſa (29), che paſſa il rin-
chiuſo, e rannicchiato vivente per varj ordini di gran-
dezze,

(29) Non v'ha dubbio, figliuol mio, che'l ſiſtema dello ſviluppo è'l più proprio a ſpiegar le apparenze della generazione ; ma
egli è ancora circondato di ſpine. Tutto il germe ſta in punto ri-
ſtretto : in queſto punto ſtanno in piccolo tutte le parti dell'animale, le quali, ſviluppandoſi, divengon ſempre maggiori. Nell'idea
dunque dello ſviluppo, altro non è, che quelch'era piccolo, poco
a poco creſcendo, compariſce maggiore. Secondo queſto ſiſtema,
nell'ovario d'Eva, furon tutti gli uomini paſſati, preſeti, e futuri,
e dall'uomo non dee altro, che uomo ſvilupparſi ; tuttavolta, ſtu-
penti Noi, oſſerviamo alcune fiate, uſcir dalla donna alcuni
corpi in tutto dagli uomini differenti. Nell'anno 41. del ſe-
col corrente, nel meſe di Giugno, una oneſtiſſima gentil Donna,
madre di più figli, in età d'anni 35. partorì dopo d'un maschio,

una

dezze , e di sviluppi a renderfi col tempo nella fua propor-
zionata grandezza . La femplicità , e l'uniformità nell'
operare della Natura favorisce oltremodo il fistema delle
uova ; conciofiacche i femi , o fiano uova delle piante ,
nelle quali ancora in riftretto tutta la pianta delineata , ed
iscolpita
una Lepre . Eccone la ftoria (*) : Nel quinto mese della gravidanza , ftando ella d'ottima salute , le fu innanzi portata una Lepre ,
dalla cui veduta fortemente turbossi , e piena di collera ordinò ,
che glie la togliessero preftamente di Casa . Cadde intanto in una
profonda tetraggine , spesso dicendo , che quella Lepre dovea esser
cagion della sua morte . Nel profeguimento della pregnezza , co-
minciò lamentarsi d'un dolor mordente nella parte siniftra dell'addomine , co'sfinimenti di cuore , accompagnato : rimase intanto
inabile a poter di casa uscire . Nell'ottavo mese , a tanti mali s'ag-
giunse una perdita di sangue dall'utero smoderata , e fi vide da sfinimenti più spessi , accompagnata ; dopo due giorni di flusso , cacciò
un bambino perfettamente formato , ma morto ; reftò nondimeno
nella finistra parte dell'addomine una dura elevazione ; stando
l'infelice Puerpera tutta raffreddata .
Dopo dodici ore per la vagina un altro corpo comparve , il
quale l'accorta Levatrice fuori tirando, trasse una Lepre, Leprissima:
avea i denti , e peli , specialmente que' lunghi a' confini della bocca , la coda , gli orecchi , e tutto ciò che in una Lepre si vede . Fu
sul fatto chiamato il Signor Pietro Ferrara , Medico molto accorto ,
il quale stava in altra stanza aspettando , che la Levatrice quel corpo fuori tirasse. Crebbono tutti i mali alla Puerpera , e'l giorno dopo se ne morì . Stette questa Lepre molto tempo in casa del Sig.
Casimiro de Alteriis , il quale avea più volte la sua vicina Puerpera
visitato . Quivi tutta Napoli la vide : *tu quoque Brute fili mi* . La
vide il Sig. Sarao , e nel mezzo delle meraviglie proruppe: *è troppo lepre* . Io che per l'addietro avea il Pareo , il Liceto , e gli altri Scrittori de' mostri favolosi reputati , non volli credere il fatto; perciocchè mi sconvolgea il cervello , la storia della generazione , e'l fistema dello sviluppo. Osservai più volte la Lepre , ed avendo fatto una
scrupolosa ricerca delle circostanze del caso , da Medici molto accor-
ti , che l'assisterono , fui , *volente* , *nolente* , a crederlo costretto .
Or via figliuolo , non perdiam tempo : o'l fistema dello sviluppo a
terra ,

(*) Quéfta ftoria non è presa dal *credulo Pareo* , o dal *Boriofo Li-*
ceto.

iſcolpita ritrovaſi , innaffiate , e coperte in fecondo inu
midito terreno , ed alterate dalla calda luce del Sole ,
d'altro non han biſogno , per apparire , e manifeſtarſi ,
che del ſolo ſviluppo : lo ſteſſo principio , e la ſteſſa mecanica (30) ſi ammira negli animali , che nel modo di generarſi poco ſi diſtinguono dalle piante.

Tutta

terra , o la fantaſia in campo. Scegli , e preſto ; qual delle due coſe
vuoi, che ferma rimanga?

I Difenſori dello ſviluppo , ch'ammettono l'immaginazione ,
come cagion produttiva de' moſtri , anno queſta uſcita , e reſta
ſaldo il di lor ſiſtema : ma tu avendo all'immaginazion tanta potenza negato , che riſponderai ? Sviluppa queſto gomitolo ? Sciogli, ſe puoi, queſto nodo ? A che penſi ? Altro ſcampo non hai , che
negar la ſtoria , e coſì facendo , tu opereresti contro la propria co-
ſcienza , contro la verità ; poiche il caſo è più che vero , ed i teſti-
monj di veduta , quai ſi trovarono all'eſtrazione della Lepre dalla
vagina , ſon molto oneſti , e ſinceri , niuna cagione avendo d'im-
porre , d'ingannare , e mentire . E quando tu credere a coſtoro non
voleſſi ; come dubitar potreſti del Signor Ferrara?

(30)   Molto , figliuol mio , differiſce la meccanica delle piante da quella dell'Embrione degli animali. La pianta ſta mirabil-
mente in piccolo nel ſeme delineata , come in molti ſemi , ſenza
microſcopj , appariſce , non eſſendo altro il ſeme , ch'una piccola
pianta : ma la macchinetta del futuro vivente nell'uovo rinchiuſa ,
non è coſì ordinata , e diſegnata . Di queſta materia non ſappiam
altro che quello , ch'è ſtato nell'uova delle galline oſſervato . Nella
cicatricola dell'uovo , anche per più giorni ſtato al calor della chioc-
cia , ſi raſſembra un corpo , il quale nulla ſomiglia al pulcino

Il cervello è per cinque veſciche rappreſentato ; il cuore per un
tubo in ſette cavità diviſo , tre grandi , e quattro piccole ; ſe coſì ,
come a polli accade , a' vivipari ancora avveniſſe ; noi nol ſap-
piamo figliuolo : l'argomento ſarebbe preſo dalla ſomiglianza ; ma
gli argomenti a ſimili, io non molto gli prezzo , nè in eſſi mi ripoſo.
Non perche l'aria rinchiuſa , ed enormemente compreſſa , ſcoppia ,
dee qualunque ſcoppio eſſer dall'aria prodotto ; poiche la polvere da
ſchioppo , e l'oro fulminante , l'iſteſſo effetto partiriſcono . Una
ſtilla d'acqua , ſe per avventura nel metallo fonduto cadeſſe , quale
ſtrepito , e ſcoppio , ſenza paragone più grande della polvere da

ſchop-

Tutta queſtà ſerie regolatiſſima, ed uniforme ſuole
talvolta da non poche accidentali cagioni ſconvolgerſi, e
perturbarſi, dal che con agevolezza gli Animali moſtruoſi
traggono il lor naſcimento; imperoche fecondate, e po-
ſte in movimento dall'attività della ſpiritoſa ſeminale ſo-
ſtanza, non uno, ma due uova (31), per eſempio d'una
vacca; ed amendue calate, e ricevute nella cavità della
Matrice, ſe per qualche ignota cagione accada, che ſi
accozzino, e ſi avvicinino inſieme nel luogo appunto delle menomiſſime cicatrici, dove ſta delineata per delicati
impercettibili ſtami la fabbrica de' Vitelli; e la maggior
compreſſione; e combaciamento ſucceda dal collo in giù,
ne avverrà, che mancando affatto lo ſviluppo in una delle
cicatrici più premuta, darà queſta luogo all'accreſcimento
d'un ſolo buſto, e d'un ſolo unico corpo; di modo che
lo ſvolgerſi, e'l diſpiegarſi riman libero, e franco nell'attacco delle due teſte.

Nè ſembra ſpinoſo, e difficile sì fatto ſiſtema, qualora ſerioſamente ſi riflette alla menomezza delle uova,
e delle cicatrici, alla molle, e pieghevoliſſima teſſitura
                                                      delle

schioppo non produrrebbe? Chi ſa, quanti altri corpi vi ſono,
i quali, o ſoli, o con altri maritati, anno quella proprietà di vio-
lentemente, rarefacendoſi, ſcoppiare. Dì: è la ſteſſa meccanica?
   Ma torniam là, donde partimmo. Niſſuno finalmente ha
veduto davvero l'uovo de' vivipari, dopo molte ore, nonche inan-
zi la fecondazione. Il germe degli ovipari è accompagnato da
chiare, tuorli, calaze, membrane, e cortecce, delle quali coſe il
germe de' vivipari è privo, come ſuperflue. Or ſe niuna ſomiglianza ſi nota, tra'l germe del pollo, e quello delle piante, come
ardiſci tu paragonar il germe delle piante a quello de' vivipari,
di cui non abbiamo conoſcenza, ma congetturando, ne ragio-
niamo?
   (31) Se così andaſſe, come tu dì, la faccenda, i moſtri ſa-
rebbono più ordinarj, e frequenti, ſopra tutto in quei animali,
                                                      i quali

delle fila, che le compongono (32), onde poſſono prenta-
mente attaccarſi, e comprimerſi alcune parti, altri rima-
nere imperfettamente diſpiegate, alcune celarſi affatto,
e coſì di mano in mano talmente mutarſi, ſchiacciarſi,
o in altra guiſa apparire, che moſtri ſtravagantiſſimi ne
dipendano.

Ed invero giuſta il penſamento del Valliſnieri poſſono naſcere i Moſtri da due, o più capi, o con altre membra, e parti moltiplicate, e inſieme, come ramo con ramo
attaccate, o incaſtrate, e fatto di due tronchi un ſolo tronco; perciocchè due, o più germi, o due, o più uova mature poſſono in uno reſtringerſi, o acccozzarſi, e coſì
ſtrettamente combaciarſi, che col tempo s'attacchino, ſi

D

com-

i quali partoriſcono molti figli; come ſono le cagne, le ſcrofe, ed
altri animali. Ha la *gran Madre* in eſſi fatto altrimente gli uteri,
avendoli non di una cavità formati, ma in due lunghi tubi, *Corna*
dagli Anatomici chiamati. Quivi molte uova fecondate, diſcenden-
do, ſi ſituano in tanti lochetti, uno ſeparato dall'altro. Se tu aveſſi qualche volta notomizzato una cagna, un gatto, una ſcrofa gravida, avreſti ſenza dubbio veduto, come ſtanno coſì bene ordinati,
e l'uno dall'altro ſtaccato. Se dunque nelle Corna di que' uteri, molte uova in ogni gravidanza diſcendono, ed i moſtri, in coteſti animali, ſono rariſſimi, allora quando dovrebbon eſſer frequentiſſimi;
conchiuder biſogna, che i moſtri non avvengono da due uova, per
accidentali cagioni inſieme accoppiate. Ma io ſtupiſco, *Sig. Accademico*, quando rifletto a' topi, i quali piccoli di corpo eſſendo, tuttavolta in ogni parto danno moltiſſimi topini alla luce, tutti ben
fatti, e non moſtruoſi. Se i moſtri naſceſſero per accoppiamento di
due uova, ſenza dubbio l'anguſtie degli uteri riguardando, in
ogni parto dovrebbon da topi moſtri fuora cacciarſi. Nell'uomo
i gemelli ſono molto frequenti, ed i moſtri troppo rari; creder perciò biſogna, che i moſtri, altro principio abbino, che quello, che
tu oſtinatamente difendi.

(32) Tutte coteſte circoſtanze figliuolo; *erravi*: dir dovea, *Sig.
Accademico delle Scienze*, ſono tutte incluſive per la quotidiana comparenza de' moſtri, ſpecialmente negli animali moltipari; ma ciò
non avverandoſi, nè men quelche tu dì, ſarà vero.

Sig.

compenetrino, s'intrighino, e un folo corpo confuso,
e addoppiato compongono (33). Ciò appar manifefto nelle
uova delle galline, che anno due, o più tuorli, donde
nafcono polli con due, o più capi, o con le membra moltiplicate.

Se poi al contrario qualche Moftro nafca fenza il capo, fenza cervello, fenza braccia, o gambe, tutto dipende
dal non efferfi sviluppato quel membro, o quella parte;
o per cagion comprimente a lui efterna, o interna non di-
la-

(33) *Sig.Accademico*, invidio la tua franchezza nel decidere un
punto tanto difficile, tanto da' fenfi lontano, tanto mifterioso. La
franchezza nel decidere, senza dubbio nasce, o dal saper a fondo
di quella cosa, o dal saperne nulla. Chi è colui, *Sig.Accademico*, che
ha in tutte le parti conosciuto il mistero della generazion naturale? E se quefta non è chiara, non evidente, tuttoche ordinaria;
come tu pretendi saper, in che modo vada la faccenda ne' cafi
ftraordinarj; cioè nella morbosa, o sia mostruosa generazione?
Sarà dunque vera la seconda parte; poichè di nulla sai, francamente decidi: eccone le pruove così chiare, così evidenti, che maggiori
non si poffono defiderare.
*Ciò appar manifefto nelle uova delle galline, che anno due, o più
tuorli, donde nafcono polli con due, o più capi, o con le membra moltiplicate.* Ben si vede, *Sig.Accademico*, che tu non hai Logica ftudiato; perciocchè sì spesso cadi ne' paralogismi. Così va ne' polli:
dunque così va nell'uomo. E dove hai tu mai letto, che l'uovo
della donna tien le chiare, e'l tuorlo? Sai tu a che servono que' liquidi, e per qual motivo l'infinita Sapienza l'abbia infieme chiufi
nella corteccia? Ciò appar manifefto. Che cosa appar manifefto? Tu
non sai di quefta voce il valore. *Manifeftum (*) pro eo fumitur, quod
ita clarum, ut manibus quafi palpari poffit.* Vuol dire cosa chiara,
senza dubbio, evidente. E fuor di dubbio, che due tuorli faccian due
tefte? Signorsì, è fuor di dubbio, *Sig.Accademico*, che tu non
sai nulla della ftoria della generazione. Senti un poco, che dice
Ariftotele dell'uova gemellifere.
Egli fu di parere, che schiudono due pulcini, de' quali
uno è maggiore, l'altro minore, e quefti non è mai vitale;

(*) *Vofsius hac voce.*

Ova

Ova (*) gemina binis conflant vitellis, qui in aliquibus tenui albuminis
diffepimento feparantur, quo minus inter se confuli fint ; in aliis nullum
eft, fed fe mutuo contingunt . Sunt nonnullæ gallinæ, quæ omnia ge-
mellifera pariunt, in quibus quod evenire vitello diximus, perfpectum
eft ; quædam enim cum duodeviginti peperiffet, exclufit geminos, nifi
quæ irrita fuerunt . Verum ita fit, ut ex gemellis alter major fit,
alter minor, & tandem in monftrum degeneret, qui noviffime pro-
venit .

Non t'appigliafti, *Sig. Accademico delle Scienze*, a quel *tandem in*
monftrum degeneret . Già vedi, che parla del minor pulcino, non del
maggiore; se moftruoso diviene, non è per la congiunzione di due
tuorli, qualmente tu hai scritto . Chi *domine* dunque te l'ha pofto in
mente ? .... Chi chi? La Nonna tua tel diffe ? E tu sì fatte dicerie al
Prencipe, iftruirlo volendo, racconti ? Senti me, piuttofto dì ; quel
gran Fabricio lo scriffe;non quegli dico,che saldo ftette,e punto non
fi commoffe dalla profferta dell'oro fattagli dal Re Pirro,e cotanto in-
trepido all'impensato barrito dell'Elefante moftroffi ; ma Geronimo
Fabricio Aquapendente,il quale scriffe così(**):*Quod fi interdum ovum*
duos obtineat vitellos intra fe pullum cum quatuor cruribus, vel alis,
duobusque capitibus, & id genus monftra pariat ; numquam tamen duo
invicem separati (ut duo dici poffint) pulli funt, fed unus dumtaxat
corporis truncus eft, qui duo capita, quatuor crura, aliaque hujusmo-
di annexa habeat . Di quefta opinione fu dal di lui scolare Arveo
corretto, il quale nell'esercitazione XIII. (***) contro al maeftro
scrive, che da due tuorli nascono due pulcini, comeche non amendue
vitali, ma uno mai sempre perisce. E nell'esercitazione XXVI. *de*
ovis gemellivicis più a lungo, e più a fondo va quefto punto esami-
nando, e per iscemarti la fatica, se mai voglia ti veniffe di riscon-
trarlo, vo dirti come comincia, e qual finisce l'esercitazione vigefi-
ma fefta . Il principio è quefto : *Gemellifica ova funt è quibus gemelli*
prodeunt pulli . Il fine : *Veruntamen ubi duo vitelli diftincti fuerint,*
duabus tunicis propriis diffepti, & grandinibus fuis, albuminibus, cæ-
terisque ad fœtus generationem neceffariis inftructi, cum Ariftotele
concludendum cenfeo tale ovum, ut partes omnes (præter corticem)
duorum ovorum habet, ita, & potentias quoque obtinere, ac nifi infœcun-
dum, aut urinum fuerit, DUOS PLERUMQUE FŒTUS PRODUC-
TURUM; rarò autem monftrum fingulare. Vedi dunque, *Sig.Accademi-*
co delle Scienze, quanto sei scarso di notizie; quanto sei novello nella
ftoria della generazione . Dovevi tutt'i cafi diftinguere, ne' quali

D 2   poffo-

(*) *De hift. Animal. lib.6. cap.III.*
(**) *De format. ovi, & pulli pag. 19.*
(***) *Degenerat. Animal.*

posson̄o i moſtri generarſi ; e queſto il primo caso sarebbe .

Se in un tuorlo ſiano due macchiette , due cicatricole , potrebbono queſte fecondate , nel dilatarſi, confonderſi , e farsene un follicolo contenente due germi , ma confuſi , ed imbrogliati . E poiche nel tempo , che quella confuſione accade, i germi sono teneriſſimi (*) , liquidi , poſſono allora facilmente le parti unirſi , e di due pulcini formarsene uno moſtruoso , o con due teſte , o con quattro piedi , o con quattro ale .

Secondo : se l'uovo due tuorli contiene , due chiare solamente , due gallature ; diviſi dagli albumi non eſſendo i tuorli , posſono le cicatricole , crescendo , incontrarſi , e congiungerſi : potrebbe allora la cennata confuſione de' germi facilmente avvenire ; come conobbelo Ariſtotele(**), Fabricio (***) , Arveo (**,*) , ed altri .

Terzo : se saran due tuorli , e ogni tuorlo abbia la cicatricola , due chiare avvolte , due calaze ; cioè se ſi daſſe , come infatti ſi danno , un novo , che conteneſſe due tuorli , quattro chiare , quattro calaze, ſi formaranno allora due pulcini , de' quali uno sarà vitale, l'altro no, come sopra, per oſſervazion d'Arveo,e d'Ariſtotele *abbiam provato* .

Il quarto caso sarebbe , quando il germe nella cicatricola contenuto , foſſe moſtruoso ; lo che più diſtesamente appreſſo dimoſtreremo.

Se tu aveſſi coſì ragionato , avreſti ben fatto , nè potreſti, *Sig. Accademico delle Scienze* , eſſerne ripreso . Ma guarda bene : queſti raziocinj, non sono dimoſtrazioni, anno anch'eſſi i loro nei , nulla di ſmanifeſto , d'evidente avendo , come tu , sconſideratamente hai scritto ; e dovevi ancora sapere , che sono congetture , riſpetto solamente a polli , i quali nascon dall'uovo , contenente , e tuorli , e chiare , e calaze , e membrane , delle quali cose il germe de' vivipari , provveduto non eſſendo , scriver non dovevi , che la tua bicipite vacca , dalla congiunzion di due tuorli , ſu moſtruosa formata . Tu sei di molte cose alla generazione pertinenti affatto digiuno,ed hai avuto il cuore di far in pubblico su di queſta materia una maeſtrevole comparenza . V' è tuttavolta chi;è ſì cieco degli occhi del corpo, e della mente, che te, per Ippocrate tiene, e bandisce,

(*) *Germen vix à vero liquido differt , tam facile diffluit . Bellin. de motu cordis prep. IV.*

(**) *De Hiſt. Animal. lib. 6. cap. III.*

(***) *De format. pulli , & ovi.*

(****) *De generat. Animal.*

latante (34) ; o pur, che impedisca l'allungamento di que'
tuboletti, o vasi, che la compongono.

I Mostri più stravaganti, e più memorabili saran
quelli, ne'quali sonosi confuse, ed intrigate nel bel princi-
cipio della calata nell'utero le cicatrici delle uova ; que'però, ne'quali, o dopo qualche tratto di tempo sonosi riunite,
e congiunte ; o pure è stata debole la di lor compressione,

non

disce. A me solamente dispiace, che tu in casa insegni a' giovani
gli elementi della Medicina. Giovani sconsegliati, ed ingannati, in
qual fonte torbido a dissetarvi andate? *Dici non potest quantam
mentibus coecitatem, quantos pariat errores, ignoratio veritatis* (*).

(34) Tu sei'l più sagace ricercatore della Verità, il più acu-
to scioglitor di problemi : ammiro la tua prontezza nel decidere
i fenomeni più intricati, ch'an fatto, e fanno torcere il muso, e gi-
rar il cervello agli uomini più savj, che sono stati, sono, e saranno.
Tutto dipende *dal non essersi sviluppato quel membro, o quella parte* :
E per qual cagione ? *O per cagione comprimente a lui esterna* : male-
dette le compressioni, e chi te l'ha ficcate nel cervello : o *interna
non dilatante*. La cagion dilatante interna è il cuore, e quando
manca, non è più vivente ; sarebbe in quel caso, un pezzo di car-
ne. Se tu mi domandi, per qual ragione, e come si generò quella
mola ; ti rispondo per vizio del germe. E chi produsse nel germe
quel morbo ? Sai tu come rispondeva quel Fisico incomparabile,
l'Etrusco Ippocrate, Lorenzo Bellini in casi simili ? *Neque scio,
neque me scire posse, fateor*. Sei tu dunque, mi dirai, un ignorante. Così non lo fossi, come io lo sono ! I talenti non sono a tutti
stati egualmente distribuiti : tu n'hai molti meritato ; perciò non ti
rincresca. *Sig. Accademico delle Scienze*, di togliermi alcuni scrupoli,
che mi seccano il cervello.

Ordinariamente i montoni, ed i castrati anno il capo armato
di due corna : spesse volte avviene, che n'abbino tre, ed altre
volte quattro : avrei un desiderio scolaresco di sapere, come ciò
avvenga. Ricorrerai alla congiunzione, e compressione di due macchiette, volendo spiegare le corna geminate ? E se così è ; quando
sono tre corna, saran, per la congiunzione d'un uovo, e mezzo,
prodotte. Che ne dì ? Non dovrebbe andar così la faccenda ? E
poiche siamo alle corna, sciogli ancora quest'altro nodo : Per qual ra-

gio-

(*) *Lactantius de vera sapientia lib. III. pag. CCCLIII.*

non coſtituiſcono l'oggetto di gran meraviglia ; come ſono
i Moſtri attaccati , o nelle parti deretane , ma perfetti in
tutto il rimanente de' loro corpi ; o vero attaccati davan-
ti : ciò , che ha dato largo , e ſpazioſo campo di filoſofa-
re,
gione que'utiliſſimi animali ſolamente ſon ſogetti alla moſtruoſità
delle corna , e le vacche no ? Non avendo io trovato alcuno , per
molti che n' abbia richieſti , d'aver vacche , bovi , o tori , con
tre , o quattro corna veduto . Sono da un Amico ſtato aſſicurato ,
che n' l borgo di Chiaja vi ſtia un ragazzo con due membri genitali.
E' quiſti ancora moſtruoso ? Senza dubbio . E come lo ſpiegheresti ?
Non altrimenti , credo , che per la congiunzione di due uova , e per
la tua dottrina delle preſſioni.
     Di tutte dunque le parti d'un germe, fu il ſolo membro genitale
fortunato , a non rimaner compreſſo . Che fortuna di queſto , e qual
diſgrazia mai fu del rimanente ? Per queſto caſo , io non dirò mai ,
che la natura ha errato ; poiche ſon certo , ch'ella ha colmato alcuni animali di tal privilegio . Il camaleonte è di due forti , e robuſti
membri generatori armato : tali ſono i ramarri, le rane , i ſerpenti ,
tra' quali alcuni l'anno in quattro diviſo (*).
     L'ordinario dell'uomo è l'aver due teſticoli, chi n'ha tre, ſecon-
do la tua definizion del moſtro , è moſtruoso . Come mai, Sig. Accademico delle Scienze, renderai ragione di coloro, ch'àn tre teſticoli, ſpecialmente di quella famiglia di Bergamo , da cui molti naſcevano ,
tre teſticoli portando (**). Dì , come fu il ſolo teſticolo eſente dalle
preſſioni ? M'indovino , Sig. Accademico, che tu dopo aver molto
penſato , le due cicatricole , e le preſſioni laſciando , riſponderai : che le corna , i membri genitali , i teſticoli , le mani a sei
dita , le lucertole a due code , ſi debban ripetere da un principio di fecondità , di luſſo della natura . Dunque i moſtri ancora dallo ſteſſo principio , ripiglierò io . Non è men artificioſo un
membro genitale , nn teſticolo , un deto , una coda , un corno ,
d'un braccio , d'un piede , d'un capo . E ſe la natura luſſureggia
nelle corna , ne' membri genitali , ne' teſticoli , per qual ragione non lo potrà nelle altre parti ? Scrutare (***) tu cauſas,
quæ tantum miraculum efficiunt , mihi abundè eſt ſi ſatis expreſſi quod
efficitur .
                                                                    Se

(*) Valliſn. notom. del Camaleonte.
(**) Graaff. de virorum organis . & Fernel. Pathol. lib. 1 cap. 8.
(***) Plin. lib. I V. Epiſtolarum XXX.

re , e determinare ((35)), se i pensieri in amendue fossero
li medesimi ; se un' anima fosse quella , che reggesse i due
corpi ; oltre a tante curiosissime inchieste Fisico.teologi-
che , le quali han chiamate in campo asprissime , e calde
quistioni .

Sappiamo ancor noi di quanta forza , e vigore ella sia
la forza de'contatti scambievoli (36) , o nelle parti de'vegetabili , o in quelle degli stessi animali: due pomi , due ci-
riegie , due pera , che nel loro principio di picciolezza
eran di molto vicine , sì fattamente dopo il decorso di
tempo si legano , si rinchiudono , e si combaciano , che
porgono bastante argomento a giudicar lo stesso de' Mostri ;

(35) Se avessi tu coteste cose con quattro , non con due
occhi veduto , senza dubbio con minor precisione , e sicurtà
parleresti . Altro non restava , che avessi fatto egualmente di Teo-
logo la comparsa , come l'hai fatta di naturalista , comeché infelice.

(36) Che'l contatto nelle frutta ne renda molte , allorche
son piccole , e tenere , mostruose ; egli è senza dubbio verissimo,
sopra tutto ne'fichi , e prugne ; frutta , le quali , perciocché a grap-
puli pendon dà picciuoli , si congiungono facilmente . Quì là cosa è piana : tutta volta nell'uve questo contatto , molte acina far-
ne dovrebbe mostruose ; nulladimeno sono rarissime , e quell'acino , che addoppiato si vede , perloppiù pende da un solo picciuolo ;
sicché manifesto apparisce(quì va bene,Sig.Accademico delle Scienze,
l'espressione) che l'acino era mostruoso fin dal tempo , ch'era un
atomo . Quella compenetrazione , che tu dì a fichi avvenire ,
non è compenetrazione ; da ciò chiaramente si conosce , che tu
sei molto semplice , e niente informato della gran madre natura .
Que' Filosofi , che qualche cosa ne sanno , chiaman fecondità ,
e lusso della Natura , quelche tu chiami mostro , ed è in tutta la
Natura manifesto . Tanti fiori , tante frutta , tanti semi , quando pochi basterebbono. Tanti animali,tanti insetti sanno quel lusso uni-
versale; puro effetto d'un infinita Potenza,e Sapienza,così nel farle,
come nel conservarle.Hai tu mai veduto,Sig.Accademico,tante specie
di Ranuncoli, di Gelsomini , di Giacinti , di Rose semidoppj , doppj , triplj ? Tu l'hai senza dubbio veduti ; ma nissuno argomento
n'hai

ſtri; porché occorre ſpeſſe ſiate oſſervar confuſi talvolta in un ſolo i picciuoli, o peduncoli, ch'eran prima diſtinti così come le ſteſſe frutta compenetrate (37), e confuſe ſino alla metà, e nelle rimanenti ultime porzioni compiute, e diſtinte.

Che poſſano le parti molli, ſpongioſe, e dilicatiſſime tra

n'hai tratto. Che ti pare, ſon moſtri, o nò? Avrai tanta fronte di ſoſtenere una generazione di moſtri, e dir ad ogni paſſo alla *gran Madre*, Signora Nonna, erraſti? Chiamar moſtri le più belle, le più giulive, le più vaghe opere della Natura? *Nihil ſentire eſt melius, quam tam prava ſentire* (*).

E' vero che'l Signor Vallisnieri, là dove de'moſtri ragiona, fa una deſcrizione d'un limone moſtruoſo, ch'ei chiama bruciforme; ma queſto non conferma il tuo parere. Sono negli agrumi quell'eſcreſcenze frequentiſſime. Ho io con meraviglia veduto un albore ben groſſo d'aranci, il quale in un anno non portava un dieci aranci buoni, comeche nella corteccia ineguali, e granelloſi; tutti gli altri eran nella buccia ſtranamente conformati: chi rappreſentava un animale, altri molti al vivo quella parte, che più d'ogni altra, tengon celata le donne: altri quella dell'uomo, e dentro quel corno i ſpicchi con de' ſemi. Tu detto l'avreſti per certo, un arancio cornuto. Il mirabil era, *Sig. Accademico*, che coteſte produzioni, non eran al gambo attaccate, ma ricreſcevan dalla corteccia; que'piccoli ſpicchi avean ſolamente alcune corde, per le quali communicavano co'vaſi deferenti del nutrimento ne'ſpicchi grandi. Dì, ti fidereſti colla *congiunzione* de' germi, o colla dottrina delle *preſſioni* ſpiegar coteſta ſtrana apparenza? Non vedi che ſono produzioni di germi da germi, e ſi fanno in un modo da noi non conoſciuto; almen io, come che corſo abbia molti, e molti anni, e qualche coſa veduto delle grand'opere dell'infinita ſapienza, e potenza, non pertanto nella conſidazione di sì fatte coſe, come di altre moltiſſime, baſſo la teſta, chiudo gli occhi, mi umilio, e la mia ignoranza confeſſo. *Nec me pudet, ut iſto, fateri neſcire, quod neſciam* (**).

(37) Io non ſo coſa tu vogli, che s'intenda per *compenetrate*. Queſta voce fiſicamente preſa, vuol dir, entrare, ficcare, perforare

(*) *Cic. Academ. queſt. lib. II.*
(**) *Tuſcul. 1.*

tra loro intrigarfi , e , quafi difsi , inferirfi , o incaftrarfi ,
può fenz'altro dubbio vederfi in coloro , che han fortito
dall'utero il labro detto di lepre , val quanto dire aper-
to con grande sfenditura nel mezzo a fomiglianza delle
lepri : alla quale organica affezione la Chirurgia efficace
preftamente rimedia , con efcojare gli orli incalliti , i
quali artifiziofamente unifce , affetta , e ftrettamente con-
giugne , ed in tale novello contatto per mezzo di ceroti ,
e di fafcie per alcun tempo rafferma , e raffoda , onde una
perfettiffima inferzione , e quafi continuazione maravi-
gliofamente fi fcorge (38) . Lo fteffo avvenir fuole a i

E lem-

re , &c : : come per efempio l'acqua ha penetrato la vefte ; cioè l'ha
paffata , e fimili : ma tu la prendi quì nel fignificato di *rimefcola-*
re , e confufe . Rimefcolato , e confufo diciamo il vino coll'acqua ,
ma fenza moftruofità .

Veniamo al cafo de'fichi , i quali tralle altre frutta , fogliono
frequentemente offervarfi geminati : lafciamo quei , che appariscon
congiunti di picciuolo , e di corpo , e que' folamente confideriamo ,
ch'anno un folo gambo , ma in circa dalla metà del fico par che
sbucci un altro mezzo , e talvolta il terzo ancora ; e quelche degno ,
Signor Accademico delle Scienze, a me fembra d'offervazione , fi , che
cotefto fenomeno è molto frequente , ed ordinario in quella fpezie di fichi , che volgarmente chiaman *Ottati* , negli altri rara effendo . Vuoi tu dunque che quella metà , al gambo attaccata , fia com-
penetrata , e confufa coll'altro fico : ma dì , con qual microfcopio
l'hai tu veduto ? *Sunt hæc delirantium fomnia , non phil fofantium*
judicia. Signor Accademico mio , tu per certo deliri .

Ma ftà faldo : torna in te fteffo , e dì , que' fichi fono femidop-
pj , non altimente che de' fiori diciamo ; e ficcome nel feme , o ra-
dice , ftà quella Potenza di produr fiore da fiore ; così nel fico , ed
altre frutta evvi una Potenza di produr fico da fico ; tantoppiù ,
che sì fatte cofe fpeffo fpeffo offervanfi ne' terreni graffi , e fera-
ci . Luffureggia , *Signor Accademico mio* , la Natura nelle piante ,
ne' fiori , nelle frutta , ne' femi , negli animali , nelle pietre , ne'
minerali .

(38) *Signor Accademico mio* , or sì conofco , che fai a fondo
la Chirurgia efficace . Per qual ragione laffù nella Cattedra non
apri-

lembi jnterni delle dita impiagate , qualora per poca ac-
cortezza si sta lungo tempo , senza spesso disgiugnerle ,
e separarle.

Or , se tutto ciò si divisa nelle parti più dure , più
resistenti , ed all'accesso dell'aere sempremai sottoposte ,
con quanto più fondato giudizio possiamo conchiudere
essere agevolissimi cotali innesti, ed attacchi , e mostruosi
tà nelle molli picciolissime cicatrici(39) dell'uova per qualche cagione accidentale congiunte , ed in alcuni luoghi
fortemente compresse , nelle quali lo sviluppo più libero , e più impetuoso opprime , e distrugge il più premu-
to , e'l più debole . Nè perciò sarà malagevole il determinare , che intanto , o son favolosi , o rarissimi li Mostri di quattro , o più teste , o pure somigliantemente
moltiplicati nelle altre parti , in quanto che l'impedimen-
to dello svillupparsi , la massima scambievole compressione , e la disadatta cavità della Matrice (40) tutto il pro-
gresso , ed accrescimento impedisce .

Io
apristi allora cotesta vena chirurgica ? Dio tel perdoni ! Con coteste
fasce , e ceroti , avresti intenerito que' cuori marmorei , e senza
dubbio in tuo favore ligati · Saresti ora Cattedratico.Chirurgi-
co efficace · Ma sta zitto : studia bene , e per diritto : fa provvisione
di cose buone , che sapendole nella prima occasione smaltire , ti da-
rem la Cattedra ; e te , e'l tuo Precone consolaremo.
  (39) Cosa credi tu , che sieno le cicatrici ? Tu per certo le
credi rammarginamento di qualche parte · Sarai , se così vuoi , un
gran Chirurgo , ma non gran Fisico · Sono le macchie , le cicatricole un sacchetto , un follicolo contenente il germe di quell'animale , di cui sono · Quel germe stà chiuso , ed impriggionato tra
più membrane , le quali formano il bozzolo . Non vedi tu , che tanto facile non è la congiunzione de' germi, e la pressione delle di loro
parti ; poiche sono molto frequenti i gemelli , ed i mostri troppo
rari . *Ubi est acumen tuum* (*) ?
  (40) Ch'è domine tu di : io giurerei , che nulla sai di Notomia

(*) *Tuscul. quæst. lib.II.*

In fine non deve porfi fotto filenzio il penfamento ingegnofo del Signor du Vernei il giovane , a cui piacque in occafione d'un Moftro geminato efpofto all'Accademia Reale delle Scienze nel 1706. , ributtar con veemenza (41) di fpirito tutto ciò , che fi è detto intorno ai Moftri fol generati dalle uova infieme accozzate variamen,

E 2

mia , o per lo meno t'è uscita di memoria . E' l'utero un viscere di membrane compofto ,molto arrendevoli,e dilatabili. Perviene alle volte l'utero in un punto di dilatazione,che tre,quattro,e cinque feti contiene, tutti l'un dall'altro ftaccati, non congiunti, non compreffi,non moftruofi.E fe cinque uova nell'utero non han fatto un moftro, chi farà mai cotanto ignorante , che vorrà farti buona la tua propofizione, che i Moftri fi fanno per la congiunzione di due uova , e per la diloro compreffione ? Io tengo per fermo , che la vera cagione , per cui non fi sono congiunti , e fatti moftruofi , sia, ch'eran tre , quattro , o cinque germi , ma tutti ben orditi , e compofti .

(41) Quefto tuo risentimento , Sig. Accademico delle Scienze, pecca un po , non vò dir altro, di temerità . Eh chi sei tu , che vuoi correggere un de'più dotti uomini della più illuftre,e veneranda Società dell'Europa, e sopra quelle cose, che non ha mai penfate,nè fcritte? Dovevi almeno farti carico, che iftruendo un Prencipe di una sì chiara, e gloriosa Stirpe, bisognava,che favellaffi con un pò di maggior civiltà, e ritenuezza. Se cotefta tua lezione nelle mani del Segretario di quell'Accademia, come facil cosa sarà , perveniffe, che diranno ? Che faranno nel veder a torto, e così rufticamente ripreso, e calunniato un uomo, il quale è ftato uno de' più illuftri membri della di loro società ? Che bel giudizio faranno de' Medici Napoletani , effendo tu , tra tutti , ftato trascelto per ammaeftrare un tanto faggio Monarca sopra la materia de' Moftri geminati? Diran,che tu sei'l più dotto Naturalifta,il maggior Medico, il maggior Filofofo di quanti ne sono presentemente in Città, effendo tu ftato il più abile reputato . Quando poi la leggeranno , diran senza dubbio:oh che gran Medici:oh che gran Filosofi sono in Napoli ! Ed ecco ragionevolmente , per te, Signor Accademico delle Scienze , avvilita tutta la Repubblica Medica Napoletana . Egli è giufto dunque, che innanzi, che quella Veneranda Società giudichi, dalla tua lezione , finiftramente de' Medici Napoletani , un d'effi face

mente nel principio della generazione per diverfiffime accidentali cagioni ; affermando egli , che la via più fem-
plice , e più fpedita a dare adequata ragione de' Moftri

                                       fia

faccia loro vedere, chi sei tu, quale è quanta opinione s'abbia di te,
e quanto male hai fatto nel censurare il Sig. Verney, il di cui parere, Sig. Accademico dello Scienze , non hai letto , o compreso. Ecco
l'occafione , che impegnò quel gran Uomo a ragionar de' Moftri.
    A dì 19. Settembre del 1706. Caterina Fevillet , moglie di Mi-
chele Alebert , giardiniere nel Villaggio di Vitry vicino a Parigi ,
per la sesta volta gravida , partorì, con qualche stento, nel principio del nono mese , due gemelli , i quali formavano un corpo con-
tinuato , ed eran infieme congiunti nel fondo dell'addomine . Così
che , le cofte destre , e finiftre eran nel di loro principio unite . Nel
confine dell'uno addomine, e dell'altro, uno era il bellico egualmente
dalle due tefte diftante , e da cui un funicolo sorgeva d'un uraco , di
due vene , e tre arterie composte . Uno dunque era il cordone um-
bilicale, una la placenta, ma molto più dell'ordinario grandi: aveau
le membrane , l'agnina , e'l corion comuni . Non avean forame
alcuno nell'ano , ma due membri maschili co' loro testicoli : dalle
piccole verghe , l'una pofta a destra , l'altra a finiftra , cacciavan
l'orina, e sterco infieme rimescolati , e sciolti. Vissero fin al giorno
26. dello stesso mese d'Agosto. Il più forte morì tre ore prima dell'altro , e morti essendo, notomizzolli. Tutto il mirabile ftava nell'addomine. Ciascuno i proprj visceri conteneva, se non che le inteftina tenui terminavano in un colon comune, e questo in un sacco delle due
vesciche orinarie, tra di loro communicanti, compofto. Mettevan capo in effe quattro ureteri, da' quattro rognoni staccati, portandovi
dentro l'orina, la quale ftemprava , e correnti rendeva l'efcremen-
ti intestinali; sicchè aveffer potuto per l'uretre, pisciando, uscire: ed
ecco il caso dell'uomo fatto gallina.
    Un fimile artificio dovette avere quella Vacca nella Città di
Perinto , di cui Aristotele (*) de' Moftri ragionando , fa menzione : *Nam & Vaccam fuiffe Perinthi accepimus , cui cibi excrementum*
extenuatum per vesicam transmittebatur , diffectufque anus dentio pro-
pere coalefcebat , nec refecanda evincere vitium poterant .
    Il Sig. Lunadei (**) in una lettera al Signor Bianchi di Rimini
diretta , per non dir d'altre molte , riferisce la storia di due gemel-
le,
                                            le,

(*)   Lib. IV. de Gen. Animal. cap. IV.
(**) Racc. di opusc. fcient. to. 22.

fia quella di creder le uova nella loro origine Moftruofe :
che non v'abbia di bifogno di due , o più uova , ma che
un folo a tal foggetto baftaffe , pur che foffe nella fua ci-
E 3
ca-

le , le quali aveano due pulmoni , un cüore ; ma grande , due ventricoli , da' quali due duodeni fi ftaccavano , e tra poco tratto , un
inteftino molto grande fin all'ano componevano .

Il fecondo mirabil lavorio fi vedeva nell'offa , la gran conca
offea nel fondo dell'addomine formanti . Non eran al folito in quefti gemelli le offa della pube a diritto fotto al bellico , ma ne'fianchi
fituate in modo tale , che i gemelli non avean una conca offea fepa-
ratamente l'uno dall'altro , ma di tutte le offa n'era una pelvi comune ben grande , molto artificiofamente formata . Le offa deftre
dell'uno eran per mezzo delle cartilagini colle deftre dell'altro congiunte , le finiftre colle finiftre . I muscoli quindi ne'fianchi piegando ,
andavano a terminare nelle offa della pube , e lafciavan quello fpa-
zio là dove dovean effer le offa della pube coverte d'una aponeuro-
fe , con di mezzo l'unico bellico , che quei due corpi fi
potessono alzare , e baffare , accoftare , e fcoftare . Di quefta favia ,
ed artificiofa conneffione delle offa , il dotto Signor Verney favel-
lando , foggiugne . *Se quefta conformazione delle offa dipendeffe
dall'unione di due uova , e dall'incontro cafuale , bifognava , che
foffe ftata molto felice ; poiche per poco che l'eftremità delle offa ,
le quali an poco di larghezza , fi fituavan l'uno fopra l'altro , quafi
tutte le parti , tanto folide , che molli , la conca del baffo addomine componenti , farebbono ftate indifpenfabilmente delle di loro
funzioni private .* Ma io non entrerò in quefta particolarità , che
troppo in lungo condurrebbe . Dov'è , *Sig. Accademico delle Scienze*, quel ributtar con veemenza di fpirito tutto ciò , che fi è detto intorno a' *Moftri fol generati dalle uova infeme accozzate?* Dove fono
le *uova nella loro origine moftruofe?* Potes con maggior avvedutezza ,
con maggior modeftia , e riverenza del Pubblico un favio Filofofo
ragionare ? In quel paragrafo egli fa il Signor Verney faviamente
vedere quali inconvenienti farebbon nati , fe le offa non aveffero
avuta quella conneffione , quella fituazione , ch'ebbono ; e non potendo una tale conformazione tanto ben ordinata effer fatta dal cafo ,
o dall'incontro cafuale di due uova , o dalla confufione , e preffio-
ne delle cicatricole , nafcerebbe una legittima confeguenza , che
quella organizzazione particolare , foffe tale nel germe , o come tu

catrice per origine Moſtruoſo . Quivi dunque eſſendo il corpo organico delineato per Moſtro , toſto che ne' canali menomiſſimi cominciavano il di lor movimento i li-

co.

dì nell'uovo ; Il diſcretiſſimo Signor Verney non dedusse , com'ei nerboſamente potea , la concluſione ; laſciolla gentilmente nell'arbitrio del Lettore . Qual motivo hai tu dunque avuto , *Signor Accademico delle Scienze* , di coſì ruſticamente cenſurare , e maltrattare un de' più illuſtri Medici di quella ſtimabiliſſima Società , e tanto benemerita nella Republica Letteraria ? Dopo molte altre notomiche oſſervazioni , coſì il dotto Franceſe conchiude .

S'attribuiſce ordinariamente la produzion de' moſtri or al caſo , or a moti puramente naturali , ma sregolati , or agli errori d'una virtù formatrice cieca , come ſuol dirſi , anche nelle ſue opere , le più regolate , e che tra tanto agiſce , come aveſſe intelligenza ; ma il moſtro , di cui abbiamo fatta la deſcrizione , e'l rapporto della di lui interna conformazione , alla figura eſteriore , fanno ben vedere , ch'egli non ha potuto eſſere opra del caſo , o d'una virtù formatrice cieca , nè l'effetto d'un diſordine caſuale de'moti naturali .

Dalle ſpoglie ſin al più profondo delle viſcere , tutto è d'un lavorio , in quel punto condotto da una intelligenza libera nel di lei fine , onnipotente nell'eſecuzione , e ſempre ſavia , ed ordinata ne'modi de' quali s'avvale .

Seguitando l'ordine comune gli uomini , e gli animali a quattro piedi , anno due uſcite per l'evacuazione degli eſcrementi della prima digeſtione , l'una per i ſolidi , e l'altra per i liquidi . Nel moſtro deſcritto , l'intelligenza ha voluto produrre due corpi umani inſieme uniti , i quali ſtar poteſſero ritti , aſſettarſi , approſſimare , o allontanare i tronchi de' loro corpi l'uno dall'altro , fino ad un certo punto . Ella ha voluto condurre per un ſol canale gli eſcrementi ſolidi in un comune ricettacolo , là dove ſi meſcolaſſero co'liquidi , affinche ciaſcuno de' gemelli , ſeparatamente per la verga render li poteſſe . Non poſſiam diſpenſarci di ſupporre queſta volontà , poiche ſe ne vede chiaramente l'eſecuzione . Io laſcio a Teologi di ricercarne le ragioni : ma coteſta volontà eſſendo ſuppoſta , io dico , che l'iſpezione di queſto moſtro fa vedere la ricchezza della meccanica del Creatore , almeno riſpetto alle produzioni le più regolate ; poiche a tutte le pruove , che noi n'abbiamo , ella aggiunge ancora queſt'altra tanto più forte , e convincente , ch'eſſendo fuor le regole comuni , ella moſtra meglio , e la libertà , e la fecondità dell'Autore di queſta meccanica cotanto varia in queſta ſorta d'opere ; poiche egli è certo , che tutte le ſpecie de'moſtri comparſi , eſaminati , o no , anne

sem-

cori, ordinatamente manifestavanſi i Moſtri nella medeſima guiſa, con la quale ſi rinvenivano originalmente delineati.

Ma ſempre *avuto una ſtruttura interna coſì ſtraordinaria, che la di loro eſteriore figura, ha paruto differente da quella degli altri animali della ſteſſa ſpecie.* Dov'è la veemenza di ſpirito, *Sig. Accademico delle Scienze? Dove ſono le uova, nella di loro origine moſtruoſe? Barbam, & pallium video, non Philoſophum.*

Impara dunque, come ragionano i Filoſofi Veterani, e per quanto la debolezza dell'umano ſapere, permette, addottrinati. Qual delle riſleſſioni trovi tu mal fondata, e che merita eſſer corretta? Chi ha fatto un colon comune? E forame nell'ano non eſſendo, ſcaricar le fecce nella veſcica oranaria? Chi ha poſto le oſſa della pube ne'lati a deſtra, ed a ſiniſtra, da mezzo togliendole, per facilitar i moti di quei corpi? Chi ha quelle oſſa con tanta maeſtria, ſituate, ed ordinate? Le due cicatrici? Il caſo? Le compreſſioni? Le confuſioni? O finalmente l'idea archetipa di Platone? Quella infinita Sapienza, *Signor Accademico delle Scienze,* che fè tante coſe, ha ſimilmente la tua vacca con due teſte prodotto; ha fatto ancora, che per un forame dell'oſſo dell'occipite da due cervelli una medolla nel forame delle vertebre s'immetteſſe; e ſiccome non poſſiamo dire, che que' due gemelli del Signor Verney nacquero da due uova, coſì nè meno la tua bicipite vacca. Nacque dunque da un uovo, nella cui cicatricola ſtava il teneriſſimo germe bicipite. Coſì nacque il ſerpentello a due teſte del Redi; coſì naſcono ogni giornata le lucertole con due code, le mani con ſei dita, le chele de' gambari duplicate, le corna, i membri genitali, ed i tre teſticoli.

Io dunque, *Signor Accademico delle Scienze,* delle oſſervazioni, e riſleſſioni ſaviſſime del Signor Verney profittando, dico, e ſtimo, che per lo più i moſtri ſien tali, anche ne' germi; cioè, che naſcono dalle uova moſtruoſi, e finche tu, non trovi argomento in contrario, ma concludente, io ripoſerò nel ſentimento del Signor Verney, e ſon certo che tu fin al *die judicii* faticando, non ſarai giammai capace di trovar coſa, per cui ſarò aſtretto di mutar parere.

Caro, *Signor Accademico,* ſenti un'altra ſtoria d'un moſtro, che a dì 27. Novembre dell'anno 17... nella Città di Converſano nacque da una donna primipara in età d'anni diciotto in circa. Nel nono meſe tra dolori, e ſpaſimi, preſentò per la vagina i piedi
quel

Ma qual erroneo , e vano difegno , farebbe ſtato quel-

quel moſtro , dall'ùtero uſcir volendo . Si sbigottì a queſta ſtraordinaria ſituazione la Levatrice : fù perciò chiamato il Chirurgo Signor Nicola Griſeto , il quale coll'ajuto dello ſpecolo, una figliuola
con due teſte fuori morta à biſtento eſtraſſe , e poco dopo morì ancora la madre . Era di peſo rotola cinque , ed un terzo ; cioè once 176.
La difficoltà dell'uſcire , non ſolamente dalle due teſte dipendeva ,
ma dalla groſſezza del feto , e per eſſer la donna primipara . Sopra
d'un buſto molto ben formato s'alzavan due colli con due teſte ,
una dall'altra diſtinta , e ſeparata.

Corſero là tutti li Medici , e Curioſi della Città , in preſenza
de' quali fe il Signor Griſeto di quella bambina la Notomia . Una
era la cavità dell'addomine , con indentro i ſoliti viſceri ; uno il
ventricolo , ma due le fiſtole cibarie dalle due teſte venienti ; uno il
condotto inteſtinale , ma molto lato ; una la veſcica orinaria ; uno
l'utero ; una la vagina ; uno il fegato ben grande con due ciſtifel-
lee ; una la milza ſimilmente grande ; due i rognoni con due ureteri ; tutto era più lato , e grande del convenevole ; un diaframma
divideva dall'addomine il petto ; due ſpine , ma uno ſterno ; due
pulmoni diſtinti , e pel mediaſtino ſeparati ; due cuori nelle due cavità del petto : avea ciaſcuno gli orecchi , li ventricoli , le vene , le
arterie ; tutto era perfettamente formato ; i due colli , e le due teſte
avean tutto ciò che naturalmente anno ; uſcivan le due medolle de'
nervi , e ciaſcuna nella ſua ſpina ſen calava , ed i nervi a deſtra , e ſiniſtra diramava.

Signor Accademico delle Scienze, penſa bene , e riſpondi , ſe pur
ti piace , alle domande ch'io ti fo . Chi fe creſcere i due colli , e le
due teſte ſopra d'un ſolo buſto , l'una dall'altra ſtaccata ? Chi poſe
i due pulmoni nelle due cavità dal mediaſtino formate ? Chi ſituò
coſì bene in quelle i due cuori ? Chi le due fiſtole cibarie in un ſolo
ventricolo congiunſe ? Chi fe in un ſolo fegato le due veſcichette
del fiele ? *Signor Accademico*, tu non riſpondi ? E'l caſo ? Le due
macchiette ? Le compreſſioni ? L'idea archetipa di Platone ? Co-
raggio , *Signor Accademico*, su riſpondi ? *Ubi eſt acumen tuum?* Dio
tel perdoni ! Per qual ragione hai tu ſcritte tante coſe , o falſe , o
non provate , e con tanta franchezza ? *Quid* (*) *tam temerarium ,
tamque indignum ſapientis gravitate , atque conſtantia , quam aut
falſum ſentire , aut quod non ſatis explorate perceptum ſit , & cogni-
tum ſine ulla dubitatione defendere ?*

P oi-

(*) *De Natura Deor. lib. I.*

quello della Natura, l'aver fatte macchine (42), che non
possano conservarsi: che non reggono, o conducono a
qualche fine, e che alle vere, ed armoniche leggi (43)
della medesima si ravvisa intieramente contrario? Sarebbe invero riputato stupido, e dappoco quell'Artefi-
ce, il quale sapendo a fondo il mestiere, che ha tra le
mani, facesse ogni sforzo, ed impiegasse tutta la dili-
genza a fare artificiosamente scomposti (44), e mal connessi i quotidiani lavori.

(45) Rimane adunque a riguardare le macchine mostruose, come opere miserabili, ed imperfette della Natura da non poche accidentali cagioni attraversata, e in-
terrotta; ciò compruovandosi da i germi, e dalle gem-
me de' vegetabili in diverse forme compresse, o attaccate, e da moltissime altre ragioni, che la chiarezza del si-
stema delle uova ha felicemente pensate, e dimostrate.

(42) Poiche tu non sai a qual fine son fatte; perciò non sono
per te possibili. Sei tu Segretario della Natura, che sai tutti gli
arcani, e fini, quali tiene nell'operare, e quel de' mostri non
trovi?

(43) Saran fatte coteste leggi a suon di flauto, di liuto, o di
qualche numerosa banda di sonatori?

(44). Quali mostri hai tu, *Signor Accademico delle Scienze*,
notomizzato, che l'hai *artificiosamente scomposti, e mal connessi*
trovati? Io credo più al Signor Verney, che a te. Quegli, i mostri notomizzando, notò, che la struttura interna è straordinaria,
e risponde all'esterna. Non sono dunque *artificiosamente scomposti*.
Tutto è ben composto quelche la Natura produce; e'l volerla chiu-
dere, e limitare in poche cose, è non sapere l'estensione della gran
potenza di lei. *Ignorat* (*) *Naturæ potentiam, qui illi non putat ali-
quando licere, nisi quod sæpius fecit.*

(45) *Rimane adunque a riguardare* la tua lezione, *Signor Accademico delle Scienze, come opera miserabile, ed imperfetta* del tuo
gran cervello, *da non poche essenziali cagioni* guasto, e corrotto; *ciò
comprovandosi* dallo stile, dalle false dottrine, e dalle buone malamen-
te

(*) *Seneca lib. VII. natural. quæst.*

te efpreffe, o attaccate, e da moltiffime altre ragioni, che la chiarezza del fiftema delle uova ha felicemente penfate, e dimoftrate. Signor Accademico delle Scienze, chi domine t'ha persuaso dar cotefte
inezie alle luce? Chi tel configliò?

Ah . . . . à . . . . quæ te dementia cœpit?

Quanto bene avrefti fatto, *Signor Accademico delle Scienze*, aver
ad altri la moftruosa impresa lasciato, quando ben conoscevi la
tua insufficienza, e l'alto valore di colui, che altre volte richie-
fto, ha tutto l'Erario della Natura votato. T'anno, *Signor Accademico mio*, i tuoi Consultori ingannato. E che sanno quei gran
Maeftri di quefte cose umili, terreni, succide? Egli o son mai
sempre intefi, ed improfondati nella confiderazione di cose sublimi
a' senfi, ed al vulgo degli uomini nascofte. Avrai tu, *Signor
Accademico delle Scienze*, più volte nel Molo, a di porto calando, veduto verso il Porto qualche Nave da lontani Paefi venire, ed in
effa i Marinari agili, e snelli, quai topi inerpicarfi, e salir per le
corde solleciti, e ficuri, su per le antenne camminare ad amma-
inar le vele. Come poi quella ciurma in terra discende, vacilla,
casca, e come ebbra fi foffe, cammina. Rifletti bene, *Signor Accademico mio*, come è fatto l'uomo: quegli, che sollecito, e ficuro
sopra punti, e linee, anche ad occhi chiufi cammina, per la ftrada
larga, e piana vacilla, e cade.

Un'altra volta dunque non attenerti al parere di cotefti *Funam-
boli*, ma di coloro, i quali sono nell'offervazione dell'opere della
Natura, cioè dell'infinita Sapienza invecchiati. Cotefti fiano i tuoi
Maeftri, e direttori. Rispetta i vecchi, figliuol mio, sopratutto
coloro, i quali sono dal Pubblico ftimati, e reputati; e sappi che
l'unica ftrada d'effere ftimato è quella di ftimar gli altri, come
d'amare, volendo effer amato. Deponi tanta superbia, effendo quefta legittima figliuola dell' ignoranza (*). *Quæ tanta gravitas?
Quæ tanta Sapientia? Arrogantia? Sinifteritas? Ac potius amentia?
In hoc totum diem impendere, ut offendas, ut inimicum relinquas?
Ad quem tanquam amiciffimum Veneris? Nofce te ipfum.* Tu sei il
novello Ippia, che sai tutto, e di tutto; ma sappi, ch'egli fu
da tutti i veri Sapienti deriso; e Socrate di nulla sapere, dicendo,
fu dall'Oracolo per Savio pubblicato.

L'uom savio cofta di poca sapienza, e molta ignoranza. Senti ciocchè molto a propofito scrive Lattanzio de'falfi sapienti (**).
*Alii putarunt fcire poffe omnia, hi fapientes utique non fuerunt.
Alii nihil, ne hi quidem fapientes fuerunt: illi quia plus homini de-
derunt, hi quia minus, utrifque in utramque partem modus defuit.*

Ubi

(*) *Plin. lib. V. Epift. XVII.*
(**) *De falfa Sapientia lib. III. pag. 285.*

Uòi ergo Sapientia est ? Ut neque te omnia scire putes, quod est Dei, neque omnia nescire, quod pecudis; est enim aliquod medium, quod sit hominis : idest scientia cum ignoratione conjuncta, & temperata

Io intendo, *Caro Signor Accademico delle Scienze*, averti fatto un regalo, qual nissuno de' tuoi Amici fatto t'avrebbe; sappi dunque profittare. Tu hai voluto far in pubblico una comparsa, dalla turba de' Medicanti emergendo; perciò non devi entrar in collera d'esser corretto, avendo ciascuno del Pubblico il dritto di ciò fare; ed io non ad altro fine questa fatica ho intrapreso, se non che per tuo beneficio, ed acciò tu finalmente te stesso conoscendo, ne facci pubblicamente l'ammenda. Ti sian d'esempio tanti Uomini dotti, i quali degli errori commessi essendo stati corretti, si sono pubblicamente ritrattati. Che dissi! Tu non hai di che ritrattarti.

Allegramente, *Signor Accademico delle Scienze*, allegramente. Già si pubblicano a suon di tromba le tue lodi per Italia tutta. I giornalisti di Roma t'han fatto l'onor grande di darti luoco nel Giornale del mese Gennajo, ultimamente uscito. Kappi, non si burla! Tu sei stato decorato del titolo specioso di Letterato, essendo tra quelli stato annoverato. Così va il Mondo, *Signor Accademico delle Scienze*: bisogna dire che'l gusto varia, come varian le Nazioni. Comeche l'Articolo terzo, che contiene l'estratto della tua lezione, sia stato fatto da un cima d'Uomo, ma non Medico, ha non pertanto il valore delle tue proposizioni conosciuto; e perciò non ha voluto aicuna garantirne.

E degno di lode l'accorto Relatore per quella figura di reticenza, che a bella posta non ha una sola parola sputato sulla critica del parere del Signor Verney, da te con tanta dottrina rapportata. Egli ben sapea il peso delle ragioni del dotto Francese, che dimostrano non esser possibile, che i mostri traggan l'origine dall'accozamento di due uova; perciò per non farti una *intemerata*, si è di favellarne astenuto. Quindi nasce un ben fondato sospetto, che il Signor Giornalista per compiacere a qualcuno, che di ciò l'ha pregato, t'ha, contro sua voglia, dato luoco nel giornale; ma l'ha con tanta prudenza fatto, che tu non avrai di che gloriarti. Non vedi tu, che tratto maestro è mai quello, ch'ei ti fa nella fine dell' Articolo? Per farti toccar colle mani, che tu non eri ben informato della storia de' Mostri, ti ha un passo di Aristotele (*) ricordato, il quale in quel capitolo, tutto ciocchè tu hai scritto de'Mostri, dice, e molte altre cose ancora : per esempio : che dall'uovo con due tuorli nascan due pulcini, qualora sono dalla membrana separati.

F 2   *Quod*

(*) De generat. animal. lib. IV, cap. IV.

Quod ſi Vitelli diſtinguntur membrana , gemini pulli diſcreti, ſine ulla ſupervacanea parte generantur . Che ti pare, *Signor Accademico delle Scienze?* Ariſtotele, che nacque ne' *ſecoli pregiudicati, e tenebroſi,* ſeppe quelche tu, nel secolo illuminato venuto eſſendo , non sapevi, che il contatto faccia talvolta i polli moſtruoſi . *Cohœrent enim conceptus, quoniam in propinquo alter alteri eſt , quo modo interdum fructus arborum complures .* Ecco delle frutta l'esempio non tuo . In queſto ſteſſo capitolo riferisce quel gran Sapiente l'opinion di Democrito , il quale i moſtri generarſi credette per la confuſione di due semi l'un dopo dell'altro nell'utero cacciati . Tal era l'opinione di quei tempi intorno alla generazione , come da Ipocrate ſi ricoglie , il quale se non fu di lui scolare (*) , fu senza dubbio di lui contemporaneo, ad Amico . Dimmi or che ſiamo a quattro orecchi la verità ; leggeſti mai Ariſtotele , o no , quando t'accingeſti all'onorata impresa ? Se lo leggeſti , per qual ragione non l'hai citato ? Ti vergognavi forse di far menzione di quell'Uomo , il quale , tranne Platone , a tutti i Greci Sapienti fu dal gran Cicerone antepoſto . Se non lo leggeſti , come porre la penna in carta , e la carta in pubblico , non avendo prima letto que' Scrittori , i quali anno de' moſtri trattato ? Ben ſi vede , che tu sei un Dottor di Gazzette . Ma tu dirai: mi son contentato de' rivi , e non mi son curato del fonte : ho letto il Signor Vallisnieri , da cui ho tutta la lezione copiato , eſſendo queſti un Autor più Moderno , e che scrive in Lingua Italiana, Ed un *Accademico delle Scienze* non sa'l conſiglio , che dava Cicerone (**) agli Amici ? Sentilo , e profitta : *Sed meos amicos , in quibus eſt ſtudium , in Grœciam mitto , ideſt ad Grœcos ire jubeo , ut ea à fontibus potius hauriant , quam rivulos conſectentur .* Studia *Sig. Accademico delle Scienze .* Addio .

(*) *Celſ. Prœfat. lib. I.*
(**) *Quœſt. Academicar. lib. I.*

THE
Pleasures and *Felicity*
OF
MARRIAGE,

Display'd in Ten BOOKS:

I. The Lady's Confent, meeting of their Relations to adjuft the Portion, the Invitation of Guefts, the Wedding, &c.

II. The arifing of the happy Pair, their Choice of Houfehold Furniture, wherein the Bride manifefts the Greatnefs of her Genius.

III. Their Vifits; how they are carefs'd ev'ry where; their Journey into the Country, and Adventures there.

IV. Their Return; her Goffiping among her Neighbours, to whom fhe complains fhe is not breeding; and applies to a Doctor, with other Matters too engaging to be overlook'd.

V. Joyful News! fhe proves with Child; the Pleafure of Longing, with a Number of Incidents entirely new.

VI. The providing Childbed Linnen, choice of a Midwife and Nurfe, vaftly important as well to the Mother as Child.

VII. Her falling in Labour; with fuch Variety of Incidents, as are no lefs true than amazing.

VIII. Her Delivery; the Beauty of the Child; ftrange Stories told by the Goffips, no lefs ufeful than entertaining.

XI. The Chrift'ning; Mirth of the good Company; with Stories ftill more wonderful, and fit to be treafur'd in Memory.

X. The Coating of the Child; great Difficulties furmounted on that Occafion; in which Madam fhews vaft Ability, well worth Recording.

The whole illuftrated with eleven Cuts, humoroufly defign'd.

By *LEMUEL GULLIVER.*

The Second Edition.

L O N D O N,

Printed: and fold by J. ROBINSON, Publifher, at the *Golden-Lion,* in *Ludgate-ftreet.* 1745.

[Price One Shilling and Six-pence.]

TO THE
AUTHOR.

AD I, dear Sir, a thousand *Hands*,
    A thousand *Pens* and *Inky Stands* ;
    A thousand *Tongues*, profuse in
       Tropes ?
A thousand *Wits*, as rich as *Pope's* ,
A thousand Years to write——what then ?
Thy Praise should charm a Million Men.

  Thy *poinant Wit*, and *humourous Vein*,
Make my *rais'd Spirits dance* again ;
Dame Nature in thy rich Array,
Smiles like a Bride, and shines as Gay,
In flowing Robes, apt, sweet, and newer,
Than Verse, or Prose, before, e'er drew her ;

a   Strange !

Strange! *all*, th' inviting *Scenes* fhould leave,
For thee to paint, which charm'd fince *Eve*!

The * *Poet fweet*, of *Sulmo*'s *Groves*,
Whofe *Lays* adorn *polluted Loves*,
Of *Nuptial Pleafures*, fcarce could *dream*!
Whilft *Proftitution* was his *Theam*!
His *Mufe*, like a fair *Harlot*'s *Arms*,
Lulls to Deftruction, *whom* fhe *charms*!
Ev'n *he*, her doleful *Victim* fell!
In *fad Exile* his *Woes* to tell.

But ev'ry *Mufe*, and *Grace*, combine,
In this enchanting *Work* of *thine*;
Thou paints *Love's Joys*, but does not feek,
To raife a *Blufh*, on *Beauty's Cheek*;
Yet *Nymphs* as cold as *Cynthia*'s *Train*,
Shall, Reading, *glow* in ev'ry *Vein*,
And wifh, now whilft their Beauty's fpringing,
Their own Epithalamium finging;
For fair, fond, coy, and fcornful Dames,
Catch all, and quench alike, Love's Flames;

---

* *Ovid*, who was born at *Sulmo*, Author of the Art
of Love; for the Leudnefs of which, he complains that
Auguftus banifh'd him to *Pontus*, where he languifh'd till
his Death.

But

But thofe demure in outward Show,
Are, at their Hearts, all Fire and Tow!
Which kindl'd, in their foft Bofoms preys,
Till Love, the Flames he rais'd, allays.

Thy *Audience* want no † *Flappers* here,
Attention thirfts in ev'ry *Ear*,
And *there* imbibes thy *Strain*, which flows
Harmonious, as *young Lovers Vows* !

We *fhare* with Joy, *thy fumptuous Feaft*,
But can *we* too, regale *thy Tafte* ?
How *Penury* does the *grateful* vex !
Ah ! Fly then, to the charming Sex !
And like a jocund Fairy, fpring
Amid'ft their foft, fweet, magick Ring !
They'll fhow'r on thee, with fmiling Look,
Ev'n all the Pleafures in thy Book ;
Then Revel, Banquet, Bill, and Coo,
Whilft Heart can wifh, —— and after too !

---

† See *Gulliver's* Travels to *Laputa*, where the Author found Flappers were of great Importance.

In fine, *my Friend*, thy *witty Page*,
Soars far above the *Critic's* Rage.

May *Fate*, (where *Wit* is no Defence,)
Preferve *it* from the *Foes of Senfe*,
From Prudes, Coquets, Fops, Bully-Rocks,
Louts, Witlings, and meer *Human-Blocks*;
And *it* fhall *Charm* whilft *Cupid* plys,
His keeneft Darts from *brighteft Eyes*;
And *thy fair Fame*, immortal prove,
As *Hymen's Rites*, or *Joys of Love!*

1 AP 64

DEDICA-

DEDICATION,

To the Fair Sex.

THIS little Perform-
ance implores your Pro-
tection ; fuffer it not
to languifh for your
Favour ; the Infant Wanderer is
juft turn'd loofe in the World,
abandon'd by its Parent ; fhew
your wonted Compaffion to Innocence in Diftrefs, and with your
lovely Hands raife it from your
Feet, that encourag'd by your
Smiles, it may prefume to claim
fome Affinity to your beautiful
felves, who, as you are the Source
of all human Felicity, gave *Being*
to this proftrate *Supplicant,* whofe

Linea-

Lineaments are copied from your bright Originals, which are embellifh'd with fuch num'rous Charms, that it is no wonder the Refemblance is fo faint; for who could ever draw the Sun in all its Glory! this Painter confcious of his Inability to reprefent you in the Fulnefs of your Splendor, prefumes only to delineate a few of your Features, and commemorate a fmall Portion of that Happinefs you fo bountifully fhow'r on your Adorers; and will be fortunate enough if the Picture retains fome Likenefs of a Profpect fo agreeable and delightful; for alas! what Colours have Luftre enough to fet Beauty in a proper Light? or what Eloquence can exprefs exceffive Felicity? the Awe of the former, intimidates the Artift, who lets fall his Pencil in Defpair of ever accomplifhing the bold

bold Design ; and the latter, tran-
sports the Orator to run on in Ex-
clamations, till he is at length forc'd
to stop with a full Note of Admiration ! A Wit as piercing as your
Eyes, and infinite as your Perfections, would only give a Specimen of Arrogance in pretending
to represent you more amiable than
you are ; your Lovers themselves,
who, become mute in your Presence, are eager to acknowledge to
all others their Inability to extol
you sufficiently, and continually
feel their Idea's surpass their Expressions ; this, Ladies, has been
the Misfortune of your Limner ;
your Virtues rose faster in his Mind,
than his Pen could record, and your
Charms languish'd in the Description ; and nothing but the Impossi-
bility of doing you Justice, together with that compassionate Disposition so natural to your soft Sex,
could

could make him hope for a Pardon,
who has succeeded no better in
your Encomium, and yet presumes
to rank himself amongst your
num'rous Admirers.

L. GULLIVER.

I AP 64

INTRO-

INTRODUCTION.

Dear Cousin,

 Receiv'd your Letter, in which you consult with me in so delicate a Point, as the giving your Hand to the beautiful Creature, who already possesses your Heart. The great Deference you have for my Judgment, perplexes me extreamly; for whilst you rely on my Skill, should I like an ignorant Pilot steer among Rocks and Quicksands, and ship-wreck your Vessel, with what might you not accuse me? For tho' Marriage, like the Ocean, is often calm, smooth,

c   and

and vaſtly delightful, in the Proſpect, yet whoever embarks in either, will be very fortunate if he eſcapes all the Perils ſo many encounter. Your Stile informs me how much Love has inflam'd your Heart, and how willingly you would follow a Guide, which leads to the Accompliſhment of your preſent Wiſhes; but who can tell how the Scene may change on the other Side the nuptial Ceremony! This is what occaſions all my Anxiety; ſhould I adviſe you to unite your Deſtiny with the dear Charmer, I am ſure of your Applauſe for the preſent, the overflowing of your Joy would load me with the kindeſt Epithets, you would admire with what Ardency I intereſt my ſelf in your Felicity, and indeed in the laſt Article you would but do me Juſtice; having your Hapineſs ſo much at Heart, occaſions my Diffidence; to others on the ſame Occaſion, I have generally giv'n my Opinion agreeable to the Bent of their Inclination, without heſitating in the leaſt, and thought it a Point of Politeneſs to obſerve they could not be too ſpeedy, ſince all agree *Cupid* has Wings;

to

to intimate, with what Rapidity the Lover fhould haften to the Arms of his Miftrefs. But, what fhall I fay to you for whom I have fuch infinite Friendfhip and Affection, fhall I repeat the fame Doctrine? doubtlefs it will be moft exceptable: But how if I advife the contrary? O hateful Thought; let it be buried in Oblivion; it fhall never efcape my Lips; for befides, that I hate to be peremptory, I think it the faireft for you to judge for yourfelf; and for that Purpofe have fent you a Portraiture of *the Pleafures of Marriage*, drawn fo impartially, that I can no Way anfwer your Letter fo pertinently, as by recommending them to your Perufal; after which, determine how you will, I fhall not be apprehenfive of your Reproach. Confider them therefore attentively, nor doubt of your experimenting every one of them in the full Extent here reprefented; nay, you may reafonably expect your Share of fome here omitted: But I will detain you no longer, for hark, the Lady is juft going to give her Confent; I recommend you to give your Affiftance in celebrating the

Wedding,

Wedding, you will be better qualify'd
to prepare for your own, I cannot
attend you, my Blood is not fpirited
enough to be there. Adieu, dear Coufin,
referve a fmall Corner of your Heart,
for,

LEM. GULLIVER.

I AP 64

THE

THE
PLEASURES
OF
MARRIAGE.

BOOK I.

*The Confent is given, the Time appointed,
the Marriage folemniz'd, and Wedding kept.*

T HE youthful Lover, till now
has been fighing, hoping and
begging to draw from thofe
charming tardy Lips, that
long-wifhed for Word of Confent: It is at length come
forth, and acts upon his love-
fick Mind, as a rich Cordial
upon a languifhing Patient. · Fortunate Lover!
You have now vanquifhed, and are triumphing o-

B   ver

ver all your potent Rivals, who can imagine your
Joy! Whatever you are employ'd about, your
Thoughts continually glance upon the near Approach of your Happiness. --- Your beautiful Mistress is now willing; Denials are laid aside; nothing remains but a small Degree of Shame and
Fear, which a little Time will eradicate. What
Mortal can desire a greater Happiness than you now
participate! Your Will and Desires are hers, and
her Desires augment your Pleasure. Now may
you tumble and regale yourself in a Bed of Lillies
and Roses; for her disdainful Looks are exchanged
for inviting Smiles. Those panting, snow-white
Breasts, which before you hardly could presume to
look upon, much less to touch with one Finger,
you may now survey all o'er with eager Eyes, and
imprint with burning Kisses. What shall I add!
The delightful Place, the Haven of all your Joys,
which heretofore you hardly durst approach in
Thought, much less express in Words, you have
now an uncontrollable Liberty to visit, embrace
and enjoy, while you have any Capacity for that
most ravishing Exercise. But, O victorious Lover, let not however your exulting Mind rumi-
nate too much upon these dazling Enjoyments;
be a little temperate in your Pleasures; because
there may possibly happen in the Course of Things
some cross-gain'd Obstructions: For I have frequently experienced, that those imaginary Joys,
which you are now indulging, introduce a numerous Train of Anxieties. Perhaps the very Mouth
upon which you are bestowing so many rapturous
Kisses, and amorous Epithets, and which now
flows with the sweetest Language, may hereafter
oftener open to overwhelm you with Reproach.
Those heaving Breasts, which now you fondly call
the *Hills of Nectar*, and *Banquet of the Gods*, may
perhaps hereafter sink in the Comparison. Moderate therefore your extatic Descriptions, and amorous

rous Praifes, till you have been longer accuftom'd to the delicious Banquet *Hymen* has prepared for you.

Neverthelefs, you have great Reafon to be jocund, at leaft for this Week; for a Meeting is appointed to clofe up the Match; and it's requifite that you in Perfon fhould wait upon your Friends, to know what Day and Hour their Affairs will permit them to attend this important Bufinefs. To do this, you muft, perhaps, traverfe the City through; and who knows after all your Pains, whether the major Part of 'em, may not be abfent from Home. Thofe that you are fo fortunate as to meet with, cannot agree about the Time: One can attend to Day, another to Morrow, a third not 'till the Week following: So that by this firft Pleafure, you have a little Feeling of Trouble; which may have its Advantage; becaufe it gives you an Earneft of, and, if rightly improv'd, may help to inure you the better to fuftain what's to follow.

But how does your Joy increafe, when after all your Labour and Fatigue, you fee your Friends and Relations happily met together with a Defign to adjuft all Matters; to the End that you may throw yourfelf into the Arms of your expecting Charmer. But here again alfo, moderate a little your Tranfport, for tho' you, thro' the Eagernefs of your youthful Defires, are prompted to take her for better or worfe, yet your fagacious Parents, or Guardians, having now no Relifh for the amorous Combat, are contriving all probable Methods to deceive, impofe upon, and over-reach each other, with regard to their refpective Difburfements.

In the mean Time however, and what an unfpeakable Felicity is that! You may be *kiffing*, *toying* and *dallying* with your Miftrefs, in the next Room; or contriving and agreeing together what

is

is to be done, both before and at the Wedding;
tho' perhaps, thro' the Discord of your Friends
and Relations, it may not be long before you are
disturb'd in your ravishing Employment, by the
disagreeable Sound of their clamorous Differences,
as the Fortune of one is disproportionate to that
of the other : Or else, that by some subtle Matrimonial Contract, they endeavour to make the
Goods of each disinheritable by the other.   In
short, as Parents and Friends know very well from
Experience, that Matrimony, of all others, is the
greatest and most delusory Contract : So their
own Disagreements are Motives powerful enough
to induce them, to dissuade the young Couple
from the Match.

But tho' on each Side they use the most plausible
Arguments, they are to no purpose ; for our Lovers are both by this Time in an amorous Blaze,
and therefore, let what will happen, the Fire must
be quench'd.   Besides this, Madam reasons with
herself thus : The Familiarities which I have grant-
ed to my LOVER, tho' they are not absolutely
criminal in themselves, yet if his Disappointment
should provoke him to a Discovery, my Reputation is ruin'd and I'm undone.   The young Lo-
VER is so enamoured at the inflexible Constancy
of his adorable Angel, that he is resolved, tho'
he should be reduced to the utmost Necessity, never to abandon her.   Let the Contract therefore,
says he, fir'd with Love, be what it will, tho'
Infamy and Destruction are inserted, I am resolv'd to sign it.   Their tender mercenary Parents, discerning the Resolution of their Darlings,
at length come to an Agreement.   The Attorney
very circumstantially draws up the Marriage Contract, which both Parties sign, and the Knot is immediately tied. Oh Heavens ! this is a Burthen from
my Heart, and a Milstone taken off from my Neck,
                                                      Here's

Here's now Matter for superlative Mirth and Re-joicing indeed; all the Friends wish the young Couple much Joy; ---- About goes a Health, to the good Success of the Marriage; every one wishing them a Profusion of every sublunary En-joyment. As Drinking is generally an Introduc-tion to Talking, so one of the Company begins to entertain the rest, with a Relation of what hap-pened to himself, in his Courtship, at his Wed-ing, and in his Marriage-state, and concludes with remarking that at first he thought of nothing but wantonning in the Arms of his Spouse; but he soon found, from the Multiplicity of Crosses, Vexations and Disappointments which Matrimony introduced, that he had Time little enough upon his Hands to prevent his Reputation from sinking, and his Substance from being totally exhausted.

But however, Mr. Bridegroom, you may now regale your Fancy to the utmost, and rejoice in-ordinately; for the Ceremony is over. You are secure of your Bride, the Chain which links you together, is so durable, nothing but Death can set you free.

And you Mrs. Bride, whose Countenance betrays such inward Satisfaction, be merry; for 'tis you, 'tis only you who occasions all this Musick, Mirth and Dancing: You have now a Husband, and a Pro-tector too, whose welcome Embraces will fill your Soul with the highest Degree of Extasy and Rap-tures. Nay, more, he'll be your Physician, to cure your pale Face, to remove the Pains from the Reins of your Back, and from your Heart, and all other Distempers whatsoever; he'll dry up your Tears with Kisses, and by his Endeavours to please, he'll anticipate every Wish.

Therefore, Mrs. Bride, make yourself merry; and since your Desire is accomplish'd in being married before any of your Bride-maids, it is un-reasonable

reasonable that you should be interrupted with any Thing that don't relate to your own Happiness. Here is Work enough indeed of that Kind. Your Apparel is as yet unmade, and your Linnens, Laces, and numberless other Things are yet to be bought. Well, who can see an End to it! Here's one Piece too light, another too dark, a third has no Gloss, a fourth is too cheap: Here's three or four Days gone, and very little Progress made.

The worst is, that while you are so industriously contriving for Dispatch, you are every Moment interrupted by one and another, who are continually bringing in either Ornaments or Necessaries to credit the approaching Solemnity.

Well, Mrs. *Bride,* your Head must certainly be extreamly disorder'd with attending to so many fatiguing Affairs at once; you'll be glad, no doubt on't, when the Confusion is well over: But comfort yourself with this, that for these few troublesome Days, you'll be rewarded with many delicious Nights. But it is not your Case alone, for the Bridegroom has had his Share of the Trouble, in providing the best *Canary, Madeira,* and *Champain,* that those Friends who come to wish the Bride and Bridegroom Joy, may be presented with a delicate Glass of Wine; but chiefly, that those who are employ'd in ornamenting the Bride, may taste the Bride's *Tears.*

But really, Friends, if you come to taste the Bride's Tears now, you are much too soon; in a Month or two, you may be certain of meeting with Plenty of unfeigned ones.

But, O Mr. *Bridegroom,* what shall we say to you? You, certainly are entitled to our Pity, on account of that Variety of Fatigue you undergo. There, you have just now miss'd the Jeweller; perhaps he's shewing some of his most costly Curiosities

to

to the *Bride* ; the more exceſſive the Price, the fonder will ſhe be of 'em ; but 'tis you that muſt have the Pleaſure of paying for 'em : However, 'tis Time enough to conſider of that when the Wedding is over ; for as yet you have not done with the *Draper, Mercer, Taylor* and *Sempſtreſs.*

But let the Thoughts of the Pleaſures that are haſtening, ſupport you under all. You'll e'er long be honoured with the beſt Place in the Chancel, and before you will be ſpread a rich Tapeſtry, your Ears alſo will be delighted with the harmonious Sound of the Bride's Aſſent, confirmed by theſe Words, *I will!* Unſpeakable Pleaſures. In the mean Time it is neceſſary that you conſult with your Friends on both Sides, who ſhall be invited, and who not ; and in this you muſt be careful to prevent Broils and Diſturbances, which very frequently happen. The next thing is, to conſider of the Grandeur or Frugality of the *Wedding-Entertainment.* But this you muſt leave to the Management of a Steward ; who, that he may oblige the ſeveral Tradeſmen concern'd, and at the ſame Time procure ſome Advantage to himſelf, will order in a Profuſion of the moſt delicate and coſtly Materials, perſuading you to believe that your Credit therein is greatly concern'd. And this muſt convey to you moſt exquiſite Delight, eſpecially as the *Bride* ſignifies her intire Approbation thereof.

But who can imagine that any Uneaſineſs ſhould ariſe about placing the Friends of the *Bride* and *Bridegroom* at Table. The ordering of this creates ſuch Diſputes, that our young Couple begin to repent, that they made any *Wedding* at all : Inſomuch, that ſighing to each other, they ſay, alas, what a thick Shell this *Marriage-Nut* has ! O, when ſhall we come to taſte its delicious Kernel !

In

In the Interim, let the *Bridegroom*, attended
with his *Bride*, go to taste the *Wedding-Wine*, and
difpel thofe Cares, that obfcure his Relifh of approaching Joys, and at the fame Time fee that it
has a delicate Flavour and Relifh, fit to entertain
fuch a Number of curious Palates.

Now *Bride*, and *Bride-maids*, look to it, for
you may expect the *Bridegroom*, and *Bride-men*,
to be fuperabundantly jolly, and much more
wanton than witty; the Wine-Merchant, a true
Son of *Bacchus*, declaring that no one fhall efcape
him, till he has drank as many Glaffes as there
are Hoops upon a Wine-Hogfhead.

Adieu to Care, and every gloomy Thought!
The Wedding's now at Hand: Let Mirth in all
its pleafing Forms be indulged to the utmoft. A-
way with all your dull, phlegmatic Satyrifts, who
prate inceffantly, that the Marriage-State brings
nothing elfe but Trouble. See here to the contrary; for the Mind and Intention of every one is
united, to pafs away thefe Days in the moft exquifite Pleafures and Delights. Away then with
Sorrow, for fhe's no Wedding-gueft; but let every Thought be employ'd to affift our young Lovers, that they may with the greater Relifh enjoy this the firft Pleafure of the *Matrimonial-
Heaven*.

But hark! there's poor *Molly* the Maid, almoft
diftracted with Expectation; fhe thinks every
Minute an Hour till the *Wedding-Night* is over,
that fhe may wait upon and congratulate the happy
Pair, to the End that fhe may experience their
Liberality for her careful Attendance and inceffant
Fatigue ---- No-Body deferves it better, thinks fhe,
for I have employ'd both Day and Night to ferve
'em, their Secrets I have kept, and their *Love-
Letters* convey'd with the greateft Care and Dif-
patch. Poor Girl, fhe has as yet liv'd upon the

Bridegroom's

Bridegroom's Promises; but he'll be generous.

Well, the charming Bride is now put to Bed; and you may divert yourself among the rest of the Wedding-guests: Who can tell but that some brave Gentleman's Coachman, Footman, or Postilion, may fall in Love with you; for one *Wedding* often begets another. Udsbuds, *Molly!* You'll then experience as well as your Mistress, the unspeakable Raptures of the first Matrimonial Entertainment, and be as well qualified to expect the second.

BOOK II.

Madam goes to buy Houshold-Furniture; the Ingratitude of some of the Wedding-Guests, and Thankfulness of others; with other no less entertaining Particulars.

WHAT tho' the Sun has been risen long ago, yet our wedded Pair are still aBed; Well, young Couple, you must needs be highly delighted, now the *Wedding* is over, and all Noise and Confusion at an End. You may now regale yourselves till the Day is far spent; and to raise your youthful Desires to the highest Pitch; you may, and I doubt not but you will, instruct one another in the School of *Venus*, and gratify your youthful Desires and Appetites to the utmost. *What Pleasures are these!*

After which, you may rejoice in the sweet Remembrance of your sumptuous Apparel and Ornaments, first invented by Madam *Squanderall*, and in the Delicacy and Elegancy of your Wed-

C   ding

ding-Feaft. Now may you pleafe your Fancies, with Ideas of the Mafquerading, Dancing,
Singing, and every other Gambol that Youth, in-
vigorated by *Bacchus*, either perform'd out of
Mirth, or Wantonnefs.

O, how merry were all the Guefts! how de-
licioufly were the Difhes. dreffed and garnifh'd!
what Credit to the Cook and Steward! The Wine
excellent! in a Word, every Thing Noble and
Grand. Well, they all eat plentifully and drank liberally; and is not the Demembrance of thefe Things,
the higheft Degree of Delight and Satisfaction?

And you, O Mrs. *Bride*, you are now not only
Wife, but Miftrefs. You are now beyond the
Power and Authority of your domineering, fnarling, mercenary Guardians, thofe Emiffaries of
Satan. ---- You are now fubject to no other Law,
but that of your own Will; and may without Referve, Shame, or Scandal, receive the fond Embraces of your vigorous Beloved. And you, O
Hufband, of the firft Edition, how do you revel
and folace in all the Delights and Extafies of new-
invented Wantonnefs! How willingly does your
liberal *Venus*, of her own Accord, open and difplay
each fecret Charm before your ravifhed Eyes;
Charms and Delights that none but thofe that feel
can comprehend! Well, make good Ufe of your
Time; fet no Bounds at prefent to your Defires,
but clafp, embrace, and carefs, thofe fnowy tender
Limbs while nothing interrupts; becaufe the
Time may be drawing near, when the Curtains of
your Bed being opened, you may difcern fuch long
Accounts from the *Jeweller*, *Goldfmith*, *Mercer*,
Draper, *Vintner*, and others, as may find you a very
different Employment.

But then, on the other Hand, you will be delighted to hear your Spoufe every Moment talk of
going with her Sifter and Aunt, to order in fuch
　　　　　　　　　　　　　　　　Furniture.

Furniture as may reflect Dignity and Grandeur upon the Owner. What Pleasure will you receive, and how will you applaud the happy Choice you have made, when your Darling gives you a Specimen of the Delicacy of her Taste in *Down-Beds, Rich-Counterpains, costly Hangings,* Venetian *Looking-Glasses, enamel'd China, Velvet Chairs,* Turkey *Carpets, Capital Paintings, Side-board of wrought Plate, curious in-laid Cabinets, rich Child-bed Linen,* Flanders *Lace,* and many other valuable Particulars. Certainly, the Joy of your Heart will far exceed the Chinking of your Purse, when your House, by the indefatigable Pains of your Spouse, is thus grandly adorn'd.

And should you, O happiest of Men! not discern the absolute Necessity of all the above Particulars, and be from thence inclin'd to indulge a gloomy Thought, or assume a doubtful Brow, you will be soon releas'd from both ; for your prudent Spouse, to your great Satisfaction, will inform you, that they, and many others, are no more than what's needful, both for Use and Credit, unless you design to banish all reputable Company from your House; and your Joy is certainly at the highest, when she kindly insinuates, that 'tis your Province to procure Money, and hers to see it expended to Advantage.

Who can describe your Pleasure, when you hear your Charmer, ever and anon expatiating upon the Portion she has brought to you ! And as it consists of Immoveables, as Houses, Lands, &c. what Joy does it diffuse, when she fondly prompts you to take a Journey thither twice a Year with her to receive your Rents.

Here your Tenants and others, salute you with the Title of Squire ; and, according to their Customs and Capacities, endeavour to exceed each other in Acts of Respect and Kindness ; nor will they be

backward

backward in amusing you with all Manner of rural Exercises and Diversions.

But here you'll meet with some Alloy to your Pleasures; your Tenants are full of Complaints about the Badness and Scarcity of the preceding Years; the ill Effects of the War, and the like; so that you must needs be content with Promises instead of Payments; for where it is not to be had, the King must lose his Right.

However, you may comfort yourself with this, that, thro' this your advantageous Match, you are sole Proprietor of so many Acres, so many Orchards, and so many Houses; and altho' you have not as yet reap'd any Advantage, but have rather been out of Pocket; that must by no Means lessen your Mirth and Joy; for would you trouble yourself about such trivial Matters as these, you need have no other Employment. If your Wife's Portion had been paid down in ready Money, you would have been extremely perplex'd, where to have dispos'd of it to Advantage, without Danger; but you know that Houses and Land are always secure, and when the War is happily at an End, will sufficiently reward your Patience and Forbearance.

You must therefore drive all gloomy Thoughts from your Breast, with calling to Mind, the extraordinary Commendations which your Friends bestow'd upon your late magnificent Entertainment; and also that two or three Days hence, a Visit is intended to be pay'd you by some of 'em, in Order to return you Thanks in Form, for the Honour you have done 'em; and this they will do in such a polite and affectionate Manner, that it will be impossible for you to avoid inviting them to sup, and spend the Evening with you; which will not only be a great Addition to your Mirth and Happiness, but will be a Means of establishing a lasting Friendship between you.

'Tis

'Tis true, you may possibly hear that some at the *Wedding* were displeas'd, not being, as they imagin'd, entertain'd according to their Rank and Deserts. Perhaps your Uncle and his new-married Niece, were not seated and waited upon to their Minds. If *Timothy* too assiduously waited upon some, while he neglected Miss *Lack-it* and her *Mamma*, or if Squire *Squeeze-up* put Miss *Betty*'s Hoop out of Shape, or *Dolly Slammikin* could not reach any Sweet-meats for herself and Companion Miss *Tawdry*, this must not diminish your Joy; 'tis impossible to satisfy all: 'Tis enough for you that the Expence was equivalent to its Grandeur.

'Tis a thousand Pities that they ever were invited, since all your Endeavours to please have proved abortive. Comfort yourself however, and a great Comfort it is, that whenever it happens again, you will not purchase Ingratitude at such an extravagant Price. 'Tis now too late to advise; but it would have been much better to have invited such Guests as those, at two or three several Times before hand, to partake of a chearful Glass and away; and then you would have had but a small Company at the *Wedding*, which are much easier to govern and please.

Tho' this for the present may give some Uneasiness, yet Pleasure and Joy again return, and will constantly attend you while your Table is spread and your Cellar open, for that will banish every Appearance of Discontent among your Friends and Relations, and will wonderfully delight also the Wife of your Bosom: And not only so, but it will exempt you from being reproached by her, with entertaining her Friends and Acquaintance in a covetous niggardly Manner; this will encourage Returns on their Side, and will be the happy Means of a most comfortable and friendly Correspondence: So that in the Season you will be gratefully presented

ed with Grapes, Nuts, Apricots, and Peaches, which being cold, must be warm'd with a Glass or two of generous Wine; at other Times Venison, Hares, Partridges, or *Colchester*-Oysters, but neither will these be agreeable without the Attendance of *Bacchus.* Oh Quintessence of all Mirth and Delight! what Expence can be too great to purchase the good Will of such generous Friends, and kind Relations!

If therefore, you by chance should meet with one of your Spouse's liberal Relations, let it be your Care to press him to accompany you Home, and their regale him with a Glass of exhilerating Wine. How pleasing will it be to her, to see her Friends treated with such extraordinary Respect; especially as by your Means he is introduced into the Company of Variety of pretty Ladies, your Spouse's Companions. And if he be single, 'tis highly probable, that you may be the happy Instrument of another Wedding. If this should be the Case, what Pleasure will you be the Author of to your Darling; for nothing pleases the Female Sex more, than to see the Work of Generation go on. By this you will make an Addition to your Wife's Associates and Favourites, who may be very useful to drive Fancies from her Brain, and extract Money from your Pocket.

If your Spouse's Judgment should fail her in the Choice of Houshold Furniture; doubt not but she will meet with variety of skilful Instructors, who will be always at hand to describe to her every Alteration in the Fashions, and point out to her, where she may lay out your Money to the best Advantage. These Ladies are extremely skilful in the Art of furnishing a House, so that you never need to dispute with your Spouse, about the Hanging of a Picture: They'll presently insinuate, that 'tis much more genteel and elegant to have

that

that Place ador'd with China. Can any tender Hufband deny it? Then the Furniture of this, that, and the other Room, is of a very low Tafte, or intirely out of Fafhion; Madam falls in with their Judgment, has them all taken down, to make Room for fuch as will better fuit with her Fortune and Dignity. Thus, like privy Counfellors about a minor Prince, do they kindly exert their Talents for the Inftruction and Pleafure of your Spoufe. Happy Man, what canft thou wifh for more!

Doft thou regret the Money! Pifh, that's a Trifle; give it liberally; Madam knows how to lay it out. But if Cafh runs fhort, be filent about it, left it happen to create Uneafinefs in the tender Breaft of your Beloved, and thereby endanger her Health. ---- Poor Creature, 'tis Trouble and Fatigue enough for her, and oftentimes breaks in upon her neceffary Repofe, to confider of, and contrive the. moft expeditious Methods of introducing Plenty and Variety.

And now, O *tender Hufband*, you are conducted to the firft Step of the inftructive School of Patience; it is therefore highly unbecoming to give the leaft Hint of Thriftinefs or Frugality: Or that Trading decays, and Money is hard to come at; that Notes, Bonds, and Bills muft be difcharg'd; No, by no Means. Smother your Concern and counterfeit Serenity; unlefs you are difpos'd to draw down upon your Head the heavy Refentment of a juftly provoked Wife.

Rather let *Socrates* be your Inftructor, to teach you Silence, and patiently to fubmit yourfelf to the Guidance and Direction of your Wife; fo fhall you poffefs the Quinteffence of this fuperlative Pleafure, and with joyful Steps enter upon the following.

BOOK

BOOK. III.

Our young Couple walk abroad; are courte-
ously treated by all their Acquaintance; with
their Journey into the Country for Pleasure;
and other Things of great Importance to
know.

AS it is true, that there is a fpacious Field of
Mirth and Pleafure for the young married
Couple to range in, fo it is equally certain, that
the Way thither is as fertile of unknown Joys and
Delights. --- Seeing it was impoffible to invite every
one to the *Wedding*, therefore our fweet VENUS
muft be conducted Abroad with all the Splendor and
Pomp of coftly Drefs and Equipage, to be fhewn
to our Bridegroom's Friends and Acquaintance:
Nay, the whole Town muft be Witnefs to the
Beauty of her Perfon, and the Harmony of their
Behaviour. To this Purpofe fhe exalts her Voice
thro' every Street to be heard, and eagerly ftares
into every Houfe to obferve her Admirers.

What fuperlative Joy is here! they can hardly
go half the Length of a Street, but they are faluted
by fome or other of their Friends, with ten Thou-
fand Wifhes for their Health, Happinefs and Profperity; with fuch a Profufion of Praifes upon the
Bride, as create an unfpeakable Pleafure in the
Mind of her Spoufe. Others invite them to walk
in, where after the ufual Wifhes and Salutations,
the Bowl goes round, attended with frequent Re-
petitions of Health, long Life and Happinefs.

Well, thinks the young unmarried Lady, what

3   a fur-

a furprizing Difference there is between a married Woman and a Maid! Every one refpe

cts, treats, and honours her. ---- She's every Day vifiting and taking her Pleafures; and is embraced and carefs'd with all the Tokens of the moft ardent and inviolable Friendfhip. Her Wonder ceafes at the eager Defires Women have to Matrimony; nor is fhe at a Lofs to account for their rufhing a fecond 'and a third Time into the Eftate, even before their former Hufbands are cold in the Grave. Oh, fays fhe, what a Fulnefs of Joy and Felicity there is in a married Life!

But this, great as it is, is only an Introduction to more Delight: Frefh Invitations are crouding in from every Quarter to Entertainments; many of which being as coftly and grand as that of their Wedding, our Couple are not a little delighted, that they are always preferr'd to the Head of the Table. If Madam is out of Order next Morning, her tender Spoufe knowing her Conftitution, propofes a Journey into the Air, or a Voyage upon the *Thames :* If the Latter is approved of, there's immediately a Pleafure-Barge ready, with brawny Slaves to execute her Will. Thrice happy State! Oh, that the grand Luminary would now ftand ftill to view the happy Pair, and thereby add fome few Hours more to the declining Day! Well, he's certainly blind who can't fee the abundant Pleafures of Matrimony.

Invitations from Friends being at a Stand, and the young Couple having had fome few Days Refpite, Madam propofes taking a Country-Journey together; firft to Places adjacent, afterwards to fome more remote: And having heard great Commendations of *Oxford* and *Cambridge*, fhe intends them a Vifit; and afterwards, my Dear, fays fhe, we will go to *York, Glocefter* and *Briftol*, for I have been credibly inform'd, that the Coun-

D tries

trics there about are exceeding pleasant, and all Accommodations extraordinary cheap. Nor would I for all the World, adds she, miss *Herefordshire*; pray therefore, my Dear, indulge me with an Opportunity of tasting some unadulterated Cyder and Perry, which is no where else to be had ; and as to *Kent*, tho' I must make one Journey thither, yet that I'll defer till after our Return to *London*. Ah, my Dear, says she, pray let us set out next Week at farthest.

Certain it is, that the good Man hears these his Spouse's Proposals with great Reluctancy, having no Inclination to be so long absent from Business, for what with Courting, Wedding, Feasting, and taking Pleasure, he finds his Substance already considerably diminish'd ; but alas, all his Attempts to dissuade her are fruitless, for, you may as well

> *Controul the Wind, and calm the Ocean's Foam,*
> *As make a tattling Gossip stay at Home ;*
> *Some Men to Business, some to Pleasure fall,*
> *But Women at their Hearts, are Rakish all.*

She dreams of her intended Journey by Night, and incessantly talks on it by Day; this is her Language : If we don't take our Pleasure now we are young, when shall we ? You know, my Dear, that a Year hence, I may have a Child, and then I must bid adieu to all Diversion, I then shall be ty'd by the Leg ; and truly, I don't see why we should not take our Pleasure as well as Mrs. *Gad-out* and her Husband, or Mrs. *Hate-home* and her Husband, I am sure we can as well afford it ; they were abroad two Months together this Summer ; you know my Dear, that my Mother, or my Cousin *Save-all*, will look to the House in our Absence ; therefore, let us away ; for the first Year you know will never return.

Well, what shall the good Man do ? if he consults his Peace, his Wife must have her Will. He loves her too well to oppose her Desires with Violence ; his Father taught him this Sentence for a Marriage Lesson, *Beware of making the first Difference.* He is not willing therefore, to give his Spouse harsh Language, lest that should occasion it, and be an Interruption to the Pleasures of the Matrimonial State.

The good Man no sooner complies, but Madam immediately orders a new laced Riding Habit, Hat, Wig, and several other Necessaries, as she calls 'em, for the Journey. Their best Apparel is pack'd up and sent before by the Carrier, that they may appear before their Friends in the Country with Credit and Reputation.

Well, away they go, every one wishing them Health, Prosperity, and a safe Return. But see ! they are hardly ten Miles from *London*, before our Traveller is so ill with the bounding of her Horse, that every Thing about her seems to be in a circular Motion, which affects so strongly her tender Stomach, that she's just ready to disgorge all its Contents. Down jumps her Spouse, to give her some Assistance ; but what can he do, no House being near ? At last the poor Lady falls into a Swoon : Oh Heavens ! who suffers most ? Madam's insensible, and he poor Creature, frantick with Surprize ; he sighs and laments excessively, calls upon her, she hears him not, which throws him into inexpressible Torments and Agonies. Well, at last his Angel begins to shew some Indications of Life, and soon after recovers Strength enough to walk a few Yards to and again, to his unspeakable Joy. After a while they remount, and ride softly on for fear of a Relapse ; the good Man thinking every Step a Mile 'till he arrives at some Inn, where his dearly beloved may perfect her Recovery.

Truly

Truly, I muſt confeſs, that if this is one of the Pleaſures of Matrimony, 'tis but a very ſorry one : But ſtay a little, yonders the Steeple, we ſhall be there preſently ; the Trouble and Vexation you have met with, will ſoon be ſufficiently recompenced by the beautiful Situation of the Place, and the kind Reception you meet with. The young Lady's Stomach being cleans'd by her Diſorder, will with the Help of the open Air, ſtrongly ſolicite her to recruit ; the good Man the mean while is contriving to pay the firſt Viſit, where he thinks his poor wearied Spouſe will receive the warmeſt Careſſes and beſt Entertainment ; this, he hopes, will effectually baniſh from her Mind all Ideas of the Sickneſs and Fatigue of her Journey. They walk abroad, ſee the Rarities, viſit his Friends and Relations, every one wiſhing them Joy, emulating each other in Acts of Kindneſs and Hoſpitality, which I aſſure is you no ſmall Pleaſure ; but every Thing muſt have an End : Madam now begins to talk of viſiting ſome other City ; but ſhe'll travel no further on Horſeback, leſt the ſame Calamity ſhould befall her again.

Well, our indulgent Huſband provides her a Coach, and the great Trunk is faſtned behind ; and that they may go off with the greater State and Grandeur, the Coach is order'd to their Friends Door. Well, in they get amidſt a thouſand Wiſhes, that Content, Pleaſure and Delight, may attend upon them thro' the whole of their Journey. Then drive on Coachman is the Word, and away fly the poor Jades thro' the Street, ſtriking Fire out of the lifeleſs Stones, as tho' the God *Pluto* was upon his Flight with his beloved *Proſerpine,*

But, O thoughtleſs Couple, conſider what a vaſt Expence will attend this needleſs Ramble ! And tho' the young Enamorata is convinced that a few ſuch Journeys as theſe will make him a Bankrupt ; yet

yet he prudently prefers Peace, Quietness, and the Pleasure of his Spouse to all other Considerations. Nay, as these are the *first Fruits and Pleasures of Marriage*, Madam thinks they are greatly obstructed by every Thought of Home, and therefore endeavours to divert the Mind of her Spouse, from attending to any Thing beyond the present Enjoyments. In the mean Time, the Servants at Home are following the Example of the young Couple Abroad. For, as they are under no Restraint, they keep open House to all their Companions and Associates; and at every Visit that they receive, down goes the Spit, and on goes the Pot; and if *Beer*, *Wine*, *Brandy*, or any Thing else in the House are wanting; the most secure Locks are made to give Way to their pretty Devices and Stratagems: This I could illustrate by numberless Examples, but they would be useless, especially to those who for any Length of Time, have committed their Affairs to Servants: Thus every Hand is some Way or other, employed to render this loving Couple superlatively Happy.

These are also some of the *Delights* of *Marriage*; and tho' the Helps that the Servants of our young Couple afford, to bring on the End, to which they both with speedy Steps are hastening, may seem trifling and but of small Importance; yet they are no less sure and certain, as many have felt to their Cost.

What Matter of Surprize is it therefore, if your House-Rent has been great, your *pleasuring frequent*, your *Servants unnecessary, wasteful and expensive*, and all this to please and recreate the Darling of your Heart; what Wonder is it, I say, if at the Year's End, the Decrease of your Substance sounds loudly in your Ears, *Oh miserable Pleasure!*

But, the greatest Calamity in this Delight, appears immediately upon your Return Home. Observe your
Spouse,

Spouse, alas! She's so prodigiously fatigued with travelling from Place to Place, that her very Bones are almost dislocated; her Back, poor Creature, is in such violent Pain, that she is not able to walk a-cross her Chamber; 'tis impossible for her to rise before Noon, nor even then, unless there is ready provided for her some costly Delicacy, to please her disorder'd Appetite. ———— In the mean Time your Servants are simpering, giggling, and rejoicing; desiring nothing more than that Madam may always continue as she is, that they may have the more Liberty to indulge themselves and Confederates, at the Family-Expence. The Eyes of *Argus* are not numerous, or quick enough to detect 'em; for should you suspect their Conduct, they have Excuses at all Times ready to delude you. But these Things are more frequent and predominant, when a cunning Slut of a Maid has got the Length of her Mistresses Foot. In such Cases, you must have two Maids, when one is sufficient, and often a Chairwoman; the one to do your Maids Work, the other to go of her Errands, that Business may the sooner be dispatch'd, and that she may be ready the sooner to go a gadding with her Mistress. ————

And as *Peggy* is so well acquainted with her Mistresses Humour, and Method of Managing the Family; she poor Creature is released from a World of Trouble and Fatigue, and may therefore with the greatest Security indulge herself in Rest, Dressing, or Reading of Plays at her Pleasure. If the Husband, upon his Return from the *Exchange*, should seem any Ways uneasy at the Disorder that appears in every Apartment; *Peggy* immediately complains, that her poor Mistress has been afflicted with such unsufferable Pains in her Head, Belly and Back, that all their Time has been employ'd in endeavouring to procure her some Relief; and that is the

Reason

Reason Sir, says the Huſſy, that Things are in this Confuſion and Diſorder; this at once ſtops the good Man's Mouth.

If at any Time he inſinuates that the Chairwoman puts them to an unneceſſary Expence. She anſwers thus: *Prithee, My Dear, give yourſelf no Trouble about theſe Things; ---- I am ſurpriz'd at you; they are entirely out of your Province; pray leave them to me; I warrant you I am able to manage the Affairs of my Family without your Directions; ſurely 'tis a Woman's Buſineſs, and not a Man's, to intermeddle with the Affairs of the Maids; beſides, my Dear, the Expence of a Chairwoman or Semſtreſs* three or four Days in a Week, is not *worth Notice.*

This female Harangue, if he values his Peace, muſt give him entire Satisfaction; and being made in the Preſence of *Peggy,* who communicates it to the reſt, they are thereby encouraged to call him in their Miſtreſſes hearing, *a Cott,* Tom *peep in the Pot,· Goodman Buſy-body,* and the like.

At Dinner, *Peggy* takes Occaſion to aſk *Madam* if ſhe won't go by and by, and pay Mrs. *Moody* a Viſit, or chat a little with Madam *Eleanor ?* 'Twill divert you Madam, ſays ſhe, as you ſeem to be not very well; ſhe'll be vaſtly delighted to hear the Story of the *North-Country* Gentleman, you having ſuch a charming, lively Manner of telling it; and I am certain, ſhe wants greatly to ſee you. Dinner is no ſooner over, but a Coach is call'd, and away go *Madam,* and her Maid *Peggy.*

It certainly affords no ſmall Pleaſure to the Huſband, to obſerve the Harmony and Agreement ſubſiſting in his Family, a ſtrong Proof of the complying Temper of his Spouſe. But the Advantage he reaps by it is great, for *Peggy* by her cunning Inſinuations and Inſtructions, has ſufficiently convinced her Miſtreſs, that the Pleaſures of the Town are vaſtly ſuperior to thoſe of the Country; ſo that

the

the good Man is under no Apprehensions of the Expence of a second Country Journey.

Behold, O LOVERS, what a Multiplicity of Roses, Lillies, and delicious Fruits spring up in the very Entrance of the spacious Garden of Marriage! Ponder well then, what the Middle of that fertile Plat may produce!

BOOK IV.

The buxom Dame gossips with her Neighbours, complains she is not with Child, consults the Doctor, is order'd Physick, with other Matters too engaging to be overlook'd.

OUR young Couple, having abundantly enjoy'd the Pleasures that flow from being feasted and caress'd; from travelling about, and viewing Curiosities; from shewing themselves to each others Relations; but especially, *O ravishing Delight!* in discerning how grandly and sumptuously they can be entertain'd for their Money; they come at last, surprizing Alteration! to discover the Emptiness and Vanity of all; and have therefore longing Desires to be at Home again to pursue their respective Employments. Verily, this is the happy Period, that the Husband has been long expecting: Now he begins to hope that his Affairs will be thoroughly regulated, and that his loving Spouse also, will, like a good Housewife, attend to the Management of the Houshold Concerns with double Diligence; which, when it is the Case, what Joy does the good Man experience?

But

But O, kind Husband, set some Bounds, some reasonable Limits to your new experienc'd Happiness ; ----- don't imagine that you are now in the high Road to all Fulness of Joy ; wait but a few Days; and Experience will undeceive you.

For the Wife has not been long at Home, before she begins to be terribly uneasy ; not knowing how to accommodate herself to this unexperienced Way of Life ; nor can she comfort herself to converse with this new Maid ; 'tis exceeding irksome to be shewing her this, commanding her that ; and far worse to be at the Pains of examining into Affairs, which she never before in her Life gave herself any Trouble about ; then the Strangeness of her new Habitation, and the Remembrance of her Father's House, are ready to distract her ; insomuch that our fond Husband has Work enough upon his Hands to chase these imaginary Difficulties from her Brain, and with Kisses to dry up those Tears, which are incessantly flowing. The poor Man has scarcely pacify'd her, and brought her to Temper, but another Cloud approaches, and eclipses all his Joys.

Madam, by this Time, has got some Acquaintance in the Neighbourhood, which she so carefully cultivates, that in a short Time, her Visits are so frequent, that she is much more Abroad than at Home. Here she becomes acquainted with Mrs. *Wanton,* who introduces her to Mrs. *Breed-well,* who is very busy in getting up her *Child-bed Linen,* her Reckoning being near expir'd. Then she is also very intimate with modest Mrs. *Long-for't,* whose want of a great Belly fills her Mouth with Complaints, and her Eyes with Tears ; nor is she a Stranger to Mrs. *Young-at-it,* who is always bragging that she dates her Reckoning from the very first Embrace. Lord, says she to herself, I have been now a Wife full three Months, and am still an utter

E Stranger

Stranger to the Pleasures these Women enjoy; what can possibly be the Reason of it?

This extreamly afflicts our young Gentlewoman, and sets her Invention to work to discover the genuine Cause: And woe be to the good Man, if he has been deficient. To the End therefore that she may satisfy her Curiosity, she in a full Assembly of her female Associates, mighty modestly relates every Circumstance of what pass'd between her and her Husband; not only the first Time they bedded, but ever since, in order that she may draw from them the like Confession; this answers her End, for they one after another begin to expatiate upon the Furniture and Performances of their Husbands; in which Relations, the disconsolate Lady easily discovers several Particulars, which far exceed what she herself ever experienced, which shocks her extreamly.

However they not only pity her, but they advise her frequently to provide for the good Man, *Eggs, Oysters, Cockscombs, Sweet-breads, Lambs-Stones, Eryngo Root,* &c. at the same Time he must be persuaded to restrain from *Tobacco, Coffee,* and every Thing else that *dries the Body,* or *cools the Kidneys*; nor must he omit going to the *Coffee-House* every Morning, to drink plentifully of *Chocolate.* They conclude with advising Madam, to be continually dallying with him, to expose before him her *naked Bosom,* and by every *wanton Posture* endeavour to solicite him to embrace her, not only more frequently, but with the greater Vigour.

Who can doubt, but she will soon put this into Execution? O happy Man, who art every Day regaled with the most luxurious and delicious Dainties! and hast the Liberty of attending the *Coffee-House* every Morning, without those bitter Reflections, with which many are loaded by their Wives.

Wives. And not only so, but your Wife beautiful as an Angel, is continually embracing and kissing you with unspeakable Eagerness and Rapture!

But alas! if after all this, Madam finds not the desired Alteration, her Countenance falls, her whole Behaviour is rude and abrupt, and she soon begins, by expatiating upon her own Youth, Willingness, Health, and promising Appearance, to call in Question the *Virility* of her Husband. Astonished with this unexpected Accusation, the poor despised Husband endeavours his own Vindication, *&c.* calling in to his Assistance, *Aristotle*, *Culpeper*, *Salmon*, and others: But all to no Purpose, she still complains, and must have a Child soon, or she shall run distracted. From this Time, the House is more a Burthen to her than ever; being always Abroad, and continually kissing, hugging and embracing her Neighbours Children to such a Degree, that many of 'em are more fond of her than of their own Mothers.

This gadding Abroad, does undoubtedly a little trouble her Spouse; but then, he considers that by this Means she will be acquainted with nursing, and the Management of young Children without any Charge; but he is the better reconcil'd to her Absence, in that he is freed from her Groans, Sighs and Complaints; for besides these, when she's at Home, his Ears are saluted with nothing but a Description of the Beauty and pretty Actions of some Neighbour's Child; and generally sums up the whole, with declaring that she'd part with all she is worth in the World, could she but be Mother of such a one.

The good Man, almost distracted at his Wife's Affliction, and finding all his Attempts to pacify her, only encreases the Disorder; he is determin'd at last to consult a Physician for himself, and to

recommend

recommend Madam to the Affiftance of fome old Doctreffes and Midwives. He therefore applies him to a *French* Doctor, eminently renown'd for removing the Caufes of Barrennefs in Women, and Impotency in Men. And why fhould he doubt of Succefs, when *Monfieur* by ftrengthening the generative Faculties, has been the happy Inftrument of giving Exiftence to fome Scores of fmiling Infants, who, without his Affiftance, had never had a Being ? The good Woman alfo confults with her Female Phyficians, that if the Fault is on her Side, it may be happily removed.

To this End, there are as many Phials and Gallypots fent in, as would ftock an Apothecary's Shop : And her Ladyfhip is made the Receptacle of a thoufand Medicaments, the better to difpofe her for Conception.

The good Man, that he may have nothing to accufe himfelf of, is very exact in taking inwardly, every three Hours, a certain Number of Chymical Drops, upon which the *French* Doctor beftowed the higheft Encomiums.

Well, if all this will not anfwer Madam's End, what fhall the poor Man have Recourfe to next ? If coftly Apparel will content her, he'll buy them for her : And altho' her Pride and Ambition many Times, are not confiftent with the Conftitution of his Pocket, yet he will not oppofe her, hoping that while fhe is exercifing her Thoughts about Finery and Grandeur, fhe will, at leaft for fome Time, lay afide her Reproaches and Lamentations for the Want of a Child ; and if in this Interim his earneft Wifhes and vigorous Endeavours, fhould be crown'd with Fertility, what Mortal could add to his Felicity, or conceive his Joy ?

BOOK

BOOK V.

*Joyful News, Madam proves with Child, and
longs; with the Pleasures that attend both:
Also some remarkable Accidents, not taken
Notice of by any other Author.*

WELL, the Clouds that have long obstructed
the Happiness of our loving Couple, are
dispell'd, and the Sun-shine of as yet unknown
Joys is breaking forth upon 'em. *Madam* has at
last conceived. Of what infinite Service are
Doctors and *Midwives?* Now, O young Woman,
is the Time for you to be extreamly cautious and
careful, lest 'inadvertently you occasion the Fruit
to fall before 'tis thorough Ripe : The Consequences of which, as all good Women affirm, are
much more to be dreaded, than the most violent
Pains of *Childbearing*. As for you, her kind indulgent Husband, who have behav'd yourself so
vigorously, continue now to reap the delightful
Reward of your Labour. If you are still desirous
of Pleasure, Joy and Happiness, disdain to take
notice of small Matters. You must now view
every Thing at a Distance, as thro' a Glass. And
as your Beloved possesses infinitely more Charms
than ever she did before, so must your Care, Tenderness and Concern for her, vastly exceed any
you ever before express'd. Does she *sigh*, *groan*,
or *grumble*; or, does she fretfully and peevishly
insult the Servants, or yourself; pass it by as the
necessary and unavoidable Consequences of her
Pregnancy. But rejoice, and be exceeding glad

if

if this happen only in the Day; becaufe you may then frequently avoid it. But generally the good Woman is worft in the Night; therefore be fure to have always at Hand the beft *Citron, Clove,* *Cinnamon* and *Plague-Waters,* that you may expre your Love, by being prepar'd to affift her. If your deareft fhould difturb you in the Night, which is often the Cafe, with Complaints of Pains in the Back, Head, Dizzinefs and Lownefs of Spirits, tho' it be never fo cold, you muft rife with all Speed, to call all the Servants about to her Affift-ance. And this is a new Pleafure, and it muft be acknowledged a great one.

But tho' the foregoing be a very great Pleafure to every tender Hufband, yet the following one is infinitely greater.

At every Entertainment that the young Couple are invited to, the big-belly'd Woman, before any Perfon prefumes to touch a Bit, muft, with a thou-fand genteel Compliments be prevail'd upon to help her felf of what fhe beft likes; and tho' fhe excufes herfelf, and declares that fhe has no Fancy to any Thing in particular, yet it only ferves to make the Company more urgent: And if fhe by chance cafts her Eye upon the Plate of one of the Guefts, 'tis immediately prefum'd that fhe Longs; and who would be fo brutifh, as not to oblige her to accept it? By this Means the poor Lady is oftentimes o-bliged to rife from Table, and being over-charged, is almoft ready to faint. Here all Hands are em-ploy'd: One loofens her Stays, another chafes her Temples, a third applies *Sal Volatile,* or *Hartfhorn* to her Noftrils, and all the Company are crouding themfelves clofe together, that Madam may have Air; thefe, with the Help of a Glafs of Brandy, reftores her fleeting Spirits. And tho' fhe finds that this Practice has generally the fame Effect upon her, yet fhe frequently repeats it, to the

great

great Joy and Confolation of her Hufband.

Madam having fufficiently indulged herfelf this Way; fhe now takes it into her Head, that fitting too much will hinder the Growth of the Child. The good Man willing to have the Credit of a jolly Boy, gives in to his Spoufe's Opinion; upon which fhe goes every Day a Pratling and Goffiping from one Place to another, leaving her Hufband without a Wife, and the Family without a Miftrefs.

As every Thing grows tirefome by Degrees, fo Madam begins to defire a Change : She pretends that fhe's too heavy to walk without Affiftance, and therefore her Spoufe muft accompany her, that fhe may lean upon his Arm. How tenderly he complies with the Motion! She longs for Fruit, but it muft be of her own gathering. Well, out they fet, but in a little Time fhe becomes fo exceffively weary, that if her Life was to lye at Stake, fhe can't fet one Foot farther. Well, what's to be done now? fhe muft not venture on Horfeback for the World, that might occafion a Mifcarriage; and a Coach, if it might be fafe, is perhaps not to be had. If you are near the River, why the Water may be rough; and that would furprize her indeed : But if it is intirely calm, perhaps there's never a Waterman : If you find a Waterman, who knows but he may be in Liquor, and who would then entruft him with fuch a valuable Cargoe? Well, if thefe are not exquifite Pleafures, what are?

However, if after all any happy Expedient may be found, to convey your lovely Charge fafe Home, it will be no fmall Joy. Well, make yourfelf as eafy as you can, to the End that other Troubles may have the lefs Effect upon you.

The good Woman growing pretty big, afferts her Privilege, which is to be fupply'd with all fhe

afks,

asks, or longs for. And what Man that loves a
Woman, and has any Tenderness for the Fruit of
her Womb, can be cruel enough to oppose her?
What, tho' her Longings are frequent and expen-
five, is not every Husband sufficiently rewarded,
by that secret inexpressible Pleasure which always
attend him, while he is generously supplying her
Wants. Miserable is that Husband, whosoever
he be, whose Soul is not susceptible of these
tender Impressions; 'tis very certain that these
Longings vary with the Seasons, as in the Summer for *Oranges*, *Asparagus*, *Strawberries* and
Wine, *Cherries*, *Plumbs*, *Peaches*, *Apricots*, &c.

Now let Madam long for any, or all of these,
tho' they should be ever so difficult to come at,
or expensive to purchase, she must have her Fill,
for who would hazard the Loss, or Disfigurement
of a Child, and the first Child too, got also with
so much Charge and Difficulty, for such Trifles.

When the later Fruits are in Season, Madam
sings over-again the same Tune; poor Creature,
how can she help it? If this Hour she longs for
Catherine Pears, the next Hour she is equally
desirous of *Golden-Pippins*; then she has a Mind
to *Filberds*, and an Hour after to *Walnuts* or
Grapes. Do what you will, there's no Help for
it, her longing must be satisfied. Thus is the
poor young Creature harrass'd from one Thing to
another.

There is no Season of the Year that exempts our
breeding Women from these Difficulties ---- In
Winter they long for *Pomgranates*, *Chesnuts and
Wine*; then *Colchester*-Oysters; anon for *Green
Geese*, or *Young Chickens*; with a thousand other
Delicacies, that present themselves to their dif-
order'd Imaginations ----

The poor Woman, whose Longing is the Consequence of her *Pregnancy*, is *O indulgent Spouse*,
the

the Object of thy tender Compassion and Regard ; but how often does she hanker after the same, nay, frequently more expensive Things, that she may indulge her luxurious Appetite, when her Pretensions to Pregnancy are either precarious, or whimsical. ---- This liquorish Palate of her's, frequently drives the good Man out of Bed in the middle of the Night ; and tho' it rains, blows, or snows ever so excessively, he goes thro' all, with the greatest Eagerness and Pleasure imaginable. And when, the good Woman finds to her Sorrow, that she is not with Child, she immediately, to keep up her Credit with her Husband, pretends to be taken very ill, and in a Day or two after miscarries, charging all upon her Spouse's not furnishing her with something that she long'd for.

However, if Madam is really with Child, what with her eating excessively of raw Fruits, Multiplicity of Sweetmeats, swallowing down Quarts of Cyder, and Wine of various Qualities ; she begins at last, to be violently afflicted with the Cholick, and other very grievous and lamentable Pains. This introduces a Train of unexperienced Pleasures : The Doctor is immediately sent for, who orders Cordials and other exhilarating Draughts to be taken, which, however, she is soon weary of. And as his Prescriptions are not so agreeable to her, as something that may give Pleasure to her Palate ; she declares, that she is certain that the Doctor has mistaken her Case, her Modesty preventing her from telling him the whole of her Complaints. The Midwife therefore, my Dear, must be sent for ; she's better acquainted than he, with Women's Affairs. *Mother Midnight* immediately appears, and having very minutely enter'd into the Nature of Madam's Disorders, advises her to be of good Cheer, assuring her that Lowness of Spirits is the only Cause and Origin of all. Let us but remove that, Child, says

F   she,

she, and all your other Complaints will vanish of course. Provide yourself therefore with the best *White-wine*, simmer it with *Spices*, *Orange-Peel*, and *Lump-Sugar*, over the Fire, and as often as you find yourself in Pain, sickish, or faint, drink plentifully : And as to more solid Medicines, the most effectual in your Case, are to be met with at the *Confectioners*, or *Pastry-cooks* ; but be sure, above all Things, indulge yourself every two or three Hours with a Glass of the best *Sack* ; this strengthens and invigorates the Child in the Womb, and will greatly facilitate its Passage out of it.

Who doubts, but that Madam prefers the Advice of her *Midwife* to that of the Doctor, her Directions being such that may be comply'd with, by the most delicate and tender Constitution ; but as to physical Remedies, it is observable, she has often heard Doctor *Drink-all* say, that Medicines taken with Reluctancy, or Antipathy, are never of Advantage to the Patient.

Thus, *O approaching Father*, you are ascended one Step higher towards the Pinnacle of true Glory and solid Happiness. Your heroick Deeds, in the Field of Love, immortalize your Fame, and the fond Embraces, and tender Glances of your now contented Spouse, serve to augment your Joy ! Her Language is now expressive of the most ardent Love, and indicates her great Approbation of, and Delight in your masculine Embraces. ----

Hide not then from others, the Pleasures and Felicities thou art happily advanced to ; rejoyce also, that the greatest and most substantial are yet in Reserve : Pleasures which will not only lighten your Heart, but your Purse also, much more effectually than those you have already experienc'd.

Comfort yourself also with this, that thro' the timely Assistance of the Doctor, the Midwife, and your own Endeavours, you may at length be the happy
Parent

Parent of a numerous and beautiful Iſſue; not only.
to the aggrandizing of your Name and Ability
Abroad, but to the Honour of your Family, and
Delight of your Spouſe at Home.

BOOK VI.

Childbed Linen is to be provided ; the Care of
the Infant ; Choice of a Midwife and
Nurſe ; vaſtly important as well to the Huſ-
band as his Spouſe and Child.

DElightful Sight! Our good Woman's Petticoats
and Aprons are ſhortning a great Pace; which,
with an engaging Fall in the Back, diſplays to the
raviſh'd Beholder a Pair of Legs, not ſwell'd in the
leaſt, but attended with all the Advantage of
Symetry and juſt Proportion : Now, the Virility and
Vigour of the Huſband, and the Healthfulneſs and
Docility of the Wife, are expreſs'd in evident and
undeniable Characteriſticks.

Now, Oh happieſt of Mortals, you are under no terrifying Apprehenſions of a fatal Miſcarriage to damp
your Joys, or ſubject you to the Deriſion of your
ſcoffing Neighbours, who are apt to imagine a
Miſcarriage to be nothing elſe but a *Matrimonial-*
Cloak for Barrenneſs or Impotency. Your Manhood has alſo delivered you from the unjuſt Suſ-
picions, and heart-breaking Reflections that you
have heretofore labour'd under, from your miſtaken
Wife; which you was obliged then to ſubmit to,
and hide, till Madam's Pregnancy ſhould declare
your Praiſe.

These Dangers are now all over, and you, O

Source

Source of Joys unknown, will soon be saluted with the welcome Name, *Pappa !* pleasing and acceptable as *Bridegroom* was before.

In the mean Time your Spirits are greatly elated, with hearing the exact Account your Darling keeps of every Week and Day. How heavily the Time rowls on, he cries ; yet it must be very amusing to consider, that the nearer she approaches to the Time of her Delivery, the more frequent and loving are her Kisses and Embraces. ---- Now you begin to perceive that a fruitful Womb cements Affection, and kindles fresh Desires.

Well, our good Woman now begins to employ her whole Care and Attention towards preparing her Baby-Things ; and, tho' there are in the Family and House, many other Affairs that seem to demand her Attention ; yet, poor Creature, her Spirits are so fatigued with the former, that she can't bestow a single Thought upon the latter. Indeed 'tis no Wonder ; for she has besides this, her Visitors to entertain with copious Discourses of her Condition, through the whole Course of her Pregnancy, which she relates very circumstantially ; and as this, together with the Expiration of her Reckoning, are Subjects of a very extensive Nature ; so nothing is more common than for Madam herein to spend three or four Hours at a Time, to the great Edification of a very attentive Auditory. How happy would it be, were our Clergy so seriously attended ! This is a very great Consolation to the Maids ; the Subject before between Madam and her Neighbours, being chiefly about the Wages, Housewifry, Dress, Vices, &c. but seldom about the Virtues of those female Domesticks ----

How entertaining it must be to the Husband, to observe the Care of his Dearest, in contriving and calculating with Mrs. *Stitch-quick* the Milliner, about the necessary Quantity of Linen for *Baby-Things.*

Things. How diligent she is in taking the exact Dimensions of every different Piece of *Childbed-Furniture*, to the End that she may not run her *Husband* to unnecessary Charges.

Well, away she goes to buy two or three Pieces of *Holland* and *Cambrick*, not forgetting a proportionate Quantity of *Laces* and *Edgings* ; the Contents, or Expence of which, what Husband would obliterate his Joy and Felicity to enquire into ?

Certainly our *Husband* is unspeakably happy, in having a Wife so indefatigable, in procuring every Thing in Time that she may stand in need off. See how solicitous she is, that nothing may be omitted, and how uneasy is she, now the Materials are bought, to provide the most expert and expeditious Persons to make them up.

But as this requires Time to be effected, so before 'tis accomplish'd, you'll find your ever careful Spouse equally embarassed about the Choice of a *Midwife* and Nurse, because upon this, depend very much the Life both of the dear Infant and its Mother. Let it not, therefore, in the least disturb you, but rather be pleasing and acceptable, if she be continually teazing you, and craving your Opinion and Advice in the Choice of this, that, or the other Person : for hereby, you will have an Occasion to observe her great Care ---- And this will be farther illustrated, that among the great Variety of *Midwives* recommended to her, she is very cautious in chusing ; for one is too young and unexperienc'd, another is *too old and fumbling*, a third is very *clumsey Fisted*, the fourth is always Drinking and Smoaking, and the fifth will deafen you with her Noise --- In short, there are so many Defects in each, that the poor Woman stands greatly in need of Counsellors.

The like Trouble has she in the Choice of a *Nurse*, for, after having spent a Month in enquiring among her Neighbours, she can hear of none without Faults ; and some of 'em very great ones ; for one is *very nasty and sluttish*, another is *idle and sauntering*, another *too dainty*, a fourth *is pert and saucy* ; one *eats too much*, another *drinks too much* ; one is *too free with the Maids*, or *too great with the Men*. There is one or two indeed, that she could fancy very well ; but then, they have not a good Knack in tossing up a little Delicacy, in a Manner suitable to the Weakness of Madam's Appetite ; which is a Matter of very great Importance.

Behold ! then, how the poor Creature is surrounded with Difficulties. And, notwithstanding she is so heavy and cumbersome, that 'tis with the utmost Difficulty that she moves from Chair to Chair ; yet her Care to manage her Concerns with Reputation to her Spouse, are in no Degree lessened ; what an industrious Wife you have ! ----

Well, she has at last, tho' with immense Difficulty, provided herself with a *Midwife* and *Nurse* ; yet still she finds no End to her Care. She now recollects some Necessaries that were omitted in the Hurry of her former Affairs ; as, a *Cradle* for the Child ; a *Skreen* to environ the Chimney ; then again, she must have new *Hangings*, and *Window-Curtains*, a *Down-Bed* for her Ease ; a *Silver Caudle-Cup*, *Candlesticks*, and a curious *Mantle*, for the *Christening* ---- so that the good Man need not fear the Circulation of his Money. How happy will your good Wife be, when once these troublesome Affairs are over, that she may have Time to give Orders, for the clearing the House from Top to Bottom ; for what a Scandal will it be should she be taken in Labour, and the House in such Confusion and Disorder, at such a Time as that, the Gossips being very busy in making ill-natur'd Observations.

These

Thefe Things do fo exceffively difturb her, that
they engrofs all her Thoughts by Day, and frequently break in upon her Repofe at Night ; fo
that fhe is often obliged to lye in Bed till Noon, in
order to fupply that Deficiency ; and if fhe happens
at any Time to be employing her Thoughts too
intenfely, about her approaching Labour-Pains,
poor Creature, how it fhocks her ; fhe feems to
be turning infide out, and has not Spirits fufficient
to declare to thofe about her, the Nature and
Caufe of her Diforder. ---- If fhe is thus feiz'd in
the Night, her *Hufband*, diftracted with Grief and
Concern, jumps out of Bed, tho' in the Depth of
Winter ; rouzes all his Servants in order to procure fome *Cinnamon, Annis-feed,* or *Plague-Water,*
to recover his *Dearest* from fuch fudden and
threatning Symptoms ; and if by a timely Admini-
ftration of fome of thefe, her Complaints are either
remov'd or mitigated, what rapturous Pleafures are
the Confequence !

Happy, thrice happy Man, whofe Happinefs is
thus vifibly augmented, with the Increafe of his
Experience. ----

Well, Madam has not a Moment to reckon ;
and the Time is now at Hand, when the higheft
Encomiums will be beftow'd upon you, for the infinite Care you have taken of, and affectionate Regard you expreffed to the Wife of your Bofom,
thro' the whole Courfe of her Pregnancy : Now
will your Labours meet with a fuperabundant Reward, your Relations will e'er long come and congratulate you alfo, upon the Augmentation of
your Happinefs, and upon the Dignity of *Father,*
to which you are happily arriv'd ; and will requeft
it as the greateft Honour you can do them, that
you fuffer them to be Sponfors in Behalf of the
charming Infant ; and as an Acknowledgement of
fo great a Favour conferr'd upon them above others,

their

their Liberality to their *God-Child* will know no
Bounds. ----

Who then, in his Senfes, but would gladly fuffer
the Ill-conveniencies of a teeming Wife, and chear-
fully fuftain all the Expences attending, to be fo
greatly honoured, efteem'd and refpected by all his
Friends and Relations ?

'Tis high Time therefore, for you, (as you
have fufficiently ftock'd your Cellar with Wine,
and other Liquors) to go and felect out fome of
the moft delicious, to the End that your Spoufe's
Vifitants may be entertain'd in a Manner that may
exprefs the unbounded Joy of your Heart, at the
Dignity and Happinefs you are advanc'd to. ----

Solace yourfelf therefore for the prefent, with
the Expectation of the Pleafures that are to
follow. -----

BOOK VII.

*The good Woman falls in Labour ; with
various other entertaining Concomitants.*

BEhold, young Couple, and confider, what
Time is elapfed, and what a Sea of Pleafures
you have already waded thro', which demonftrates
to you the fuperlative Happinefs of a married Life.
You are now entering upon, as yet, an unknown
Scene of Delight ; Pleafures that know no Bounds ;
to which all your former may be confider'd as an
Introduction. ----

View *O, Hufband*, the Countenance and Behaviour

haviour of your Spouse, and see with Joy all the
Indications of approaching Labour : What *wry* and
four Faces she makes, what *Groanings* and *Squallings*
serenade your ravish'd Ears ! Well, who can help
it ! if her Time's come, let us wish her a happy
Minute. But sure she's mistaken, for a Fortnight
since, she said she had two Months to go, perhaps the
Cat has eat her Reckoning. Well, 'tis the first
Time, poor young Creature, she'll know better
with the next Child ; and as long as the Work of
Generation goes forward, the Husband must of
Necessity be highly delighted ----

Our Couple are hardly warm in their Bed, before Madam makes hideous Out-cries, and bitter
Lamentations, for fear she should want necessary
Assistants. 'Tis owing to you, says she, unkind
as you are, that I parted with *Jenny* and *Dolly* the
Sempstress: How handy and useful would they have
been about me in this my Extremity. Oh ! for
Heaven's Sake, my Dear, says she, arise and call
in some Help, or I shall be lost. Up starts our
astonished Husband, deaf with her Cries, and with
some of his Cloaths on, and the rest in his Hands,
runs down some of the Stairs and tumbles down
the rest, his Wife all the while roaring out, make
haste, make haste, make haste ! O the Midwife,
the Midwife in a Minute ! Our tender Husband,
having sent up the Maid, flies like an Arrow out
of a Bow, drown'd in Sweat, to the other End of
the Town, the Dwelling of *Mother Midnight.*
But who can describe the Anxiety and Perturbation
of his Soul, as he ran along, lest any unhappy Accident should prevent her coming. One while he's
in fear lest she should be sick ; then he's just distracted to think that possibly she may be call'd out
to some other Woman, who also may live at a
great Distance ; then she may be in the Country :
Or, if none of these may be the Case, it may be

impossible

impossible for him to procure a Coach, and that will be as bad, because the Gentlewomoman is unable to walk : And these gloomy and terrifying Apprehensions are greatly augmented, by the good Woman's declaring that she has set her Mind so much upon this *Midwife*, that if she is not to be had, she shall never be deliver'd. If another should come into the Room, immediately her Pains will go off, and who can answer for the Life of either the Infant or Mother?

But, O indulgent Spouse, moderate these your frightful and terrifying Apprehensions, 'tis possible that they may be all groundless, and only the Effects of your great Care and Sympathy for your Spouse. Who can tell, but that this necessary old Lady may be at Home, and that you may conduct her safely and speedily to your expecting Wife! What Joys will then take Place, when she is safely delivered of a fine jolly Boy, or a beautiful Daughter? Then will there be an End, at least for the Present, to your rising three or four Times a Night, in the Midst of Winter; nor will your Rest be any more disturbed with the lamentable, heart-piercing Groanings, and Grumblings of your big-belly'd Wife.

Think not much then of your present Trouble and Vexation. What tho' you are thus forced from your warm inviting Bed, and are obliged to traverse the Streets thro' Showers of heavy Rain, have you not this to comfort you, that 'tis a Work absolutely necessary to your future Honour and Happiness? And is also the proper Time to exhibit to your Friends, Neighbours and Relations, the Sincerity of your Love, and the superlative Ardency of your Affection.

But tho' you have been so fortunate, as to meet with the *Midwife*, and have introduced her to your Spouse's unspeakable Satisfaction; yet don't
vainly

vainly imagine that your Bufinefs is over, and all your Fatigue at an End. Are you fo ftupid as to believe, that good *Mother Midnight* is capable of herfelf to manage all the Affairs relating to your *Wife* and *Child*? Hafte away then with all Speed and Diligence, and collect together your *Sifters*, *Aunts* and *Coufins*, with others of your Spoufe's moft intimate Acquaintance ; hurry them quickly away ; they need not ftay to drefs, left in the mean Time their Affiftance fhould be wanted.

But be fure, that your Invitations are attended with all proper Order, Ceremony and Politenefs ; be very careful that each of thofe Ladies be invited in Order, according to Dignity, Age and Rela-tion ; becaufe a Miftake herein may introduce Confufion, and caufe much ill Blood amongft your Relations and Friends. ---- How lamentable will it be, if your Sifter fhould refufe to come to the Chriftening, becaufe your Brother's Wife was in-vited to the Labour before her ? She'll make no Allowances for the Hurry and Confufion, which your Wife's Illnefs muft neceffarily occafion in your fympathifing Breaft ; nor confider that the want of timely Help, and the terrible Symptoms of approaching Labour might induce you unthinkingly, to invite thofe firft, that were firft to be had.

'Tis true, thefe Difturbances, together with his Labour and Fatigue in running about backwards and forwards, may, at firft View, feem to damp the good Man's Joy, and decreafe his Felicity ; yet let him confider, that by thefe he is only in-itiated into the inftructive *School of Patience* ; in which he will by Degrees receive fuch agreeable Leffons, as will in the End perfect him in the Exercife of that moft valuable and ufeful Grace. Happy Tuition !

Well, the good, impatient, expecting *Daddy* is return'd, but to his inexpreffible Affliction, the

Goffips

Goſſips he has been haraſſing of himſelf to invite, are none of 'em come ; for, notwithſtanding the good Woman is ſuffering the moſt racking, excruciating Pain, and ſtands in great need of Help ; yet they muſt ſpend the precious Moments in adorning themſelves, as tho' they were going to a Wedding, fearing, tho' they are all Relations and Friends, the Obſervations and Remarks of each other.

Let us now compaſſionate a little the Diſtreſſes of our almoſt diſtracted Huſband : See how he runs to and fro, as deſtitute of all Senſe and Reflection, trampling his Hat under Feet, and tearing his inoffenſive Locks from his frantick Head ! Then he ſtands immoveable, and reſembles rather a Statue, than an animated Being. Anon, he's ſeiz'd with ſuch a violent Agitation in all his Limbs, that you would ſwear he was attack'd by a *Tertian* Ague. Then down he ſits, and hearing two or three piercing Squalls, he falls into ſuch an exceſſive Fit of crying and ſobbing, as would even melt the moſt unrelenting Heart. ---- Then comes one of the Goſſips to him, for ſome Things out of the Drawers ; and tho' he has the Keys in his Hands, he ſtarts up like one recover'd from a Trance, and runs with all the Eagerneſs of Deſparation from Place to Place, to ſeek for 'em. Another good Woman follows, to haſten the former, which ſtill heightens the poor Man's Flurry and Diſorder. He examines his Pockets with one Hand, while he holds the Key he's looking for in the other ; then putting the Key into his right Hand, he ſearches his Pockets for it with his Left : And thus he goes on backwards and forwards, 'till fortunately he at laſt drops the Key from his trembling Fingers upon the Floor, which puts an End to their Search, and reſtores him a little to his Senſes.

Well,

Well, the Drawers are examin'd, but, O shocking Disappointment ; many Things are yet wanting, and those that they find, are not in a proper Order for Use. The *Midwife* halloo's and bawls to such a Degree for the Things that she wants, that the Outcries of the labouring Woman are drown'd by her superior Noise.

Away runs fat *Marget* the Maid, puffing and blowing to their Neighbour Mrs. *Buy-all* ; in order to borrow some Necessaries for the Woman and Child ; what an unaccountable Dilemma, are the *Gossips* and our *Spouse* plung'd into afresh, by this unexpected Neglect ? Oh, that this was the End of his Sorrow !

Our venerable *Mother Midnight*, having examin'd the Premises with great Care and Circumspection, begins to discover by her Countenance, some Diffidence of Success ; which the sagacious Gossips discerning, they hover about her like a Swarm of Bees, begging and praying that if it is not her Work, she would be so merciful to the poor Gentlewoman as to declare it, to the End that they may send for superiour Assistance in Time. The prudent old Gentlewoman, thro' their Importunity, is obliged to confess, that great Difficulty attends the Case ; yet she is not without Hopes that in good Time, a happy End will be put to all their Fears, and the good Woman's Misery at once, but they must have Patience. ---- This suspicious Declaration sufficiently alarms the Apprehensions of the Gossips ; which are so evidently display'd by their melancholy gloomy Looks and doleful Accents, that the good Man is just at his Wit's End. Then one begins to pray for a happy Minute, another, that an Alteration in her Pains may soon happen, a third, that she may be strengthened and supported to go thro' it, for she, for her Part, can't see that her Labour is ever the forwarder,

forwarder, notwithstanding all that she has taken by the Advice of the *Doctor* and *Apothecary :* Nay, she is certain, (for she has had several Children herself) that unless she has some very speedy Relief, both she and the tender Infant will be lost. Doleful Spectacle !

Oh, says the Maid *Peg*, if this is the Fruits of Matrimony, I'll live and die a Maid ! I'll never venture as long as I live : And tho' I believe that it must afford a vast Degree of Delight to be caress'd, and embrac'd in the Arms of a youthful vigorous Man that one loves ; yet delicious as it may be, it can never make amends for so much Anguish and Pain. Well, Heavens send it well over with my dear Mistress, sweet good-natur'd Creature as she is, but I am afraid she'll never go thro' it.

Well, it must be own'd that the *Husband*, and *Wife*, with the *Midwife*, *Nurse* and *Gossips*, have now sufficient Reasons to summon up all their Courage and Resolution to support and assist them ; forasmuch as all their *Cries* and *Tears*, their *Cinnamon* and *Plague-Water*, the Advice of *Doctor* and *Apothecary*, have all been made Use of to no Manner of Purpose ; so that unless some happy Alteration ensues, it will be very difficult to rank *this* among the *Delights* and *Pleasures of Matrimony*.

But pray, hark a little ! a few more such Pains as those, will diffuse Joy and Rapture thro' every Heart, and display them in every Face : That's well done again ! listen, what Bustle they make within ! There, now they are quiet again ! 'Tis certainly over. Well, have a little more Patience, and your longing Eyes shall be delighted with a *smiling Infant*, and your Ears shall be saluted and ravish'd with the long-expected Title of *Father*.

BOOK

BOOK VIII.

*The good Woman is delivered ; the Beauty of
the Child ; the inſtruƈtive, and delightful
Tales of the Goſſips ; and the extravagant
Raptures of the Huſband, &c.*

DElightful Scene ! After all this Confuſion,
Diſtraƈtion and Danger, the happy Minute is
at laſt arriv'd ; the good Woman is ſafely deliver'd,
and our indulgent, loving Huſband, is not only
thereby diveſted of his former Diſtraƈtions and
Terrors, but is advanced almoſt to the higheſt
Pitch of *matrimonial Glory*, *Honour* and *Happineſs !*
O, who can comprehend his Joy !

But, as human Felicity may receive ſome Addition, from the Applauſes and Congratulations of
others ; ſo our enraptur'd Huſband, diſpatches
away *Peggy* and *Dolly*, to acquaint all his Friends
and Relations ; not in the leaſt doubting, but that
they all will be as joyful and merry as himſelf.---Be-
hold, what an Air of Mirth appears in his Face,
while he repeats his Orders to thoſe about him,
that all Things may be in Readineſs and Decorum,
to entertain his expeƈted Viſitants ! and what Delight he ſeems to take, in the Readineſs of *Miſtreſs
Do-all*, to furniſh the *Midwife* with *Clouts* and
other Appurtenances without Number ; while
Miſtreſs Swift-hand, and *Pry-well*, are turning
every Thing *topſy-turvy*, under a Pretence of
ſearching after ſome Things ſhe wanted : Not in
the leaſt imagining that they are only indulging an
imper-

impertinent female Curiosity. --- And woe be to the Character of your Spouse, if these evil Ey'd Praters should discover the least Rent-hole or Blemish in either *Table-cloths*, *Napkins* or *Clouts*. How would their ill Nature, Malice and Envy triumph, at the pleasing Discovery; one or other of 'em would be thrusting their Fingers thro' the Vacuity, and with spightful Smiles and Grins, take the first Opportunity to display these suppos'd Indications of your Wife's Negligence, to the Notice of their tattling Companions. This will afford a very copious Subject for gossiping Reflections both at Home and in the Neighbourhood; and your *poor Wife*, after all the Pains and Trouble she has been at, will be reproach'd by those *Tale-bearing Hussies*, with the opprobious Character of an ill Housewife; tho' at the same Time, could you but be admitted into the sluttish Recesses of her envious Accusers, you would find their Linen in such a tatter'd Condition, that they would be exceeded by nothing, but the antient *Standards* and *Colours* in *Westminster* or *Guild-Hall*.

Well, notwithstanding all this peeping and prying into Holes and Corners; the *young Bantling* is at last drest, and the delighted Husband call'd in to take his first View of it; upon his entering the Chamber, good *Mother Midnight* presenting his Son and Heir to him, and obliging him to take him in his Arms, utters, with all the Gravity becoming the solemn Occasion, the following emphatical Expressions; *Here Sir, there's your Child, and a thumping Boy he is; I heartily wish you much Joy of him, and Heaven send he may make as good a Man as his Father.*

Udslifo, what a tickling Pleasure is this! what excessive Delight must the Father experience now! And who can forbear Laughter, to see him stand handling

handling his Darling, as a great overgrown *Monkey* does a *young Kit' ing* ?

Our venerable old Midwife may now also in her Turn begin to rejoyce ; for the Father's Heart is so over-flow'd with Rapture and Delight at the new Honour and Dignity, that he is happily arriv'd at, that she'll soon taste of his boundless Liberality ; and this can be no Wonder, because every Child is a very great Addition to the Wealth of its Parents.

While these Things are transacting, the Cloth is laid, and the Table spread with all the Rarities and Delicacies of the Season ; which give infinite Satisfaction to the good Women, whose Spirits, by this Time, are pretty well exhausted ; tho' their Curiosity is herein also very much concern'd, for they long as much to know what is provided for their Entertainment, as they do to satisfy the Demands of their craving Appetites, ----

It would be the greatest Wonder in the World, if among such a Number of Women, there were not some to be found of a contentious dissatisfied Temper. Accordingly one finds fault with *this*, and another with *that* ; *this* is not in Season, *that* has no Relish ; with numberless other Mistakes, that either the *Caterer* or *Cook* has committed. The whole is concluded, with Madam *Cook-well's* assuring the Gossips next to her, that if she had been consulted in buying and dressing the Victuals, the Entertainment should have been much more elegant and far less expensive ; but, God help 'em, adds she, what can one expect from such young Folks ? they'll know better next Time. If her Hearers don't seem to join with her in this Elogium upon her own wonderful Abilities, she assures 'em that she has the Honour to be consulted by several Ladies of the first Rank and nicest Taste, whenever they make any grand Entertainments, which they

H   would

would not do if their Judgment was equal to
hers. ----

While thefe are engaged thus, fome at the other
End of the Table are pratling forth the tranfcendent
Virtues of *Oyfters*, *Coxcombs*, *Lamb-ftones*, *Sweet-
breads*, and the like ; for they have experienced
their Wonder-working Effects, by the repeated
Embraces of their Hufbands. You are certainly
in the Right, fays Madam *Luxury*, 'tis what I
would recommend to the Ufe of every *married
Couple*, who are defirous of tafting the higheft Degree of Nuptial Pleafure. For my own Part, fays
fhe, I freely own, that the plumper I find my Par-
tridge the fitter it is to Pott : This Kind of Difcourfe
being fo very entertaining, and continuing fo long,
the Lying-in-Woman is almoft forgot, 'till thro'
Weaknefs and want of Refrefhment fhe fwoons
away ; and had fhe not been foon recovered, the
Mirth of our goffiping Ladies would have been
greatly obftructed.

Happy for the good Man, if he has any Knowledge in the Affairs of the Kitchen ; for the Difcourfe runs fo high that Way, that if he has not,
he muft either be filent, or betray his Ignorance.
But he is foon relieved from this tirefome Dilemma ;
for, the *Woman in the Straw* ; the *fhaking of the
Sheets*, and other erefting Subjects, in which he
can bear his Part, begin now to engage the
Tongues and Attention all around the Table.

Well, let 'em go on, while *Fat Jenny* runs to
and again to fetch the Nurfe, who has not as yet,
made her Appearance. With the utmoft Difficulty,
fhe finds out the Place of her Abode ; and there fhe
hears that fhe is nurfing a Gentlewoman, at the
other End of the Town : What can fhe do ? the
Nurfe muft be had : A Curfe light on my Miftrefs,
fays fhe, as fhe runs melting in her Greafe, for being out in her Reckoning, which has given me all

4   this

this Labour and Trouble. Well, she finds her out; but fresh Difficulties attend her Embassy: The Gentlewoman will not part with her, insisting upon it, that Possession gives the best Title. *Jenny* cries and roars, and swears she'll not go without her. Thus they *pro* and *con*, 'till *Sleep-little* the Nurse begins to imagine herself to be a Person of great Importance in her Business, and that certainly, since Nurses are so plenty, it must be owing to her superior Skill, that they are each of 'em so unwilling to resign their Pretensions.

A few Days make a Discovery of our Nurse's Experience and Understanding; for, lamentable Case, our dear Infant has got the *Thrush* in its Mouth; and can by no Means be brought to take the Breast. The poor Woman is in such Agonies with the Confinement of her Milk, that she's just distracted; and is terribly affrighted lest a Tumour, or something worse should be the Consequence. And what adds to the Affliction, the Nurse's Stomach is too delicate to suffer her to draw 'em.

Now, Oh tender Husband, is the Time for you to go to an experienced Apothecary, and lay before him your beloved's Grievances, to the End that he may bring with him Remedies against the Choring of the Milk, and to heal the dreadful Clefts in her tender Nipples, till such Time as the Child is able to take to the Breast.

Certain it is, that the present Situation of your Spouse, her Complaints excepted, is Matter of great Joy; for now, she may be maintained at much less Expence, than when she was longing for all that she could could either think on, or see; the utmost Extent of her Desires, being circumscrib'd within the narrow Compass of a little *Panada*, *Caudle*, *Stew'd-Prunes*, *new laid Eggs*, or the like. ----

If the *Nostrums* of Mr. *Glister-pipe* the *Apothecary*,

cary, fhould unhappily be ineffectual, as is often the Cafe, you will neverthelefs, have no Reafon to mitigate your Mirth ; for the News of your Wife's Illnefs being rumour'd abroad, you will be foon attended by a *Poffe* of grave, elderly, female Phyficians, deeply experienced in all the various Diforders to which Lying-in-women and Infants are fubject.

There's the venerable Wife of Doctor *Needham*, how gravely fhe applies the Spectacles to her Nofe, that fhe may with the greater Certainty difcern the poor Infant's Diforder: She is certain that a Glyfter will make a perfect Cure. And as to your Wife's Breafts, fhe'll fend home for an Ointment, that at once ufing will put the Milk into fuch a Motion, as will not only take away the Pain, but infallibly prevent it from forming the leaft Tumour whatfoever.

Mrs. *Rattle-pate*, tho' fhe will not prefume to depreciate the Efficacy of Mother *Needham*'s Prepa-rations, yet fhe is fure nothing can exceed the Vir-tues of a *Sandwich-Carrot*. Take a *Carrot*, fays fhe, and after having fcraped it hollow with the Point of a Pen-knife, apply a Piece over each *Nipple :* This will attract all the ill Humours from the Breaft, without the leaft Senfe of Pain or Fear of Danger. And tho' Madam, fays fhe, this may appear, at firft View, to be a very infignificant Medicine, yet if one Chriftian may believe ano-ther, I have found the Advantage by it in fix Lyings-in, when all other Applications have fail'd.

For my Part, fays Mrs. *Tattle*, I believe what you have advis'd to be an excellent Remedy ; but as Madam's Nipples are exceeding fore and tender, I would firft of all advife her to bathe them well with fome *Aqua Vitæ*, and after that to wafh 'em with fome of the beft *Rofe-water* ; there's nothing like it. I have had 13 Children, *live-born* and *chriften'd*, *chriſten'd*, and have always been ſubject to ſore Nipples, but nothing that I could think of ever gave me ſo much Eaſe. Pray, Madam, therefore don't omit it.

Up ſtarts Mrs. *Flippant*, declaring that ſhe has often made uſe of the *Carrot*, according to her Neighbour's Directions, nor did ſhe ever omit *Aqua Vitæ* and *Roſe-water*, but never in her Life found the leaſt Benefit. Nay, ſhe has tried a thouſand other different Things recommended by one and another, beſides having the Advice of the *Apothecary*, and all to no Purpoſe ; ſtill ſhe was in Miſery, till at laſt ſhe was cur'd by only once uſing *Salvator Winter*'s Ointment.

Mrs. *Pry-in-all* begins to relate the wonderful Effects of *Oil* of *Myrrhe*, and of the famous Plaſters prepared by the noted *Gentlewoman* in the *Minories*, above all other Applications.

After which, the ſage Matron Mrs. *Poſitive* acquaints the Company, that ſhe is poſſeſs'd of a Recipe worth its Weight in Gold ; that ſhe had it from one of the ableſt Man-midvives in *London* ; and that out of an hundred Women who have made uſe of it, by her Recommendation, not one of them miſs'd of a Cure. For which Reaſon ſhe has not only carefully conſulted the Works of Dr. *Culpeper*, Dr. *Bates*, *Quincy* and others, who all ſpeak greatly in its Praiſe, but alſo that Poſterity may reap the Advantage, ſhe has committed the ſame to writing. With that ſhe pulls out a little Book, and after having carefully fixed her *Barnacles*, ſhe reads thus : *Take* Lapis Calaminaris *prepar'd, what Quantity you pleaſe, make it into the Form of an Ointment with as much* May Butter *as will ſuffice :* With this anoint your Breaſts all over four or five Times a Day ; this will not only prevent the Milk from curdling, but will alſo effectually cure and harden your Nipples. And if the Child ſhould ſuck it in with the Milk, ſo much the better, for

by

by that Means it will be cur'd of the Thrush.

Will any Body dispute, but that our Husband must be wonderfully delighted and edify'd to hear, how liberally the good Women communicate their Knowledge and Experience, for the Advantage of his Spouse and her tender Infant !

But will not his Pleasure be vastly encreased, when he is so happy as to be intirely freed from the Company of these chattering *Magpies*; who notwithstanding all their friendly Pretensions, have nothing so much in View, as the indulging their voracious Appetites at the good Man's Expence : Certainly this must be esteem'd as one of the greatest of Nuptial Delights.

These Remedies may be all very excellent, says the *Grandmother*, but 'tis impossible for my Daughter to use 'em, for *lack-a-day !* the poor Girl is so weak, and her Stomach so much disorder'd, that the very Sight of an *Ointment*, let alone the Smell, would cause her to faint away. Nor will she be ever able to suckle the Child ; for the Moment it is put to the Breast, she is in such intolerable Pain, that she's just ready to run distracted. What can we do ? To hire a wet Nurse is very chargeable ; and God help 'em, they have had Charge enough already : Besides, who knows what Distempers the poor Infant may contract by sucking a strange Woman. Nor will I ever consent to its being nurs'd abroad ; for that oftentimes destroys all natural Affection between the Mother and Child ; and not only that, how often do we see Children either half starved, or else poisoned with Nastiness, while others are eaten up with the Rickets, and so are helpless and deformed all their Lives. No, no, in God's Name let us keep it at home, and endeavour to bring it up by Hand ; for bad nursing at Home, is better than good nursing abroad.

The frugal Contrivances of this sagacious old Lady, unfortunately prove all abortive ; for the
Child,

Child, notwithstanding all the Care and tending imaginable, grows so very froward and peevish, that the whole Family is distracted, and confus'd ; and Mrs. *Sleep-little* the Nurse, is so harrass'd and fatigu'd with it, that she gives it, as her Opinion, and who can dispute it, that the Child pines for the Breast ; and that they must very soon, either procure it a Breast, or a Coffin.

This the poor tenderhearted Mother can by no means agree to : Her Love to her Child is so predominant, that she will suckle it herself, let her go through ever so much. Well, the Child is brought, and she makes several Attempts to accomplish her laudable Intentions, but all in vain ; for the Pain is so vehement, that it almost deprives her of her Senses. A *Wet-Nurse* must now be had with all Expedition, lest the poor Infant should expire ; all Hands are immediately employ'd in this Service. And after much Trouble and Difficulty, our diligent *Grandmother* succeeds : She has happily been recommended to a mighty housewifey, sober, modest young Woman, with a curious Breast of Milk as blue as a Razor ; and as her Husband is just gone a Voyage to the *East-Indies,* so there is no fear of her Milk being spoil'd. Well, this fortunate Event, creates extraordinary Joy in the Breasts of both *Father* and *Mother :* Now are their Hearts at Rest, after all their Anxiety and Solicitude ; for the *Wet-Nurse* is prodigious fond of the *Child,* and it begins to crow and thrive amain : Nor is the *Dry-Nurse* less careful of the *Mother* ; so that every Thing begins now to have a very promising Appearance. Make much of yourself, therefore, Oh happy Mother ; for now is your Time : The tormenting Pains of suckling are at an End ; nor will your needful Rest be any more disturbed, with the Cries and Lamentations of your pining Infant : Consult therefore your Ease ; indulge your Appetite, and
chear

chear up your Spirits with reviving Cordials, or
generous Wine. Now muſt you bid adieu, the
ninth Day being over, to lifeleſs inſipid *Panada,
Gruel,* &c. and enter upon a more ſtrengthning
and nouriſhing Diet ; ſuch as *roaſted Chickens,
young Pigeons, Wild-Fowl, Turkey, Lambſtones,
Fiſh,* and various other Diſhes, that your Appetite,
aſſiſted by your fruitful Invention, will eaſily ſug-
geſt. But be ſure, that altho' your Strength and
Vigour may return, you don't diſcover it too ſoon ;
on the contrary be continually expatiating, in your
Spouſe's Preſence, of your great Weakneſs and
want of Appetite ; this will excite in him the
higheſt Degree of Pity and Compaſſion, and will
prompt him to continue to you the Enjoyment of
thoſe Delicacies 'till you yourſelf are ſatiated with
the Repetition of 'em.

Well, now O *new Father,* come to an ingenuous
Confeſſion ; are there any Pleaſures equal to thoſe
you enjoy ? You are now not only ſo happy, as to
be admitted to eat and drink with your Spouſe
at her Bed-ſide ; but are alſo unſpeakably delighted
to perceive, by her chearful Behavour, that in a
very ſhort Time, you will be again admitted to
embrace and careſs her as uſual.

This is the delightful *Month,* that creates in the
Mind of every *married Woman* ſuch pleaſing Ideas
and Reflections, nor ought it ever to be eras'd from
the Memory of every *loving* and *indulgent Huſband* ;
for as by the Vigilance and Care of the *Nurſe,* the
Lying-in-Woman is not only recover'd from all the
conſequential Weakneſſes of Labour, but is alſo in-
vigorated by proper Diet, and of Courſe becomes
extreamly deſirous of her Huſband's Converſation ;
ſo he alſo, by a Participation of the ſame, is better
qualify'd to give her all imaginable Pleaſure and
Delight.

Well, what an Advantage it has been to our
Huſband,

Husband, that he met with a Nurse so well qualified; and what a Joy it is, that her Labour and Attendance have been follow'd with such wonderful Success : The very Ideas of her Pain and Travail, are quite forgot ; and instead of a wan, ghastly Countenance, she now begins again to appear with all the sprightly, inviting Charms of Vigour, Youth, and Beauty : And as Preludes to approaching Joys, she is now ever and anon throwing the Pillow at her Spouse ; patting his Cheek, and squeezing his Hand.

BOOK IX.

The Child is christen'd ; the Feast provided for the Gossips, the true Stories they relate, very delightful to read, and instructive to remember.

NOW, O happy Father, you have had the Possession of eight capital Pleasures, together with an infinite Number of concomitant Delights ; which have, no doubt on't, excited the Envy of less happy Mortals : But your Felicity knows no Bounds ; for, there is just now opening to your ravished Senses, a Scene to which you have hitherto been an utter Stranger.

The good Woman, tir'd with her Confinement, begins to express a strong Inclination to be Abroad, that she may shew to all around her, the beautiful Produce of their mutual Embraces. But before this can be effected, had not we better have the Child christen'd ? without doubt ; nothing can be

I objected

objected to a Thing so necessary, but then, it is of no small Moment to agree on its Name; various are the Desires and Opinions of the contending Parties, the Father's principal Kindred are call'd *John*'s and *William*, the Mother's *Thomas* and *Robert*; but these Names will by no Means do! but wherefore I pray! Why truly, says Madam, my Child shall not go by the nick Names of *Bob*, *Tom*, *Bill* or *Jack*! no, indeed, my dear Boy is as pretty as any, and shall have an agreeable Name; what a Duce do you tell me of your Kindred, will they be weak enough to take Exceptions at my Child's Name; you see its Godfathers have referr'd that Matter to me, and I will have his Name *Valentine*; for 'tis from that very Day I date his Being, and what can sound more delightful than *Vall.*

O dear Madam, interrupts Mrs. *Nurse*, what a charming Name you have pitch'd upon, *Valentine* was always my Favourite, but I am in terrible Pain for him, whilst he is descending the Tree to encounter his savage Brother *Orson*; but then again, how my Heart leaps when he leads him conquer'd in a String like a muzzled Bear; and shall my dear Babe be a Knight Errant, and overthrow Giants, Knights, and Monsters? *Valle*, my sweet little *Valle*, Pappa must buy it a keen Sword, and Armour as bright as Silver and harder than Flint, and in a little Time, it shall be knighted, and go and cut down that Monster the Giant of *Prussia*, and rescue the poor distressed Lady of *Hungary*. O the happy Event! methinks I see my little Hero return in Triumph, and all the World ecchoing his Fame; no more to be said, call him but *Valentine*, and let him alone for the rest. ---- Well, what can our good Man say to this? shall he tell the Nurse, his Spouse and she speak of different Persons? what will that avail, will not Madam persist, and can he do better than

submit?

submit? What can be a greater Pleasure than to come into the Sentiments of the Mistress of his Heart; besides, they are in a Manner unanimous of the Lady's Opinion, he must be cast in the End; yield therefore with Generosity, and receive the Thanks of the good Women. ---- Very well, you have certainly taken the wisest Course; nothing remains now, but to proceed to the Ceremony, the Parson attends in the next Room, and is in haste to go to a young Couple that wait for a Specimen of his Office. Well, this Affair being happily over, the good Woman gives to Nurse a Catalogue of those that she intends to invite. What a List is here! Zounds! why the poor Woman will be a Week upon her Journey. However, you need not be in Pain, lest she should omit any; for 'tis from the Multitude of Gossips, that arises her own private Advantage. Well, the Pleasure that flows from the Company of such a numerous Collection of merry agreeable Ladies, must be ravishing.

Now has poor *Sleep-little* the Nurse, an Opportunity of discovering another Branch of her Skill and Diligence: She is no sooner return'd from inviting the Guests, but she begins to bustle from Place to Place, and from one Thing to another, to the End that all her Affairs may be extreamly neat, and in Order; for she is not a Stranger to the impertinent Curiosity of the *Gossips*: She dreads therefore the least Omission of her Duty, knowing that her Reputation as a Nurse, will thereby be very much affected ---- Poor Woman, how rightly she conjectured; for there's Mistress *Order-all* and others, under a Pretence of visiting the *Necessary-House* and other Places of Retirement, only withdraw themselves, to inspect into every Hole and Corner, in order to furnish themselves with Matter of Reflection and Scandal among the Neighbours.

But

But let us turn our Eyes to a more pleasing Prospect: There's both the *Wet* and *Dry-Nurse*, fully
employ'd in decking forth the *Bantling* to the best
Advantage ; and herein may be discover'd, not only
the delicate Taste of your Wife in her Choice of
the most fashionable, and costly Ornaments, but
also the Dexterity of the Nurses, by whose Management, the natural Beauty of the Infant is set
off to the greatest Advantage. There, *Father*,
says the fond *Mother*, see how like a *little Angel he
looks !* Lord I What a beautiful Creature it is.
There *take him*, and *kiss him* : *Dear Madam*, says
Nurse, what a vast Resemblance there is between
my *Master* and the *Child*, he looks as if he was
spit out of his Mouth. What would not one go
thro', to be the Mother of such a delightful *Infant !* Well my *Dear*, says Madam, I vow Nurse
is a very good Judge ; for every Soul that has seen
your Boy, says, that he is the very *Model* of you ;
and that he is as like you, as one *Drop of Water* is
like *another*. Is'n't he, pray Madam, says she to
an old Gentlewoman that sat next to her ? Why,
really Madam, replies the Lady, I think some of
his Features are not unlike yours ; but he is vastly
like your Spouse, from the Waiste downwards :
Well faith, says another, he's a fine jolly Child,
his Father spar'd neither Stuff nor Labour I'll warrant him.

As the Delights of Conversation very much depend upon Variety, so now they make a Transition from the Child to themselves.

Our new Mother opens the Way, with giving a
very particular and pathetick Relation of all that
befel her during her Pregnancy and in her Labour,
and observes what a vast Difference there is between
one Woman and another, spinning her Discourse
out, thro' a great Variety of entertaining Particulars ; concluding the whole (for she would not but
they

they should know it for the World) with relating to them the Stratagem that her Husband made use of to come to Bed to her. Truly, says Madam *Lack-it*, if as you say, that there's a great deal of Difference in Women, I am sure there's as much in Men; for tho' I am as likely as another, and, perhaps, as willing, I am not ashamed to speak it, I neever found my Husband so ready to fire his Chace Gun.

Well, says another, I don't know how it may be with others; but my Husband I remember was once only a Fortnight from Home; and the Night he return'd I really thought he was mad. I am sure I did not lay my Eyes together till three in the Morning: And that very Time Nine Months I was brought to Bed of two as fine Boys, as ever the Sun shone on.

Have a little Patience till the *Bowl* has gone about a little, it will certainly be well worth your while.

In the mean Time observe how delighted poor *Nicholas* is, at the Health and Vivacity of his Spouse; at the Grandeur of her Dress, and Magnificence of her Chamber. Poor Creature, he is so full, that he can't tell how to give Vent to his Joys, unless by a Profusion of Wine, Sack, Punch, and other exhilerating Liquors.

See again how diligent he is in helping his voracious Guests to *Roast-Beef*, *Capons* and *Ham*, *Turkey*, *Neat's Tongue*, or other relishing Morsels, that his Liquor may be exhausted the sooner. Well stand fast *Bowls* and *Glasses*, for you have a terrible Exercise to go thro', between this and Morning.

What a vast Addition would be made to our Father's Happiness, if he could but attend to every instructive Discourse, that is deliver'd by these *nimble-Tongued* Visitants round the Table, now they begin to be warm. Mrs.

Mrs. *Sharpset* begins with lamenting that Nights should be set apart so universally for Nuptial Embraces. But for her Part, her Husband and she has so frequently broke thro' that Custom, that latterly she has always expected it about an Hour after Dinner.

Mrs. *Touch and take* is much of her Neighbour's Opinion, for being once at a Gossiping with her Spouse, where they were elegantly entertain'd, they no sooner got Home, but they both of 'em were seized with such an amorous Fit, that they could not stay to undress, but went at it with all the Spirit and Eagerness of their first Embrace. I can't say, adds she, that I was ever so delighted in my Life; and altho' I was then not very young, nor had been with Child for six Years past, yet that Day nine Months I was deliver'd of my Son *Bob*; and a beautiful Child he is, tho' I say it.

I do assure you, Ladies, says Mrs. *Courant*, that what I am going to relate, is as true as we all sit here. A certain Maid that sold Glasses about our Town, had toy'd so long with a young lusty Fellow, so that in nine Months Time her Phial was ready to burst. Her Pains coming on pretty fast, away she runs to the Town-Midwife, where she was safely delivered. About an Hour after she took home the Child, washed her Cloaths, and the Day following cried her Glasses about as usual. This surprizes the whole Company prodigiously, there's a vast Difference in Labours indeed, says another. There was a married Woman, a Neighbour of mine, who was so unmercifully us'd by an old fumble-fisted Midwife, that it would make your Hair stand an End. However, at last they sent away for Mr. *Peepin*, a noted *Man-Midwife*, and with much Difficulty he saved the poor Woman's Life, but the poor Infant was lost. Well

I really

I really think, adds she, that Whores have the best Luck.

Up starts another, declaring that it is a great Hardship that Women can't indulge themselves in lawful innocent Pleasures, without bringing upon them such a Variety of Torments and Illconveniency. However, says she, I never hear a Man-Midwife mention'd, but it brings to my Mind a very merry Affair that happen'd to one of my Husband's Relations. The Woman, you must know, at the End of her Reckoning fell into strong Labour, which continued with great Violence three Days and three Nights. The Midwife and all the Women were very much alarm'd. At last the Woman cries out aloud, *Oh I never shall be deliver'd, I can't be deliver'd, I shall die, I shall die, unless my Husband's Instrument which has caused me all this Pain, be cut off before my Eyes!* Pray Madam, says the Midwife, what a horrible Request is this? You are certainly beside yourself. Would you destroy that, and endanger your Husband's Life too, which was ordained for your Use and Pleasure! No, no, it can't be permitted; he has done no more than his Duty, and what you have often long'd for and expected. A Pain coming on at that Instant, she baul'd out: *O, don't talk to me of Use and Pleasure; I tell you I shall never be deliver'd till I see the nasty Thing cut off before my Face.* In short, Perswasions were thrown away upon her, for she did nothing but repeat the same Request for an Hour together. In the mean Time her Pains going off, the Women began to be in Fear both for her and the Child. In short, they acquainted her Husband with it, who seem'd to be very much concern'd; but as he thought she would soon change her Mind, he said with a Smile; no, no, I may get another Wife, but if I once lose my *Man Thomas,* I am

sure

fure I fhall never have another.   Finding her thus
inflexible, they laid their Heads together how they
might deceive her.   In Order to which the Hufband went to her, and with all the counterfeit
Symptoms of Grief, he affur'd her, that rather
than hazard her precious Life, he was willing to
comply with all fhe defir'd ; with which fhe
feem'd very well fatisfied.   Soon after three or
four Surgeons came in to perform the Operation,
and in her Sight, lay'd him extended upon a Table,
and bound him faft thereto with Cords.   After
which they took out their Inftruments, and laid
them one by one in Order ; her Hufband all the
Time expreffing the utmoft Dread of the approaching Operation.   Now Madam, fays one of the
Surgeons, I'll foon prefent you with the Caufe of
all your Sorrow.   Nay Sir, fays fhe, I don't want
it ; let me but fee it fairly off, 'tis all I defire.
With that he took his Knife in one Hand, and
concealing a Cow's Teat in the other, he feigned
to make a Cut, one of his Companions at the
fame Time fqueezing fome Blood out of a Sponge ;
this was follow'd by a moft terrible Squall from
the Hufband.   There it is, Madam, fays he, holding up the Teat: You'll be eafy now certainly.
The Man was immediately order'd to Bed, and the
Woman was deliver'd before the Surgeons left
the Room.   She had not been long got to Bed,
before fhe began to enquire after her Hufband's
Welfare.   Oh, he's very ill indeed, reply'd the
Midwife.   Do thofe Things ever grow again,
fays fhe to one of the Surgeons.   Grow again,
Madam, fays he ; will a Man's Leg grow again
after it's off ? No to be fure, fays fhe.   Neither
then will your Hufband's Inftrument.   Lord ! fays
fhe, furely I was bewitch'd.   But, pray, Sir, can't
you fet it on again, for methinks I would have
him to be like other Men ? No, no, fays the
Surgeon,

Surgeon; If I can save his Life, it will be well; but truly I very much doubt it. In three or four Days the good Man begins to walk about the House, but pretends that he is very weak and faint. At last, however, his Strength returns, and he don't appear to be much the worse for his Loss. The Woman's Month being expir'd, her Husband went to Bed to her, as usual, but lay very quiet. But she, wanting to be doing, puts her Hand towards her Husband's Belly, as you know we married Women love to do; but the good Man desir'd, that as she had deprived him of the Testimonials of his Manhood, that she would not put Desires into his Mind that he was not able to accomplish. The next Night, Madam was at the same Sport again, but meeting with the same Return, she said to him; why my dear, has the barbarous Man cut it quite close; has not he left a Stump behind? To be short, the good Man having fasted above a Month, could carry on the Jest no longer, but throwing himself into her Arms, he convinced her that he was still able to raise in her, the Pleasures she had often before experienc'd. The good Woman in the midst of her Raptures, says to him, Oh! my dear, I really think that the Stump is as good as the whole.

Mrs. *Lispwell* then relates a Story of a Servant-Maid that she kept some Time ago. This Baggage, says she, you must know, was always neglecting her Business upon one frivolous Pretence or another, to be gossiping her Time away at a *Stay-maker's* in the Neighbourhood. Now she must go to bespeak a new Pair; anon she must go to have them try'd on; then her old ones must be taken in; by and by she's grown fat, and they must be let out; then they hurt her under the Arms. Lord help me, I had no Mistrust of her all this while. But as true as we are alive, in a

K

few

few Months, Madam could wear no Stays at all, for her Belly was up to her Chin. After much ado, she at last confess'd that she only went there to be bon'd.

I never, says another, was so deceived in my Life as I was in *Patty Pale-face* ; I really took her to be the most modest Creature in the World ! 'Twas a great Grief to her Parents. I have frequently obferv'd her in the Fruiterer's Shop at the Corner yonder, but I thought as she feem'd to have the Green-sickness, that she went there to indulge her Appetite in Fruit, unknown to her Mother. However, the Fruiterer had been in the Saddle, for she began to be very Big, and said it was by eating of Oranges and Lemons : Doctor *Stultus* said it was the Dropsy. But her Mother, foon after, apprehending her Disorder, committed her to the Care of a good Woman at *Hackney*, who in a little Time tap'd her of a very fine Girl; which was put out to nurse, and Madam at the Month's End return'd perfectly cur'd.

Mrs. *Loud-enough* was just about beginning, when they heard a violent Knocking at the Door. Which being open'd, our Gossips Husbands were introduced, to the great Joy of Nurse, who imagined that now her Presents would be doubled : But one of the Ladies, not so well pleas'd with her Husband's Appearance, cries, what a Plague do they do here ! now our Conversation will be interrupted with their Nonsense. Nurse, however, fill about, your Master must pay for the Wine, for three or four Glasses wonderfully promotes Freedom. And I think Nurse, that it is very requisite, that you yourself should now take your Portion of it ; for you seem to be very much fatigued and low-spirited with waiting and attending; but have a Care, for it has oftentimes very odd Effects. I remember, my Sister's Nurse was
mightily

mightily addicted to drink her Master's and Mistresses Health, till at last, when she went to feed the Child, she ran the Spoon under its Chin, then into its Eye, afterwards against its Breast. And such was its wonderful Effects, that she could not distinguish a *Cap* from a *Clout*, nor a *Biggen* from a *Forehead-Cloth*.

Thrice happy Father! thou hast not only delighted thyself with entertaining the good Women with all imaginable Delicacies and Varieties, both for Eating and Drinking, for which they have return'd thee a curious Collection of instructive Relations; but you have now also the Happiness of repeating the same to their Husbands, who will not be backward in doing Honour to your unbounded Generosity, while their Corporations will contain the Contents of the often replenished Bowl. Upon my Life, says Mrs. *Laughwell*, you have a fine Child here; I think I never beheld its Fellow. Egad, says her Husband, if we, my dear, were just now alone together, I'd be hang'd if I did not get you with Child of such another. You are very merry, Child, replies the Wife, but sure you are not so sharp set, but you may easily stay still we are at Home.

Two Soldiers, says Mr. *Fill-up*, were drinking together, and talking of the Pleasures of a Female Bedfellow; one of 'em finding that the Discourse had operated below, says to his Comrade; if I had a Wife this Instant, I'd suffer my *Boltsprit* to be cut off, if I did not get her with Child. Why *Jack*, says the other, you need not be long without a Wife, if I was as strong in Hand as you, I would be hang'd, if I did not get a Girl's Consent to have me in two Hours. The other doubting the Premises; a Wager was immediately laid. Away he goes, and in a few Minutes, met with a bouncing country Lass, with a *Cream Pot* in her Hand: He directly makes an Attack; the Girl

resists

refifts ftoutly, and refenting horridly her being ftop'd
in the Street by a Foot-Soldier. Child, fays he,
don't be offended ; my utter Averfion to lewd Wo
men, induces me to feek the Acquaintance of a vir-
tuous honeft Girl ; and that you are fuch, your
Looks and Behaviour fufficiently prove. Pray,
Sir, fays the Girl, give yourfelf no farther Trouble ; I am in no great hafte for a Hufband, efpecially for one of your Cloth. I own, fays he, my
being a Soldier is no very great Recommendation ;
but that's owing to falfe Notions of us. Our
Wives are the happieft of Women. And tho'
our Pay is not large, yet whatever the Country
produces is ours, and as often as we want, we
make Ufe of it, without the Trouble of afking
Queftions. Thus Sorrow is a Stranger to our
Hearts, and all the frightful Apprehenfions of Poverty are banifhed. But as to my felf, fays he,
my Merit and Valour have rais'd me Friends,
and they are endeavouring my Promotion ; fo
that with me, in a little Time, you'll enjoy all
that your Heart can defire. In fhort, Madam
capitulates ; but defires Time to confider of it.
Confideration, fays he, is the Ruin of every Thing ;
for which Reafon a Soldier abhors it. Now Child
is your Time. Speak before that Cloud has paffed the Face of the Moon, or elfe for ever after
hold your Tongue. In fhort, before the Moon was
clear the Girl furrenders. He gives her his Tobacco-
Box for a Pledge, and fhe, in Return, prefents him
with one of her Garters, and tells him the Place
of her Abode. They parted, fhe for her Cream,
and he to his Comrade ; to whom he relates his
Succefs ; with very great Encomiums upon the
Beauty and Modefty of his Miftrefs, and finally
produces the Garter. The Soldier being aftonifhed
at what he heard, told his Companion that he
fhould be infinitely obliged to him, if he would
                                                        help

help him to juft fuch another. In troth, replies he, give me but one Week's Pay, and you fhall have *her*; for as our Contract was made in the Dark, fhe'll hardly be able to diftinguifh us afunder. They ftruck up a Bargain directly. Next Morning the enamour'd Soldier, taking the Garter with him, went to his Lady; and after having repeated to her what paffed over Night, fhe immediately leaves her Service and marries him. And he prov'd as good as he promis'd; for nine Months after fhe was brought to Bed of a fine jolly Boy.

Well, fays Mafter *Crofs-grain*, this is a moft diverting Story indeed: It pleafes me, becaufe it has fuch a happy Conclufion. I wifh what I am about to relate had been fo fuccefsful. *Will Crotchet* and *Molly Mockit* got intimately acquainted, no-body knew how, and were both of them extremely defirous of tafting the Joys of Wedlock. Their Friends on both Sides being confulted, were very well pleas'd with the Match; and accordingly Articles were drawn up, with a Penalty annexed to the Breach of 'em. Things being thus fettled, they were next afk'd in the Church, and the Marriage-Day was fix'd upon, all Parties feeming to exprefs the higheft Satisfaction and Content. But all on a fudden, the young Couple fell out to that Degree, that they loaded one another with the moft opprobrious Language imaginable, and diffolved themfelves from all Manner of Obligations whatever. The old Folks being acquainted with the fudden Alteration, called our young Couple before 'em, in order to enquire into the Caufe of it. *Crotchet* being examined, declared, he forefaw that the Match would be unhappy; for notwithftanding her Difguifes, he had found her out to be a lazy, idle, nafty Slut; that fhe was noted for the greateft Brawler in the Parifh; and that he had feen her more than once intoxicated with

Liquor,

Liquor, among a parcel of Chair-women and Washer-women : And therefore he desir'd, that unless they had a Mind to be his Ruin, they would not insist upon his having her.

The young Woman, on her Part declar'd, that he was a Drunkard, a Spendthrift and Gamester, and that he was intimately acquainted with all the nasty Whores in the Parish, and that rather than be ty'd to such a Beast of a Man, she'd be hang'd out of the Way. The good Folks were, you may be sure, very much shock'd at what they heard. However they desir'd them to be easy, telling them that they might be both of them miftaken ; and that as it was possible, some envious People had rais'd these Reports to obstruct their Happiness ; and that if they were true, yet as Matrimony was generally a Cure for such youthful Frolicks, they desired them to fulfil their Promises. But all that they could do avail'd nothing, and therefore by joint Consent they committed the Writings to the Flames. In a very short Time after, *Crotchet* married his Neighbour *Peg*, who was six Months gone with Child by a Foot-Soldier. And *Molly* ty'd herself up to a Waterman, who after he had got her Belly up, enter'd himself on Board of a Man of War.

Mr. *Lack-wit*, beginning to speak, was prevented by the Opening of Mrs. *Sweet-lips*, who began thus : There was a Gentlewoman in our Neighbourhood, very remarkable for bringing forth Twins ; her Husband was a mere Dwarf; little Birds you know, Ladies, have often very long Tails. I had the Happiness to be sent for to her Labour. In a very little Time after I had been in the Room, she was delivered of two of the finest Babies that ever my Eyes beheld. The Midwife, being willing to leave every thing safe, was busying herself about the Woman, when all

of

of a sudden she cries out, here! here! what are you all about, why don't you attend? Here's another Child for you: And so there was indeed a lovely Girl, with a Cawl over its pretty Face; it came crying into the World, with as much Strength, as a Child of a Year old. The good Woman begg'd and pray'd to leave none behind, for she thought she felt another stir: What now do you think of such a Husband as this? Well, a little Man for me; they have always a Blessing sent 'em.

What a valuable Present would it be to Posterity, could a Collection be made of all the Stories that were related: But that is impossible, where there are such a Mixture and Confusion of Tongues, both of Men and Women. The different Languages at *Babel* were almost as intelligible; here's one extending her Throat in a Horse-language, by Way of Applause to her Neighbours; smutty Songs another is bellowing in praise of the Punch, where his next Neighbour, having got his Load, is snoring in Concord, like the grunting of a Hog.

Let the Batchelor no more glory in his whimsical Notions of Happiness; and let the whole Race of Fumblers, look on, envy and despair. Now, what Pleasures are hastening! The People are up, and just ready to take their Leave; delightful Moment! what Raptures must the good Man be in, while he is receiving the Compliments and Acknowledgments of his grateful Guests! Not a Soul of 'em forgets to wish him and his Spouse much Happiness, putting up also their Prayers, that Heaven may bless them, the next Year, with as fine a Daughter, as they have got a Son; to the End, that they may again be invited to replenish their Souls at his Cost. Well, they are all gone staggering Home; let us therefore wish them a good Night.

Now,

Now, O *Father*, as these Pleasures are almost at an End; prithee confess, don't you already begin to wish, that you may soon have another Opportunity of repeating them over again?

Well *Nurse*, you have now, I hope, reaped the joyful Fruit of all your Labour and Trouble; and certainly no one ever deserved it better: Your Master has done his Part, in providing a grand Entertainment, and your Mistress has not been wanting to invite a great Number of Gossips to consume it. Well, Heaven be praised, your Fatigue is at an End: If your big Expectations are not thoroughly answer'd, you must consider that Trading is dead, by which Means Guineas and Crowns, are seldom to be seen, and seldomer given away; you must therefore, the next Job, make a better Bargain for yourself with your Mistress. And now, as your Time is but short, it behoves you at all Opportunities, to chear your Heart with a Glass of good Wine; it was bought to be drank: And now you may do it without the Fear of offending the Gossips; or, hurting your own Reputation: The more private you are the better, you'll drink never the less in public. Consider also, that it may be a great while before you are called to another Labour; and longer before you may meet with such a dainty-mouth'd Mistress and liberal Master; 'till when, you must be confin'd to a Garret, or a Cellar, and grow lean upon a miserable Diet at your own Expence.

BOOK

BOOK X.

The Child is coated ; a Feast upon the same,
very wonderful to be related.

HOW superior are the Pleasures of married
People, to those enjoy'd by single Persons !
fresh Delights and Joys, are Day after Day opening and displaying themselves to their ravish'd
Minds, that others are ignorant of. Such is their
Felicity, that the most exalted Description, conveys but a very imperfect and faint Idea to the unexperienc'd Imagination : You have already had a
View of nine prime Pleasures, attended with an
infinite Number of subordinate ones, but the out
Lines have only been exhibited ; what would they
appear, if the Advantages of Light and Shade,
were properly dispos'd by a skilful Pencil !

Happy are our young Couple, that they have
so wisely conducted themselves thro' such Scenes of
Pleasure, as not to be overpower'd and bewilder'd
in the delightful Labyrinth.

They have hardly digested the Delicacies of the
Christ'ning, but other Joys are presented to their
View : The Child must now be coated, and as it is
a Concern of vast Moment and Importance, it
would be the utmost Stupidity to pass it over un-
commemorated. What therefore, is so well
adapted to secure this Event from Oblivion, as an
Entertainment : The former was for the Midwife
and the Godfathers and Godmother, and a few
others, but this must be more comprehensive ;
therefore you need not doubt, but these Visitants

L   will

will be as delightful and entertaining in their Conversation as the former, and will be of infinite Service in helping to confume the Liquors which the others left behind 'em ; which no Queftion are an unfpeakable Burthen to you. Don't think, that the Health of you and your Family will be drank to, lefs frequently by thefe your Relations, than by thofe who were only Friends and Acquaintance. Let not therefore fuch gloomy Imaginations difturb your Joys : Be but eafy, and you'll foon fee how handily they'll empty your Difhes, and Bottles. But left their great Modefty fhou'd prevent 'em from being free ; pour yourfelf out a Bumper, and make a Beginning with, *Long Life to his facred Majefty* ; *Succefs to his Arms* ; *Confufion to the* French *and* Spaniards, *Succefs to Trade*, or the like, and I'll warrant you, they'll follow you clofe, and in return, your Ears will be charm'd with the repeated Sound of, *to you, and your Spoufe's good Health* ; *may Profperity and Happinefs attend you both*, and *that you may be bleffed nine Months hence, with a beautiful Girl to your jolly Boy*, that we then may have another Opportunity to rejoyce in the Happinefs that attends ye.

While you and the Men are thus profitably employ'd, your Spoufe and the Women will be holding a grand Confultation about the Furniture for the dear Infant, to the End that it may appear in all Refpects conformable to the Circumftances of its *Papa :* This muft be fettled to Day ; becaufe to morrow fhe goes to be Church'd, and in the Afternoon fhe'll have Work enough to go among the *Mercers*, to lay out your Money to the beft Advantage. And indeed a whole Day is full little for *Madam* to determine an Affair of fuch Moment in ; fhe can, with much more Eafe lay out your Money, than come to a Determination in what to expend it. One while this Thing will

mighty

mighty well become the Child, but then again, she thinks it too common, for she has seen several Children lately with the same. Then, she should vastly like that, but then again, she's afraid it will be too grave. Lord! Madam, says Mrs. *Eye-all*, did you never observe, your Neighbour's Child over the Way? Why what of that, says Madam? It is in the genteelest Dress that I ever saw: Well, and do you think that my Child is to be dreſt like theirs: No, I'd have you know, 'tis not come to that neither. The good Woman, however, at laſt determines that she will pitch upon nothing in particular, till she goes Abroad; she'll then, no doubt on't, see something to her Mind. And as it is for her firſt Child, and God knows whether ever she shall have any more, she's reſolved not to spoil a Ship to spare a little Tar: These Things you know, Madam, says she, are not to buy every Day; and as the moſt ordinary Thing I can buy, will be the same Charge making up, I will therefore without any more Trouble, have the very beſt that I can lay my Hands on; besides, it will be much for my Huſband's Credit, and I know he'll be highly delighted to see his Boy, (for he's vaſtly fond of him) dreſſed up like a little Angel.

Rejoyce therefore, Father, that these Charges are at an End; and pleaſe yourſelf to think, that as your Child grows up, you will every Day have freſh Occaſion to ſhew your Love to it by repeated Inſtances of Liberality: Should you indulge the leaſt penurious Thought, you will at once eraſe from your Mind the Reliſh of paſt Pleaſures, and eclipſe those that are juſt breaking in upon you. Rejoyce, alſo, that the Wife of your Boſom is not only beautiful, but fruitful, by which your Name will be perpetuated to Ages yet to come: And not only ſo, but that she is ſolicitous to equip your little

Darling

Darling in such a Manner, as to be the Delight of
every Eye, and the Joy of every Heart ; the
Credit of which, will in the End terminate upon
yourself : While, therefore, your Spouse is ruminating upon, and adjusting these important Matters
to Advantage, disturb not her prudent Cogitations,
with any Doubts, Scruples, or Objections ; but give
her all possible Assurances, that you are charm'd and
delighted with her frugal and cautious Oeconomy ;
and for the World, whatever you may think, suffer
not the Words, *Pride*, *Extravagance*, *Expence*,
or such like, to fall from your Lips in her hearing,
so shall your Joys be everlasting, and your Pleasures know no Bounds.

I know you are ready to reply, but pray speak
softly, that Merchandizing and Trading are prodigiously decay'd, that the War enhances the Price
of Commodities ; and, as a Consequence of which,
People are daily breaking in your Debt ; that
your Expences have been very great since you have
been married, and the like. But, is not this looking on the wrong Side of the Picture ; turn it therefore, and behold what an Infinity of Pleasure, Joy
and Happiness, surrounds you ; ballance the Account between 'em, and you will still find Reason
to be joyful. ---- But to comfort you, however, a
little, for I am afraid you are vapourish ; to Morrow or next Day, Nurse is to be discharged, and
you'll then not only have one less in Family, but
you'll be rid of a *wasteful*, *guttling*, *sluttish*, *tittle-
tattle*, *gossiping Hussey*.

Your *Wet-nurse*, indeed, must be with you till
the Child is wean'd ; but then you are vastly happy
in her, for she is very fond of the Boy. Besides,
both you and your Spouse are freed from the ill
Conveniencies of such a troublesome Bedfellow ;
while others, who suckle their Children themselves,
are continually disturb'd with the Squalling and
Roaring

Roaring of the turbulent Child. Nay, 'tis often the Cafe that the Woman is fickly and weak, and not able to take the Child out and put it into the Cradle ; fo that the Hufband muft be difturb'd, if it be twenty Times a Night, to give his Wife all neceffary Affiftance. Here indeed, I think the Pleafures of our Hufband are deficient.: He only enjoys them in the fuperlative Degree, who is very affiduous in rocking the Cradle, warming the Pap, and feeding the Infant, dandling it in his Arms, and in making Ufe of all proper Methods to quiet it, that his poor Wife may enjoy the Pleafures and Advantages of Reft. But fuch a Man's Happinefs feldom ends here ; for after having been rocking the Cradle three Parts of the Night, the Child, inftead of being appeas'd, grows ten Times croffer, and roars and bawls to that Degree, that Father, Mother, Maid, and all in the Houfe, muft get out of their Bed to quiet it : Nor, is this all their Pleafure, for in a few Months more, fome Teeth are ready to cut, and as this is attended with great Pain, it throws the poor Infant into a Fever, which fets it a bawling and fqualling fo violently, that it's Parents can't get a wink of Sleep for a Week together ; but are every Night counting the Clock, and wifhing with the utmoft Impatience for the Approach of Day.

But let not fuch as thefe repine at their Lot, if they intend to make any Advances in the inftructive School of Patience ; let 'em rather efteem it a Happinefs, that they have thereby frequent Opportunities of putting their Knowledge into Practice, which is the ready Way to promote its Increafe. How will their Trouble and Diligence be rewarded, when the tender Infant fhall make its grateful Returns with innocent Smiles, winning Glances, and lifping forth the chearing Sounds, *Mam*, *Dad*, *Pap*, and the like. But you, thro' the Affiftance

of

of your Nurse, being free from most of the Trouble
of the Infant, may possibly find Leisure to accomplish the kind Wishes of your Gossips, and your
Wife may enter upon a new Reckoning. And
what an unspeakable Pleasure will it be, when you
are fully satisfied, that you are about to enter upon
the second Edition, and, perhaps, with consider-
able Additions of Delight and Joy! Then will
your Character as a Workman, be sufficiently esta-
blished among the old Women, to your everlasting
Honour and Renown!

But, when you find that your Spouse has happily
conceived, beware of Country Journeys, especially
on Horseback, lest the tender Fruit should be
blasted before it is fit for *Mother Midnight* to
gather : But 'tis hop'd, that former Experience has
impress'd these Things with proper Force upon
your Memory.

But in the mean Time, turn your Eyes to the
Center of all your Joys : See your beautiful, smiling
Infant, adorn'd in all the Elegancies of the most
luxurious Fancy. See how tenderly your Spouse
views him, and embraces him by Turns ; then
views him round, and kisses him again. Charming Sight!

Well, I think it's high Time that your Spouse
should begin to return her Visits, that they may all
see and applaud her Taste, the Child's Beauty,
and your Manhood. She has a World of Business
upon her Hands, to be sure ! 'Twill take up a
Month at least : My Heart begins to ache, for the
Nurse and the Maid, who must attend her to carry
the Child, for he's really very heavy ; I'll warrant
they'll wish both Child and Mother too at the Devil,
before all the Visits are paid. But I am most of all
concern'd, on Account of the Maid ; poor Creature, she'll be tir'd to Death when the Child's
wean'd, and the Nurse is discharg'd : Her whole
Employment,

Employment, when she has done her other Business, will be rocking, dancing, dressing, and
carrying him Abroad. She'll be ty'd to the Child,
like a Bear to a Stake, and never be suffer'd to go
Abroad as usual among her Relations and Acquaintance.

Let not happy *Father*, the gadding Abroad of
your Spouse, give you the least uneasy Sensation;
for, if you have any Taste, you'll discern that this
also is a Pleasure inseparable from a married State.
The Ill-conveniencies that attend her Absence,
don't deserve the least Notice or Regard; for if
Affairs should be neglected at Home, you may
easily call to your Assistance, a Sempstress, and a
Chairwoman or two, and every Deficiency will
soon be supply'd: To this you are no Stranger:
Consider also, to your unspeakable Comfort, that
there's an absolute Necessity for the Child to be remov'd from Place to Place, in order to preserve
and promote his Health. To sit upon its Breech,
every good Woman can tell you, will soon bring
upon it the Rickets, and other no less terrible Disorders; and then, the pretty Creature is ruined
for ever. Not only this, but it's being constantly
taken Abroad, will inure it to Company, and by
Degrees it will thereby be taught to eat any Thing
that is given it; and to distinguish in an Instant
Malt-liquor, from Wine or Brandy. And are not
those most noble Accomplishments in a Child? And
you'll hereafter have the Happiness to see, that all
your Endeavours to correct those pretty Habits are
entirely useless; but, what have we to do with
Futurity: Care is the Parent of Grey-Hairs?

Besides all the above Advantages of taking the
poor little Creature Abroad, it may not be one of
the least, if it should happen to catch the Small-
Pox; because then you will have the Pleasure of
your Wife's Company at Home, as well as the Satisfaction

I

tisfaction of a Nurse to attend it in all its Illness; all which will be considerably augmented by the small Expence of a Doctor and Apothecary, and the terrifying Apprehensions of the Loss of the Beauty of the Child.

If your Spouse should now be again with Child, you must, in order to diversify your Pleasures, believe it is a Girl : And herein you may indulge your Fancy without Bounds. You must represent her to your Mind, possess'd outwardly of all that's tender, soft, and charming; and inwardly, of the highest Degree of Docility, Wit and Modesty : How will you be ravished to see the little Miss, neatly dressed, with her Work and her Book going to School without Reluctancy ! And what will be your Pleasure, when from Time to Time, she comes between your Knees, and smilingly gives you an Account of the Progress she makes in her Learning ! But, stop not here : A few Years more, and she becomes the Wonder and Admiration of all around her, for her exquisite Skill in every Accomplishment that adorns that tender Sex. How fluent and elegant does she speak the *French* Tongue; but when she sings, or gives you a Specimen of her Skill, on the Spinnet or Harpsicord, you are ravished. Add to these, an easy agreeable Air in dancing, and an exquisite Taste and Delicacy in Dress ; and all these, and many more attended with unaffected Modesty ; what Wonder is it, if all the young Ladies in the Neighbourhood, are ambitious to rank themselves among the Number of your Daughter's Associates ? With these Helps, she will soon be instructed to relish the Pleasures that flow from Alteration of Fashions ; will imbibe the highest Veneration and Esteem for the richest *Damasks* and *Brocades* ; and will humbly adore a Suit of *Pinners*, *Handkerchief* and *Ruffles*, if they are of the newest Mode, and most costly *Brussels. Lace.*

Lace. These valuable Accomplishments, you will have the Pleasure to see succeeded by others, of no less Importance to the Dignity, Honour and Prosperity of your Family. Receiving and returning of Visits, from House to House, with all the Ceremony of well-bred Ladies; frequenting the *Play-house*, *Opera*, *Masquerades*, and all other Kind of publick Diversions; you, O happiest of Mortals, will find to be the Result of your Daughter's docile and tractable Disposition. But the Joy you take in her fine Accomplishments, would be defective, if they only serv'd to make her the Delight, Wonder, or Envy of her own Sex: She begins therefore to feel an unaccountable Propensity, towards establishing an innocent Correspondence with some of the other. To effect which, she dresses and walks Abroad more frequently, and with the utmost Art she's Mistress of, is incessantly endeavouring to captivate some Youth or other, with the superior Charms of her Innocence and Beauty. And, as she has thus made the Signal, she's soon attended with Crowds of Admirers, each endeavouring to exceed the other in Demonstrations of the most durable and inviolable Affection. But while she is thus endeavouring to lay the Snare for others, she is at last entangled in it herself: She feels it; and, for want of Experience, she soon discovers it to the pleasing Object of her Wishes. He fans the Flame, and in an unguarded Moment, not only deprives her of her Chastity and Virtue, but begets upon her his Image, to grace and adorn your Family. Now are your Joys at the highest Pitch imaginable!

As you have therefore, O happy Pair, been encircled round with such an Infinity of ravishing Pleasures and Delights; let your future Time be

M   employ'd

employ'd in ruminating upon the pleasing Ideas : But bury them not there; describe to all about you, without Reserve, your blissful State ; so will many others, enchanted with the Relation, follow your Steps and join the happy Throng.

THE

CONCLUSION.

THUS, dear Cousin, I have exhibited to your View some of the first Scenes of the blissful State of Matrimony ; are they not delightful ? And do you not long to see the last Act ? But, however, be not impatient, for Marriage may not unfitly be compar'd to a Tragi-Comedy, where the Beginning promises nothing but Joy and Felicity, which nevertheless is often interspers'd with a Number of disagreeable Incidents before the Conclusion.

Consider also, that the Prospect I here send you, is taken from a Point of Sight extreamly advantageous ; the married Pair themselves are neither extreamly great or very mean, but of the midling Rank of People, (who certainly have the largest Portion of earthly Felicity) their Fortunes and Ages are suppos'd to be equal, their Tempers agreeable in themselves, and conformable to each other, their Love reciprocal and tender, together with an Uniformity in their Dispositions ; to which may be added, that hitherto Fortune has been propitious to all their Wishes.

Possibly

Possibly the View of the Contrast might not be quite so agreeable; suppose Age united with Youth, or my Lord wedded to his Chambermaid, or the Dutchess with her Footman, what Harmony might be there expected? But let us imagine Equality in Age, Birth and Fortune, can nothing else imbitter all their Joy? What shall we say to unaccountable Coldness on one Side, and Jealousy on the other, the Husband refractory, the Wife stubborn, the one a Gamester or Rake, the other perhaps both. For there are some Satyrists fond enough to accuse the Fair Sex, in these polite Times, of imitating all the modish Vices of the other. But let who will give them Credit, you and I will remain Infidels in so delicate a Point. As for you, it is enough that the beautiful Creature you adore is without Spot or Blemish, possesses an Assemblage of all the Vertues, and such Charms as can never fade; is so affable and agreeable, who can behold her without Transport? Then her Temper is so excellent and uniform, who ever saw it discompos'd? No Person certainly; have not you been as vigilant as a Spy, and yet could never make any Discovery of her Imperfections; how could she conceal them from you? Impossible! Have not you attended her like her Shadow? Could she be continually on her Guard, and always elude your Inquisition? No, no, she is doubtless a Compendium of all Perfections! And who can question your Happiness, when you are united to the dear Charmer! O the extatick Moment that gives you all you wish! All that Earth can yield to make your Joy immense. Years, Months and Days will then so swift and smoothly glide along, they will seem but Moments heretofore; and all your future Time revolve in a Circle of Delight. Dear Cousin, if this is the Case, no Wonder you
should

ſhould be eager to enter ſuch a Paradiſe ! 'Tis
true, there was a Serpent in that of old, and *Eve*
could liſten to his Tale, but what of that ? Women
now are wiſer.   Well, ſhall I hear what you reſolve in this momentous Affair ? But howſoever it
be, reſt aſſur'd your Determination will not in the
leaſt diminiſh my Affection, which ſo far reſembles *the Pleaſures of Marriage*, as only with Life
to admit

F I N I S.

1 AP 64

PART III.
WORKS ATTRIBUTED
TO MARTIN GULLIVER

THE
Art of BEAUING:
IN
IMITATION
Of *HORACE's*
Art of *POETRY.*
ADDRES'D
To a Certain LORD.

BY
MARTINUS GULLIVERIANUS.

——— *Rifum teneatis Amici ?*

The Third Edition.

LONDON Printed, And

DUBLIN: Reprinted by J. WATTS, and
W. S. ANBUREY, in *Caple-Street* ; and
fold by J. THOMPSON on *Cork-Hill.*
M, DCC, XXX.

TO

MARTIN

ON HIS

Art of *Beauing*.

A SATYR, *manag'd with an Art like thine,*
  In which thy Genius with Roscommon's *shine,*
May better claim the Drapier's *artful Lays,*
To shew thy Merit, and inhance thy Praise :
Mew'd in by College Walls — *my Wings are clip'd,*
Nor once remember Helicon *I sip'd ;*
Except you call our Pump-House *by that Name,*
And common Water, a Poetick Stream,

A 2   *Then,*

Then, I confess, I breath Parnassus Air,
And have drank many Bottles to my Share;
Nor wonder, if these Feathers sprout anew,
When they are prun'd by such a Friend as you.

C.   W.

January the
13th. 1729-30.

THE

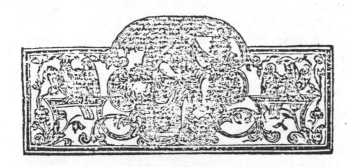

THE

Art of *Beauing,* &c.

UPPOSE *Belinda* painted to a Hair,
With her own Face, but with a Neck
    of Mare,
With Wings of ———,* and with a Tail
    of Ling,
Who could help fmiling at fo odd a Thing?
Such is, my Lord, the Figure of a *Beau,*
Toft out by Fancy, and Valet, for Shew ;
Which were it not for Powder, his Grimace
May well refemble, faith, a fick-Man's Cafe ;
Where Incoherence crowding thro' the Brain,
Declare to all Men that the Man's in Pain:
Not but that *Beaus* and *Poets* ftill are free
To ufe a vaft Extent in Nicety.

---

* *Nymphæ.*

For

For Inſtance *T——e* you'll find genteely dreſt,
In a plain Jocky, and black Velvet Veſt,
With fierce Bob-Wig, and little Nab, cut down
Moſt of your beſt dreſt Fops about the Town ;
Yet none from hence a colour'd Veſt became,
Without the outward Coat was all the ſame.

A Diſtant *Beau* will promiſe mighty Things,
Behold, approach'd his Laces turn to Strings,
And what we judg'd a Col'nel at firſt Sight,
Is metamorphos'd to a *Rainbow Knight*. *
A Miller's Nab upon a Campaign Wig,
Or Cambrick Shirt upon a Suit of Rig,
Strikes every bit as bad a Stroke as he
That would Deſign a Storm, but draws a Tree.
When you ſtrut in with ſo much Pomp and Shew,
Why in the End can't you appear a *Beau* ?
Be what you will, ſo you be ſtill the ſame,
And I'll engage my Life you purchaſe Fame.
By what I find, the grandeſt Part of *Beaus*,
For Truth of Dreſs are couzen'd by its Shews,
This would wear Ruffles not half Finger deep,
That wear them ſo, that ſcarce a Nail ſhould peep.
Some think it Art to change the ſelf ſame Hat,
To wear it monſtrous large, or monſtrous ſquat ;
For Dreſs is now to that Perfection grown,
That, few but have ſome Faſhion of their own.

My Man, *John Tom*, as far as a *Beau-Strut*,
Would give pehaps a tolerable *Cut* ;

---

* *Aliter*, a Foot-man,

But

But farther, Sir, he begs to be excus'd,
'Tis not his Trade, and you muſt be refus'd.
What is there more ridiculous for me,
Than aping that I was not born to be?
Beaus ought to ſee firſt what became them beſt,
And as they fancy, ſo I'd have them dreſt:
After a ſerious and judicious Choice,
They cannot fail to have the publick Voice.

Sir *John* muſt alſo take the greateſt Care,
When he's *toſt out*, the modiſh Time to *ſwear:*
Oaths muſt be choſen, and a *carcleſs Gate* ;
Now let alone—— now thunder'd out in State.
Gad d——n me, Sir, ſwore with unthinking Face,
May *cut down* fifty in a proper Place.

Be cautious alſo how you change the Mode,
Depart but ſeldom from the common Road ;
Yet though you be particular a while,
If Fancy like it, all again will ſmile ;
Soon will they follow Faſhions they deſpis'd,
Now grown familiar——yet to have them priz'd,
You muſt derive them from ſome ancient *Beau,*
That blaz'd in former Ages, long ago,
Some *French Coupee,* that found out what would pleaſe
The modiſh Sparks, and Moderns of his Days.
Now, if in this 'tis given on my Side,
Why ſhould your grave Philoſophers deride ?
If *Tom* is happy in an *eaſy Gate,*
Or *ſudden Laugh*—ſhould therefore *Puppies* prate,
When for *Bellair,* even *Florio,* by this Light,
Have been a Means of making Youth polite.

B   *Beaus*

Beaus ever did, and will, I may engage,
Difcourfe like *pretty Fellows* of the Age:
Words are as Leaves, in *Autumn* difappear,
And ftrait a newer come again next Year:
All things turn out, I fancy, by the L——d,
When Death's commanding Officer a-board.
Who would have thought to drink a Difh of Tea
Where Chairs and Coaches now choak up the Way? †
Or who could think to lofe a Quarter's Note
Where grifly *Charon* often row'd his Boat: *
Yet this and they, and all will be forgot,
Why then fhould not *dull Fafhions* go to pot?
And him, moft certain, I'd conclude a Fool,
Who'd fix thofe Things where Fancy is the Rule.

An *Officer* firft taught the World to fwear,
From whence we got that pretty modern Air;
And *Mourning*, *Tom* will have it firft defign'd,
To fhew the inward Colour of the Mind;
But now we wear it for this Caufe, I think,
To fhew our Friends have left behind fome *Chink*;
Yet, as to who invented *Mourning Cloaths*
Is undecided by our modern *Beaus.*
A *Spaniard* brought your Rapiers into Vogue,
And we, in Barter, gave our *Irifh* Brogue;
With this, upon your *Sawcy Sparks* we draw,
That, and few Oaths will keep the Houfe in awe.
Then to the Tavern for a hearty Glafs,
Chat with a Friend, or kifs a pretty Lafs;

---

† *Lucas's.*   * *Groom-Porter's.*

There

There it is proper to roar out a Song,
Let it be dull or witty, ſhort or long:
No matter how, ſo *Puppy's* not uncivil,
He might be there as noiſy as the D——l.
Why is he honour'd with the Name of *Beau*,
That neither would, or does one Faſhion know;
And chuſes to be ignorantly gay,
Rather than own he wears an old *Tupee?*
Let Things, for God's ſake, have their proper Place,
And wear no *Tie-Wigs* on a *Weaſle-Face*.

Swear not ſo often when a Lady's by,
Nor talk of Smut, or very roguiſhly;
Yet in ſome Company a Joke will hit,
And paſs upon the Company for Wit;
Nay, e'en your Clergy will begin ſometimes,
In ſhrewd *Entenders*, and licentious Rhymes;
And if the Cloth was off, I know it true,
Would ſpeak, themſelves, as movingly as you,
He that would be a *pretty Fellow* now,
Muſt learn to Cringe, Laugh, Ogle, Sing and Bow;
Muſt raiſe Deſires to what Pitch he will,
And that *dear Man* will ſeldom fail to kill.
If I'm at Church, and am inclin'd to pray,
That horrid Creature's always in the Way:
Firſt he begins to ſtare me in the Eyes;
Plays with his Breaſt till mine begins to riſe;
But if he ogles ill, I ſleep, or laugh
Behind my Fan, or give a ſudden Cough.
Your Looks muſt always alter with your Stile,
Or elſe the Labour's hardly worth your while;

For

For Nature forms and softens us within,
And without Nature what is worth a Pin ?
Pleasure inchants, Extaticks will transport,
And thus it is with *M*——— and *D*———.

But he whose Face and Language disagree,
Might as well go and hang himself, I see ;
For 'tis absurd to think that Man can pass
For any thing but for a silly Ass.

Observe the Character you would maintain,
Of Lord or Bishop, private Man or Dean,
But always talk that individual Strain.
If you design to turn out for a *Beau*,
Then let us see it in a tearing Shew :
If you think fit to be a Bully-hec,
Then bully it, and never value Neck :
If Widow-hunting is Sir *John*'s Delight,
Let him be chairing it all Day and Night :
And here you must not, to revive a Suit,
Tell some damn'd Lie, incredible to boot ;
No, if you ha'n't a Story ready coin'd,
Let it be from some well-known Tale purloin'd,
Disguis'd and probable, at least, what's told,
Nor Word for Word, though it is monstrous old ;
So well improv'd, that it your Suit secures,
And then with Reason it may pass for yours.

Begin not as a Friend of mine begun,
G—d d—n me, Madam, I am such a one.
In what did all this Ostentation end ?
Why, it came out at last,——he had no Friend

But

But her (alive) with whom he could trespass *
To fill his Belly, hungry as it was.
Ha, ha, ha, ha, How far is this from me!
Who bluntly told my Mistress——thus, you see,
I have not quite, faith, forty Pounds a Year
Till Dadda dies, nor then it self, I fear :
Such as it is, you're welcome to my Heart ;
If not——no Harm is done——and we may part.
How different these Courtiers Stiles appear !
One ends in nought, — *That* forty Pounds a Year:
One seems to promise *Flambeaux* at first Sight,
The other's one continu'd Stream of Light :
Short and concise in ev'ry Word he'll say,
And steals her Soul insensibly away.

Now, if you'd make the same Impression, mark
That ev'ry thing be suitable, *young Spark :*
If young, take care of your old-fashion'd Things,
Of monstrous Hats, and wearing large Seal-Rings :
If old, how well a Cue and and Suit of Lace
Become *long Spindles* and a *Leathern Face* ;
Thus Youth must not appear in Form of Age,
Nor Years appear less otherwise than sage ;
For whatsoever contradicts my Sense
I must abhor, though at my Friend's Expence.

Never presume to make a God appear,
But when there's Reason for to *curse* and *swear* ;
Nor should you *laugh* but when your Jests are dull,
And then a Chorus act it to the full :

----

* *A-la-mode de* France.

What

What Humour wants a Chorus fhould fupply,
And that will make them witty prefently ;
For 'tis furprizing, how a Chorus-Laugh
Will turn a Wizard to a very Calf.

A *Perriwig* our Anceftors firft wore,
Nor dreamt of *Tye-Wigs*, with one Leg before ;
But when our *Beaus*, Sir, travel'd into *France*,
Thy learn'd Behaviour, Drefs, and how to Dance ;
Then came rich Cloaths, and graceful Action in ;
Then Balls were giv'n, and Methods taught to win :
Then 'twas no Treafon, even in the Dark,
To hear, nay fuffer fomething from a *Spark* ;
For they diverted Ladies with fuch Truth,
As could be fcarce expected from their Youth.

The firft of thefe foon found a Temper fage
Too grave for that uncultivated Age ;
And fo an odd unthinking Air brought in,
Not rude to Virtue, nor morofe to Sin ;
But yet fo paffive as 'twas foftly brave
As oft as Decency would give it leave ;
Becaufe the Ladies, with the Mufick fir'd,
Lov'd to be prefs'd to what themfelves defir'd
But then they did not wrong themfelves fo far.
To call a *Trull*, or *Kitchen Maid* their Dear,
Defcend to a Mechanick Stile indeed,
To gain a Favour from my Lady's Maid :
No ! nor fuch fervile Courtfhip for to fhun,
Conclude my Lady —— may be won :
For Gentlemen fhould blufh as much to ftoop,
To afk a Chamber Maid without a Hoop,

As

As a grave Matron walking would be feen,
With Women of the Town on *Stephen's Green* :
Nor muſt you think that this diverting Stile,
Allow of Scandal, or Affronts the while ;
Or to ingratiate your felf with her,
To foil another Lady's Chara&er :
No ! firſt with Truth begin your Comick Tale,
And let Invention now and then prevail,
To poliſh Circumſtances here and there,
Which might attra& the liſt'ning Fair-ones Ear.
If 'tis facetious, and' run thro' with Eaſe,
Perhaps *Bob Short* may ſtrive this Way to pleaſe,
Nor without Pains be undeceiv'd, I ſing,
So much the Manner may improve the Thing.
A Monſter hurry'd from the School to Town,
Cannot expe& at once, to *knock us down* ;
And tho' his Converſation we diſlike,
It muſt not be obſcene, or boariſh like,
The better Sort Scurrility abhor,
And he'll be cenfur'd for a Country Cur.
Yet if theſe *Gothick Monſters Schollars* are,
Dublin's too forward to prote& them here :
But Gods ! to mind no earthly Thing but that,
In hopes the World will pardon *what is what*,
Is ſuch a raſh —— But I forgot, *God knows*,
That I am writing to no Men but *Beaus*.

Read Men, as well as Books, by Women bright ;
Read them all Day, and dream of them all Night :
But Bully *Plautus* was too much eſteem'd,
And e'en his Rudeneſs then, Politeneſs deem'd.

When

When *Thespis* from the Tavern reel'd away,
With *Boon Companions* at the Break of Day,
Their ghastly Faces, pale with Fumes of Wine,
Frighted the Children where they came to dine:
Rude were their Actions, dull was every Joke,
And you might trace them by the Windows broke.
This *Æschilus* with Indignation saw,
And built a *Round-House* to keep *Rakes* in awe,
Brought *Watch-Bills* in, and by those prudent Means,
Stopt Devastations caus'd by *Swords* and *Canes.*
Next *Cavan Bail* appear'd, with grand Applause,
'Til their Licentiousness abus'd the Laws;
Then it was Time to put those Laws in force,
And to suppress their Insolence of Course: .
Ergo our *Government*, and *Men of Fire*,
Deserve such Praise as Patriots should desire.

Nor should we be less infamous, I guess,
For our Victorious Arms than for our *Dress*,
But that it is so tiresome, I suppose,
We cannot bear to be *Eternal Beaus.*
Democritus his own dear Person lov'd,
And scorn'd to have it once by Art improv'd:
He Thought none *Beaus* that Nature made not so,
And this has made ten Slovens for one *Beau :*
For some there are that think themselves too fine,
In any Habit whatsoe'er, to shine.

O my unlucky Stars —— did I not live
A little faster than my Purse would give;
None would have *dash'd* with such Success, I say't,
But rest, I must now, satisfy'd with Fate,

And

And only ferve to raife the Love of Fame,
To which I willingly refign my Claim.
Yet without *Beauing*, I may teach to *Beau*,
Tell you his Duty, Ornaments, or fo;
When he's to hand a Lady from her Coach;
How to Receive a Friend at his Approach.
If *Puppy* tends the *Kettle*, (as in *France*
Some of your Courtiers will, in Complaifance)
How for to do it the politeft Way,
Or help a Lady to a *Diſh* of *Tea*.
Thefe, and the fuch like Galantries in Life,
May help a Perfon to a *Pretty Wife*.

Oft have I known a Man, by Complaifance,
Win on a Lady's Heart, and more advance
In one Day's time, than *Florio's* pretty Face
In a whole Month, with nothing but Grimace.

Frank had a Genius aptly turn'd and gay,
Our *Iriſh* Youth are bread another Way:
If the *Glad Father* can but get his Son
To multiply, with Eafe, his one and one,
That's all his Wiſh, his utmoft of Defire,
And *Dadda* glories to be term'd a Sire.
Can Men like thefe, devoted thus to Ruft,
Think e'er to foar above their native Duft,
Or once expect to have a Turn of Thought
Above their Anceftors, for Ages fought?
No! You, my Lord, that underftands a *Beau*,
Will not commend the Fop or Man of Shew;
I dare fay none your Lordſhip will commend,
But the firm Soul, the Gentleman and Friend.

C

Beaus

Beaus practice should, and give themselves the Way
To speak succinct, and tolerably gay,
Easy as clear, insensible tho' long,
Smooth without Flatness, without Bombast strong ;
For Superfluities are soon forgot,
And *Beaus* talk Nonsence when their Brains are hot.

Never be so conceited for to think
You can perswade us by a D——n and S——k,
Or bring in Ladies by the Head and Ears,
That to my Knowlege are defunct those Years.
Obscenity Old Age can never bear,
And Youth will shun what ever is austere ;
Yet he that has the Happiness to please
Both Young and Old, will flourish all his Days,
This is the Youth that gains the Daughter's Heart,
And with her Parents plays away his Part ;
And this is he that will a Fortune get,
If it is possible for human Wit.

Yet be not, Sir, too rigidly severe,
If in this Tune my Gentleman should err ;
A String may jarr, *Dubourg* is not to blame,
And the most skilful Archer miss his Aim.
But where a *Puppy* has been told by Friends,
Here you went wrong, Sir *James* — and never mends,
But still persists to throw away his *Chink*,
He's as impertinently mad, I think,
As *Tom* the *Cat-Gut Scraper*, that will play,
And never minds one Syllable we say.

If there be such abandon'd Impudence,
That stumbles sometimes on a *Girl of Sense,*
I stand amaz'd, and fret within to see
The *Black-Guard* plac'd in such good Company;
Yet where one has too many on his Hand,
He can't expect that all of them will stand ;
Philander's self has fail'd in some 'tis said,
Tho' none knew better how to gain a Maid.

Beaus *are like Pictures, most of them appear*
Some better at a Distance, others near ;
Some love the Dark, some walk in broad Day-Light,
And boldly challenge the most piercing Sight ;
Some please for once, some will for ever please,
And all is Humor that the *Puppy* says.

But you, my *Lord,* Experience tells you so,
Remember this for certain, that a *Beau*
Admits no Medium, he must always be
Bound up in *Folio,* or *Epitome.*
A Counsellor of tolerable Sense
May want Judge B——d's pow'rful Eloquence,
Or be less read than *Lord Chief Justice H——le;*
Yet this indifferent *Lawyer* may prevail ;
But no Authority, that I can see,
Allows of any Mean in *Foppery.*

As a bad *Consort,* and a coarse *Perfume,*
Disgrace the Neatness of a *Dining-Room,*
And might, with more Discretion, have been spar'd,
So *Beaus,* whose End is only bare Regard,

C 2   Admit

Admit of no Degrees, but muſt be ſtill
Toſt out in ſuch a Manner as to *kill*.

In other Things, Men have ſome Reaſon left,
And one that cannot *dance* may turn to *Theft* ;
Deſpairing of Succeſs, forbear that Way,
And ſo divert the Mob another Day,
But all without Conſideration *beau*,
And Think that *Lace* has Pow'r to dub them ſo:
But you, my *Lord*, is of too fine a Taſte
To reliſh *Florio* in the *Scarlet Beaſt*.

Old Maſter *Orpheus* kept a Dancing-School,
Nor taught, as ſome will have it, *Bears* by Rule,
But Man, as lawleſs and as wild a Thing,
And firſt diſwaded him from *Duelling*.
Thus was *Amphion* feign'd, by Comick Tunes,
To make Stone-Walls dance to his Rigadoons :
And *Fidlers* by Traditions, hence I find,
To be the earlieſt Tutors of Mankind.
Then *Homer's* and *Tyrtæus*' Martial Lays
Gave to their Hero's what great End they pleaſe.

Some think a *Courtier* may be form'd by Art,
Others maintain that Nature wins the Heart:
I neither ſee what Art without a Vein,
Or Wit, without the Help of Art, can gain.
He that intends a Voyage to the *D———l*,
Muſt uſe himſelf not to be over civil,
Drink like *Old Nick* he muſt, nor be debarr'd
A Neighbour's Wife, 'til his tan'd Buff grows hard:

───────────────────────

* *At the Gallows.*

M

My *Rake* must learn to bear the *Sulphur-Smell*
Before he trades upon the Coast of *H——ll*.

But all your little whoring Youngsters now,
Swell with vain Praises, which themselves allow,
And taking Sanctuary in the Crowd,
Brag of their Life and Impudence aloud.
A wealthy *Rake* will take more Pains to treat
A flattering Audience, than they shall to eat.
'Tis hard to find a right good-natur'd *Beau*,
That can distinguish between Friend and Foe.
And ne'er delude your self to tell a Tale
Before those Men you treat with M—h and A—e;
For they, be sure, will praise it without Laughter,
Tho' 'mong themselves they flout at you just after.
True Friends, like Men that really grieve, appear
Less mov'd, altho' it cost them not a Tear.

Wise were the Kings who never lov'd a Soul
'Til they unmask'd it with the honest Bowl:
Nor can you arm your self with too much Care
Against the Wiles of them that speak you fair.
If M——'s Advice is ask'd by any Friend,
M—— freely tells them how, and what to mend:
If they persist, —— M—— will not strive to move,
A Passion so delightful as self Love.
The prudent Care of such a Friend as this
Will give you Notice when you speak amiss ;
Will make a strict Enquiry all around
What People say, —— and where a Fault is found ;
Will tell you privately, nor fear to blame
A Friend in Fault, when he confess the same.

These

These Things which now seem Trifles, and defign'd,
Will be of ferious Confequence you'll find,
When they have turn'd you once to Ridicule,
And you become a pointed common Fool.
A mad Dog's Foam, the Plagues and Punifhment,
Which angry Powers on poor Mortals fent,
You are not fure more carefully to fhun
Than Rake-hells, when their *Drinking Bouts* are done.
On thofe the *Mob* and *Black-Guard* build a Sconce,
But dreaded and profcrib'd by Men of Senfe.
If in the Raving of a *drunken Fit*,
Any of thefe fhould fall into a Pit,
There he might roar and burft his Lungs for Help,
None would affift, or pity once the *Whelp* ;
But really think he purpofely fell in,
To fnore and wallow with his *Brother Swine*.

Hear how an old *Sicillian Rake-hell* dy'd,
Who thought, I fancy, to be deify'd,
Empedocles, you muft have known the *Squire*,
A cold young Spark, that wanted *Winter-Fire*;
He had been c——pt, Sir, fev'ral Times before,
But met his Fate at laft in one pox'd Whore :
There let him ftew, for were my *Duke* alive,
The fame old Trade *Empedocles* would drive.

Leave, Leave for *Beaus* to make themfelves away,
It is a Sin to hinder them, I fay,
Why fhould it be a greater Crime to kill,
Than to keep Men alive againft their Will ?

'Tis

'Tis hard to fay for what Unrighteoufnefs
The *Drunken Fiends* their thirfty Souls poffefs ;
But they are all moft vifibly, *I fwear*,
And like a wild and broke-loofe baited *Bear*,
Without Diftinction, feize on all they meet ;
None e'er efcape that find them in the *Street* ;
Like *Leeches* ftick unto the *Flask* of *Red*,
And never leave till they have *drank Men dead.*

F I N I S.

The *HERALDIAD*;

A *SATYR* upon a certain Philosopher.

Containing a Description of the *Grub-street* Debate held the 22d of this present Month. By MARTIN GULLIVER.

But he proclaim'd by shouting Mobb,
Like Monstrous L—— *acting Hobb,*
Exulted———— Arb——le.

I Sing the Man with shallow Head,
With Copper Skull, and Brain of Lead,
Who late appear'd in Chair of Wood,
And Schoolmen's Arguments withstood.
Ye grave and fertile sober Dames,
Who rule o'er philosophick Dreams,
Who with dark Phantoms bless the Brain
Of fav'rite Scholars bred in *Spain*,
Assist my Muse, your Works to sing,
And your great Hero's Praise to sing.
Dulness, who still preserves her Right,
Daughter of *Chaos* and dark Night,
To make her Empire brighter shine
Amongst the Schoolmen. Sons Divine;
Commands *Don Fo*—— her Off-spring bless'd,
Of all her stupid Gifts possess'd,
To stand aloft in empty Air,
And shew her Might in wooden Chair.
Him, amongst all, the Goddess chose,
Her mighty Power to expose;
For he, for many Years had read,
And with her Learning vex'd his Head
Her abstruse Darkness he made reign,
As well in *Dublin* as in *Spain*,
Her useless Trash distill'd in full,
To darken every youthful Skull;
To fill their Heads with Stuff and Nonsense,
And this had been his Province long since.
Obedient to the heavy Will,
He strait resolves to try his Skill;
Fills a whole Sheet with useless Lumber,
But Stars below point out the * Number.
These he determines to maintain,
And the dull Power prepares his Brain;
Thrice o'er his hard anointed Head,
A misty Show'r of Vapours shed.
Thrice o'er his Temples waved her Wand,
And fixed his Skull with powerful Hand.
And now the Dunce ascends the Chair,
And stands Extolled in Wooden Square,
Around his Head unseen alone,
The cloudy Goddess fix'd her Throne.
From her thick Head, with darkness Crown'd
Dull *Phantoms* issuing, hover round.
But lest he fail, or languish, lo !
Two wretched Coxcombs wait below §

With dulness bless'd with shallow Sence,
Much Pride, and more Impertinence
These two in *falso vel in Vero,*
The Goddess bids assist her Hero.
Behold a Band of Scholars mighty
With Stuff, and Dross, and Dullness weighty;
With heavy dark Objections proper
Attack the wretched Skull of *Copper* :
The wretched Skull with pond'rous Brain,
Strove to perceive, but strove in vain,
For Dullness the all-dosing Power
Of Vapours shed too large a Shower,
And forc'd it with *Lethargick Wand*,
Neither to speak, nor understand :
Objections strike the empty Air,
The heavy Dunce stood Thoughtless there,
Or if one Glimpse of Reason stole
Thro' the dark Caverns of his Soul,
All mute he stood for want of *Latin*,
Tho' he had labour'd some in *Sattin*. *
As when some Wretch on *Wooden-stage* ‖
Erect withstands the mobbish Rage:
The rotten *Eggs* about him fly,
And dash his Skull exalted high,
The white and yellow Filth besmears
His Eyes and Nose, and Chin and Ears,
Unmov'd he bears the filthy Trash
And fix'd to Wood, withstands each dash.
Scarce once, or twice, some Sence appear'd,
While the Dunce nor discern'd nor heard,
When *Pallas* seeing from afar,
The empty Dreams of learned War,
Lest her few Friends shou'd Sicken there,
Enrag'd approach'd the wooden Square ;
Thrice stopp'd the empty Dunces sound,
And breath'd her Influence around ;
Thrice struck the Dunce, and as he stood,
Transform'd him to a log of Wood,
Thrice rung a Bell to Damn the Scheme,
And break the Philosophick Dream,
Dullness with Indignation fir'd,
Confess'd her Fate, and slow retir'd ;
Enough, Enough, the Rabble cryes,
And thro' the Gate the Vision flies.

---

* *Our Hero prudently printed a full Measure of this Trash, that it might look big in the Eyes of some Colle-giars and Women there; but lest he should over-charge his Arain, determin'd no less prudently to dispute no more than five Questions, which were marked by Stars.*

§ *These two were constantly Turmoiling the Head of the young Gentleman who answered under the Pulpit, but they deliver'd him nothing but Bombast.*

* *'Twas by a special Instinct from dullness our Hero got his Questions Printed in Sattin, that the Memory of this solemn Act might live the longer : And the Ro-mantick Figures painted round the Learning, will excite the Curiosity of many to observe them.*

‖ *Who has observed the Weakness and Wretchedness of many Arguments proposed there, will see the Justness of the Comparison between them and rotten Eggs.*

Printed in the YEAR, 1730.

THE
ASINIAD:
A Second
SATIRE
Upon a certain WOODEN-MAN
revived.

By MARTIN GULLIVER.

Mendaces rerum formæ — — — —
Os humerosque homini similis sed sub specie ista
Mens asinina latet — — — —

Printed in the YEAR, 1730.

THE

ASINIAD:

A Second

SATIRE, &c.

A R M S and the Man of upper Room,
    Reviv'd by Pow'r from wooden Doom ;
    What Wonders sprung from Skill Divine
I sing. Inspire me Muses Nine.
Ye Pow'rs of Dreams and Magick Slumbers,
Once more I call you to my Numbers.

   With Head disturb'd, and Aspect sow'r,
Retir'd, the dull indignant Pow'r,
Confus'd, her cloudy Phantoms roll,
And Grief and Anguish pierce her Soul ;

Thrice

Thrice ſhook the Horrors of her Head,
Thrice ſhook her Magick Wand of Lead;
Then rail'd at all the Pow'rs Above,
But moſt at *Pallas* and at *Jove.*

    Alas, ſhe crys, my choſen Son
Is Loſt, is Ruin'd, and Undone.
And when I loſe my choſen Darling,
With him I loſe my dark, dull Learning;
My Nonſence now no more ſhall reign;
No more ſhall Time be ſpent in vain;
No more from Earth, and Native Dirt,
Shall Coxcombs riſe to Prate and Flirt,
From Cellars, Dunghils, and from T——
To learn my *Species* and dull Words;
No more . . . .
 . . . .
 . . . .
 . . . .
. , . . but here deep Sighs and Groans
Forc'd from her Breaſt, and choak'd her Moans;
Nor ſhall the cautious Muſe impart,
Some deeper Thoughts that touch'd her Heart,

    Whilſt thus She ſate with Anguiſh ſeiz'd,
Upſtarts *Ventoſo* all amaz'd;
(*Ventoſo* vain of mobbiſh Praiſe,
For oft repeated flat Eſſays,
In Voice and Mouth, like whining Bellows,
Surpaſſing ſtrangely all his Fellows)
All ſtruck at once with Grief and Ire,
To ſee the Downfall of his Sire.
With Brain diſturb'd, he rag'd and ſtorm'd
Againſt the Pow'r who thus transform'd
His Parent lov'd, his Friend, his Maſter,
And menac'd Ruin and Diſaſter;
Twice a ſad Hue of lucrid Yellow,
Dy'd his plump Cheeks and Forehead ſhallow;
Twice clipp'd his *Engliſh*, and with Sound
Affected, breath'd ſhrill Tune around;

                      Twice

Twice turn'd his Lips awry; his Eyes
Upstaring sideways to the Skies.
So stood the poor dejected Lad,
All Mute, all Helpless, and half Mad,
When from the envious Shades of Night
Sad Spleen arose, a gloomy Spright;
Parent of Calumny, and fell
Revenge brought forth in lowest Hell:
The Fiend assumes each Form and Feature
Of a brown, ill-made Female Creature.
She, to the Coxcomb in Despair,
Presents two Forms of thinnest Air:
These, These, she cry's, destroy'd your Sire;
The Coxcomb burns with sudden Fire;
Envy, Revenge, and raging Madness,
Reviv'd him from Lethargick Sadness;
To seize the Phantoms, swift he flew,
The airy Phantoms swift withdrew.
Dreaming, he runs this Way and that,
Tho' much oppress'd by pond'rous Fat.
Still by the Wings of Spleen convey'd
He runs: Still grasps an empty Shade.
The Phantoms rise: He tracks them soon
Up to the Regions of the Moon.
Pursues them there with Spight and Fury,
To drag them both to Judge and Jury.

Ah me, what Perils do Environ,
The Man that meddles with cold Iron!

Behold the Sage and blue-ey'd Power,
Sees the vain Boy from higher Tower;
Enrag'd once more to see a Tool,
Deserving Rods, elop'd from School:
Descends and speaks: " *Thou Vermin wretched,*
" *As e'er in measled Pork was hatched;*
" How dar'st thou thus from dirty Shore,
" Impudent rise, so high to soar?
" Thou silly, empty, prating Parrot,
' Fit but for Cellar, or for Garret;

" Thou

" Thou peeping Insect from the Mire,
" Raising your Snout, to aim still higher.
" But BEGGAR rais'd, shall always grow
" As insolent as he was low.
" And do'st thou Fool, pretend to Knowledge,
" Who never yet hast seen a Colledge ;
" Think thy self Mirror of the Nation,
" Whose little Skill is Affectation ;
" Of which your shallow Head is full,
" For Froth and Moonshine fill your Skull.
" Learn to be humble, nor grow Vain
" With Gab, and Cobwebs wrought in *Spain :*
" And think that Buttermilk and Beer
" Become you best, your Native Cheer.
She spoke, enflam'd——and furious hurl'd
The Wretch down to the lower World.
Spleen flies affrighted ! left alone,
All pond'rous falls the helpless Drone,
Down from the Height of Lunar Sphere,
Thro' the whole Mass of yielding Air.
And then had met a certain Fate,
Had crush'd his Limbs and shallow Pate ;
Had not the cloudy Parent-Power,
Preserv'd him in the fatal Hour ;
Forgetting now her Rage and Cholar,
To save from Death her falling Scholar.
Not far from Earth she waits to seize him,
To softest Bed of Filth conveys him,
And in a Shore supinely lays him.

So when some Poison-breathing Toad
From Ditch strides up the sleepy Road,
Pond'rous he labours up his Way,
And stalks and grovels thro' the Clay,
Till all fatigued on slimy Walls,
His weak Legs yield, and down he falls ;
Then into native Mire he sinks,
And there he lies, and there he stinks.

But *Murtagh*, in the sad Disaster,
Prepares to quarrel for his Master.

Murtagh

Murtagh! a dull Dog, empty-pated,
Murtagh! fuccefslefs and ill-fated;
Unhappy in his firft Effay,
Forc'd from thick Darknefs to the Day,
Anointed Poet! bright and fharp
As an Afs playing on the Harp:
And canft thou be unfung in Numbers,
That fing dull Dunces and thick Slumbers?
No, *Murtagh,* whilft they fee the Light,
Thou fhalt be celebrated right.
Arife, forgot, defpis'd, and dead, *
Brave Front of Brafs, and Brain of Lead.
Go, quoth the Goddefs, go my Son,
And let a facred Work be done;
Go, write fuch Verfe as ne'er was written,
Your Thoughts and Numbers be be———
Beware of Language, Rhime, and Senfe,
Write nought but bold Impertinence:
Let Falfhood, Scandal, Judgment rafh,
And Dirt befmear your wretched Trafh.
Go, be your Thoughts projected fcarce,
When they muft wipe and clean each A———
By Courfe direct from Brain abfurd
Convey'd to Sympathetick T———

 She fpoke: Then op'd with Wand of Lead
His thick, hard, empty, ftinking Head,
To dip his Brain profoundly dull,
And fit it for a leaden Skull;
Then thrice her Breath with his fhe mix'd.
And his dull fenfelefs Numbers fix'd.

 But ftill poor Log, amidft a Pack
Of Rabble, lies in Garret black;
(Him there the Goddefs had convey'd,
And in his genuine Manfion laid)
But what can't Powers divine perform,
Tho' *Phæbus* rage, and *Pallas* ftorm?

———————————————————

* *A Magick Incantation.*

That wooden Log that sleeps in Death,
Shall mix once more with Life and Breath.
The human Soul from Earth and Air
Had vanish'd to the Lunar Sphere;
But Dulness, by strong magick Dreams,
Behold, invents new wond'rous Schemes.

An Ass inur'd to Toil and Blows,
To Summer Heats and Winter Snows,
Expiring lay, his drowsy Soul
Convulsive groan'd in Kennel foul.
The Goddess with her Wand of Lead,
First prob'd each Part of Hero dead;
With Heart exulting found the whole
Proportion'd to the brutal Soul:
By Spell divine and Magick Charms,
All warm she caught it in her Arms.
Thrice to the Log she fix'd her Mouth,
Thrice turn'd to North, and thrice to South,
Perform'd her Circles thrice times Nine,
And rais'd dead Log by Power divine.
An Ass's Soul informs the Wood,
And animates new Flesh and Blood;
Then from the heavy panting Heart
Slow Heat's diffus'd to ev'ry Part:
This done, the Goddess in his Pate
Resum'd her so long wish'd-for Seat.
Hence dull Philosophers and Asses
Adore her there whene'er he passes.

So by the Will of mighty *Jove*,
A Log descended from above,
Vested with Power to reign in Bogs
O'er the whole Tribe of miry Frogs;
The croaking Nation join'd to sing,
Long live our wish'd-for *Wooden King.*

N. B. *If this meets Encouragement; a Key shall be Publish'd with the next.*

GRAFFANIO-MASTIX:

OR, A

COLLECTION

Of Curious

POEMS

ON THE

CENSOR

CONTAINING,

I. The Cenforiad.	V. Variæ Lectiones,
II. The Defence.	excerptæ ex operibus
III. The Threnodia.	Nugatoriis Bentleii,
IV. The Laft Will.	Theob. & Wellftedii.

All curioufly illuftrated with ANNOTATIONS
of divers learned Authors.

To which is prefixed the Life of MART. GULLIVER.

———Tibi Scriptus GRAFFANE Libellus   MART.

DUBLIN:

Printed, and Sold by GEORGE FAULKNER at the Pamphlet-Shop in Effex-ftreet, oppofite to the Bridge, 1730.

THE

CONTENTS.

A N

THE
CENSORIAD.
A
POEM.

Written originally by MARTIN GULLIVER.

Illuftrated with fundry curious Annotations of divers learned Commentators *Scholiafts* and *Criticks.*

—————*Fælicia tempora, quæ te*
Moribus opponunt!—————

JUV.

—————Thou Vermin wretched
As e'er in meazel'd Pork was hatched!
Thou Tail of Worfhip, that doft grow
On Rump of Juftice, as of Cow!

HUDIBRAS.

Cum variis Lectionibus excerptis
Ex eruditiffimis Commentariis Ric.
Bentleii, Lud. Theobaldi
Nec non Leonardi Welftedii.

To which is added an ANSWER.

The Fourth EDITION.

DUBLIN: Printed by GEORGE FAULKNER, (lately remov'd from *Skinner-Row*,) at the Pamphlet-fhop in *Effex-*
ftreet, oppofite to the *Bridge*, 1730.

THE
COMMENTATOR's

Proeme unto the courteous Reader.

THIS delectable Piece of Poesie having
mainly and marvelously suffer'd throug:
the Precipitation of sundry Transcriber:,
and Copyists heretofore; we deemed it mee:
(and in some sort it behoveth us) to restore it t:
its pristine Garb; partly by comparing togethe:
the several Copies, and adhereing unto such thereof as liked us most, partly on the Verity of othe:.
and finally on our own Experience, manyfu:
Observations, and profound Penetration.

And in good sooth to compyle this Commen:-
tarie, much Labour and Oyle hath been expend:
ed, albeit great Pleasance hath it ministred un:
us, inasmuch as it hath enabled us to bring in:
Light this Piece in its primal Purity, and eke t:
testifie unto the Publique our unwearied Indeavo:
for the Entertainment thereof, unto the Prepond:-
rancy of whose Judgment, we subject the Fru::
of our Toyle the Erudition,

Age, benigne Lector, his nostris contibus fave.

Vale & fru:::

Martini Gulliveri
vita ex variis Veterum testimoniis
Excerpta.

Artinus Gulliverus matrem habuit *Aliciam,* quo vero
patre natus minime inter Doctos consensum. Varias
rum conjecturas & disputationes non nostrum est hic pro-
re; sufficiat si de ipso *Martino* pauca commemoremus,
que, quum plurimis confessum, eum quendam (quicun-
modo fuit) habuisse patrem. Natus est in Anglia, Comi-
Shropshire pridiè Calendarum *Martii* Anno 1242. Inter
res Matronas matri enixè parturienti astantes, *Shiptonam*
dam prophetissam fuisse traditur, eamque (studio ma-
seu potius Divinitùs impulsam) Labiis nùnc primùm
antibus potionem quandam in cranio Coracis contentam
movisse, Cum Nonnullæ præsentium Rogitassent, cujus
hoc fecisset, *Shiptona* respondit, sibi permanifestum
e, infantem natum esse egregiæ Indolis, & modo Va-
futurum, & ut vires insitæ quam maximè adaugerentur,
c potum dedisse. Quid infans & puer gessisset, ad rem
anibus parum attinet; præclari tamen ingenii, quod
m vix prima adoleverit ætas, indicium exhibuit, tenebris
inimè obvolvendum duco. Indicium, Cui nunquam in-
r celeberrimos extitit quicquam simile aut secundum.
d quò feror? hoc certe eruditis jamdudùm innotuit, &
rrogantiæ vel stultitiæ jure arguerer, si promulgarem hester-
m fuisse solem; hoc ergò nomine, Maturioribus jam con-
, omninò prætermittendum censeo. Spectemus nunc
Martinum

Martinum anno poſt decimum quarto in Academiam C.
brigienſem delatum, ubi ſedulo in biennium literis o.,
navavit. Cum ex improviſo colloquium inter comb:
de Regimine Academiæ exortum eſſet, variæque de c.
latæ Sententiæ, dixit ſe de certò ſcire, hincè multis a.
nis, Collegium in *Ierne* extructum, & ſtatuta regim.
abhinc deducturum fore, hocque (perrexit ille) i.
fundamento, bene multos in annos provectum iri, donec
ſus quidam, circiter, vel in Anno 1728, Cenſoratum in.
rit, & ſeſe, ut qui bene mores intelligat, ad munus o.
dum obtulerit. Hinc occaſione captâ. (indignatus eſt .
innovationes cujuſcunque generis) hoc Poema Cenſo.
ſcilicet condidit, dicens ſaltem exemplar fore futuris .
bus, ſi non de omni prædicabile eſſet de *Obeſo* illo prædi.
Affirmant nonnulli identidem dixiſſe, hoc munus tan.
annum a ſingulo obeundum fore, & quod ſecundo ab i.
tione, in hoc officium eligeretur Mathematicus quidam, .
duntque præterea, alterum carmen hujus ergô compo.
ſed quùm nobis firma ſit mens nil niſi verum expre.
longe abſit aſſerere ea, quorum veritas non abunde eluc.
Sed his omiſſis ad finem propero. *Martinus* cum a.
decimum ſeptimum compleviſſet, puſtulis ſuccubuit, a.
dùm ab omnibus defletus, ſed nullis, quam nobis Liter.
flebilior, relictis plurimis vaticiniis, quorum quædam .
explentur, alia vero reſtant in poſterum explenda.

Jam vero de nobis noſtraque hac editione, pauca !.
dicamus. Poſt multas vigilias & Bibliothecarum perſc.
tiones indefeſſas hic tibi, benevole lector, obferimus C
ſoriados editionem, quam poſſumus perfectiſſimam; et ſ.
cum ſerio reputaveris, quantòpere laboravimus vindic.
a tineis & blattis, fragmenta, imò potius fruſtula chart.
quibus hæc perfecta colligitur editio, ſi quot hallucina.
inſertiones & omiſſiones, quas, aut invidia aut incuria f.
ſuccurrendæ fuerint, quantùſque fuerit pulvis decutier.d.
dulò conſideraveris, nil moror, quin gratias, tametſi non .
vocatus, rependeris. Prædictionem in vita Autoris m.
tam omnimodo expletam jam nunc vidimus, & in l.
ejus dicatur, quod ita adaptaverit poematis circumſtantia.
ſi ſuis ipſe oculis vidiſſet Cenſorem. Quid reſtat nunc .

mi.

The Author's Life.

...huic finem imponamus operi? Finiatur ergo; & quæ-
...m eamus istud Poema de Censore secundo, si tale quid-
...m reperiendum est.

Translated for the Benefit of the English Reader.

Martin *Gulliver* was born of his Mother *Alice*, but by
what Father is not agreed among the Learned. It is
...t to our Purpose to set forth here their various Conjectures
...d Disputes; let it suffice, if we mention a few things of
Martin himself, especially since it is allow'd by several that
...had a Father (be he who he will.) He was born in *England* in *Shropshire*, the Day before the Calends of *March* in
...e Year 1242. Among other Matrons, who were assisting
...s Mother in her Travail, 'tis said there was one *Shipton* a
Prophetess, and that she (thro' love of his Mother, or ra-
...er inspir'd from above) gave him his first Drink out of a
...ven's Skull. Upon being ask'd by some present, why
...e had done so, she answer'd, that it was plain to her, that
...e Babe was born with a goodly Disposition, and wou'd in
...me be a Prophet, and that she had given that Drink to im-
...ove, as much as possible, his natural Abilities. His Actions
...ile an Infant and Child are little to the Matter in hand;
...t the Indication which he gave of his great Genius, when
...e was yet scarce a Youth, ought not, as I think, be buried
in Darkness. Such an Indication, as that any of the most
...mous Men have not only not parallel'd, but fallen far short
...! But whither am I carried? It is certainly long since
...ell known to the Learned, and I shou'd be justly branded
...th Arrogance or Folly, if I shou'd tell the World, that
...e Sun was up Yesterday, therefore on this Account, upon
more mature Deliberation, I think fit to omit it intirely.

Let us now look upon *Martin* settled in *Cambridge* College
...n the fourteenth Year of his Age, where for two Years he
...ligently apply'd himself to Letters; where upon an acci-
...ental Discourse between him and his Pot-Companions con-
...erning the Government of the College; and after each had
...poken his Sentiments of it, he said, that he assuredly knew,
that many Years after a College wou'd be builded in *Ireland*,
D   which

which wou'd deduce its Statutes and Method of gover
from thence, and (continued he) being fix'd on this F
dation will advance happily for many Years, until a ce
Burly Fellow in or about the Year 1728, shall instit
a Censorship, and shall, as being well vers'd in Mo
propose to execute the Office himself. Taking an Op
tunity hence (for he cou'd not endure Innovations of
kind) he wrote this Poem, viz. Censoriad, saying tha
wou'd at least be a Copy to succeeding Bards, if it were
in every respect applicable to that same burly Fellow, be
mention'd. Some affirm that he declar'd at the same ti
that this Office was to be executed yearly by each Pers
and that in the second after its Institution, a certain Mat
matician shou'd be elected to it, and they add besides, th
he had compos'd another Poem on this Occasion; but si
we are resolv'd to publish nothing but what is real, far
it from us to assert things, whose Truth is not abundant
apparent. But passing by these things I hasten to the
Martin when he had compleated his 17th Year, died of t
Small-Pox, very much lamented of all, but by none than
Men of Letters more lamentable, having left many Proph
cies, some of which are already fulfilled, and others awa
their Completion among Posterity.

Let us now have leave to speak a few things of our sel
and this our Edition. After many Watchings and unwe
ried Searchings of Libraries, we here, Courteous Reader,
offer to thee the most perfect Edition of the Censoriad, whic
we cou'd procure; and if you seriously think with your se
how much we have labour'd in rescuing from Moths a
Worms, the Fragments or rather Crumbs of Paper, out
which this Edition is gathered, if you diligently consider
how many Hallucinations, Insertions, and Omissions, th
effects of Envy or Neglect, were to have been obviated,
and how much Dust to be shaken off, I doubt not but yo
will pay your Thanks, tho' you had not been call'd upon for
them. We even now have seen the Prediction mention'd in
the Author's Life in every respect compleated, and to his
Praise be it spoken, he has so adapted the Circumstances of
the Poem, as if he had seen the Censor with his own Eye
What

...at now remains, but that we put an end to this Work?
... then finish'd ; and let us go in quest of that Poem
...erning Censor the second, if there be any such thing to
... found.

Judicia quorundam tum veterum tum recentiorum Scriptorum in hunc nostrum Authorem.

GULLIVER ingenio quantum probitate celebris
Aöniis innavit aquis——

Muret. Lib. 2 *Poet.*

Aspice, censorem qua pinxit *Gulliver* arte.

Sclavon. de arte Poet:

Inter vates melioris notæ *Gulliver* minime rejiciendus.

Vanderglucht de Officio Poet.

Quemadmodum apud Græcos Homerum, apud Romanos
...em Virgilium, ita apud Nostrates *Alexandrum Popeum*
...Hexametris componendis cotemporaneis suis longe præsti-
...e sæpenumero *Gulliver,* cujus judicium nequaquam dubi-
...dum censeo, affirmavit.

Tan. in Logograph.

Martinus Gulliver, longissimo etiamsi intervallo *Lemuele*
...ductus, tamen inter sui Poetas sæculi rei poeticæ satis feli-
...er operam dedit.

Bibl. in cap. 10. *Comment.*

Antiquitas suos impune vates jactet, & nos non paucos
...merare possumus, quos inter *Martinus Gulliver* haud im-
...rito locum obtinuit.

Bell. in Tom. 20. *opusc.*

Vir-

Judicia quorundam, &c.

Vir tam ingenii acumine quam Sermonis elegantiâ ...
Gulliver.

Frag. incert.

Ingenuis quoniam depulfis artibus Alma
Squallet & invidiæ damnofis fentibus horret;
Nec virtutis honos ftudii nec gratia reftant,
Quin fervile jugum & vultum mentita feverum
Luxuries regnant, quin verfis omnia fatis
In pejora ruunt, an non *Martinus* hiaret,
Si foret in terris? &c.

Dunfc in Lib. 2. Somnii

FINIS

THE

CENSORIAD.

SHOU'D the old Censor of Imperial *Rome*
Raise his tremendous Presence from the *Tomb*,
How wou'd he glow with just indignant Rage!
How wou'd he pity and detest that Age,
5 Where Ideots dictate, and Buffoons turn Sage.

ANNOTATIONS.

Censoriad. So Iliad, Æneid, Dunciad, &c. But let the
Reader be satisfy'd, that it signifies no more than a Song on
the *Censor*, which Word naturally produces a Note. Certain it is, that the generality of Mankind are ever fond of
filling those Offices, for which Nature hath render'd them
most unfit.

Optat Ephippia bos piger, optat arare caballus.

Hor.

Our Hero being elected to the *Censorship*, remindeth me
of some *Germans*, who allowed an Ass to be best qualified
to distinguish the Harmony of Sounds, because it had the
longest Ears. Whence the Epidemic fondness of our
Kingdom for Musick may rationally be accounted for. ——
Nam auriculas Asini quis non habet?

Heinsius.

Ver. 5—Where Ideots. Alludes to this of *Juvenal.*

——*Quoties aliquid de moribus audent.*
Qui Curios simulant, & Baccanalia vivunt.

Q thou!

O thou! to whom these Verses I direct,
Whom *Folly* can't *secure*, nor Wit *protect*,
Too bulky grown to pass unnotic'd by,
And yet too dull, to rally and reply,
10 How wou'd that *Cato weep*, nay *Smile* to view,
Dictators ap'd by Animals like You?
Who dare confirm new Offices and Laws,
At once the Scourge and Scandal of thy Cause;

ANNOTATIONS.

Verse 8. Too bulky——*Similiter Horatius:*
——*Epicuri de grege Porcum.*
Ver 10. How wou'd that *Cato* Weep. Some *Criticks*
contend, this and the following Lines shou'd be read in
hunc modum.

How wou'd that *Cato* Weep, nay Smile to see
Dictators ap'd by Animals like *Thee?*

Either I think may serve; but here give me leave to animadvert on the Ignorance of a certain Scholiast, who assur-
eth, that *Weep* and *Smile*, applied so closely to the same
Person, imply a Contradiction in Terms: but well we may
imagine this *Critick* never knew there was such a Figure in
Rhetoric as *Epanorthosis;* or that *Weep* might refer to the
Abuse of the *Office*, and *Smile* to the *Buffoonry* of the Person, Ignorant at the same Time of that beautiful Expressi-
on in *Homer.* ——Δαχρύεν γελάσασα. Il. :
She mingled with a Smile a tender Tear.
Pope

Ver. 12. Who dare confirm——The Reverend Hero of
our *Poem*, was not only the Institutor of the *Censorship*, but
the first that, through a consciousness of his own superior
Worth and Abilities, embrac'd the honourable Office himself, and by his indefatigable Industry, hath paved a Path
worthy to be Trodden by all succeeding *Censors.*
Hunc talem spectate virum, imitamini virtutem. Dunces
W

Who teach unpolish'd Monsters to reclaim,
15 And servile Hearts to tremble at a Theme,
Where *Dread* and *Dulness* all their force unite
Where *you* give *Subjects*, and where *Freshmen*
(write.

Who least offends, himself should Censure most,
Our *Censor* seems the Object of his Poll:
20 To thinking Minds this honest Task shou'd fall.
But *Gr*——prates too much, to think at all:

ANNOTATIONS.

Ver. 14. Who teach unpolish'd, *&c. Similiter fragmen-*
tum incerti Authoris:
Ipse rudis rudibus posuit præcepta novistis.
Ver. 16. Where *Dread* and *Dulness*, &c. Tho' no Animal
is more sluggish and despicable than an *Ass*, yet nothing is
more Frightful than it's braying. *Idem.*
Ver. 18. Who least, *&c.* Directly opposite to this Rule
of our Author, is the general Practice of the World. For
the Ignorant and Vicious are ever more the most Impertinent and Censorious; and it is not doubted by the learned, that the *Hero* of this *Poem*, for being well accomplish'd
in both these Respects, was as *Milton* expresseth it on a parallel Occasion——*
namely *Satan*'s Election to the Censorship of *Tartarus*, &c.
advanc'd to that bad Eminence,
Heinsius.

Ver. 19. Our *Censor* seems
This may seem a piece of *Satire* on our *Censor*, but I must
beg Pardon, if I Argue from an opposite Principle, 'tis the
highest *Encomium* he cou'd receive, since he sacrifices his private to the publick Interest of a *Society:* This, as I take it, is
the true Spirit of a Patriot, and a notable Imitation of *Cato*
I shall strengthen this my Opinion with one Argument. Sup-
Offi-

Officious, fawning, frivolous and loud,
Awkardly Vain, and impotently Proud;
Partially strict and sneakingly Severe,
25 And sickle as the * Beast, which lives on *A.*
He can't judge right, for Triflers never can,
'Tis not the *Cause* that's odious, but the *Man*
Great is the Task, and worthy of a Mind,
Imbu'd with *Virtue,* and by Wit refin'd,
30 To point the Paths of *Piety* and *Truth,*
To curb the Sallies of licentious *Youth.*

ANNOTATIONS.

pose my Neighbour were so extremely kind, as to We..
my Garden, shall I Quarrel with him for his good Off..,
because at the same Time his own is over-run with Net..
and *Thistles?*   Li..

Ver. 21.   But *Gr*—.This Word hath occasion'd sev..
Conjectures, some imagine it to be *Griffith,* some *Gr..,*
and others peremptorily affirm it to be a Name, too ob..
ous to be mention'd.   *Casaub..*

Ibid Ver.   But *Gr*—— the Word *Prates* is very sig-
nificantly apply'd by our Author: thus we say the *Parr..*
Prates, the *Magpye,* &c.   *Similiter* λαλιϛίεραν κορῶ'ης, A-
pud Anacreontem.

                                                          Bentleius

Ver. 27.   'Tis not the Cause, *&c.*   So that we may fa..
his Office becomes him, as the Armour of *Achilles* wou..
Thersites, and on whom (according to Mr. *Young*)
              It——Shines as *Trophies* on a Post.

                                                          Gratia..
                                                              A:

* This Periphrasis signifies a Camelion
Est Animal, quoi mille duit diversa colores
Aurat species.   Paccuvii frag.

At once endeavour to *Inſtruct* and *Pleaſe,*
Adviſe with *Candour,* and *Correct* with Eaſe;
To ſuch a *Cenſor,* and in ſuch a *Cauſe,*
35 Whoſe good Example ratifies his *Laws,*
We give Attention, for Offence attone,
And make his Life, the Standard of our own:
But when this Mimic *Ape,* with Aſpect ſow'r,
Exerts the rigour of Tyrannic Pow'r,
40 We ſtart with generous Indignation back,
For who wou'd take the Potion of a Quack,

ANNOTATIONS.

Ver. 32. At once endeavour, &c.   So *Horace.*
   Aut prodeſſe volunt aut delectare———
   Aut ſimul & jucunda & id. nea dicere vitæ.
  Et paulo poſt,
     Omne tulit punctum, qui miſcuit utile dulci.

Ver. 37. and 40. And make his Life, &c. our Author here
in the Characters of a good and bad *Cenſor* concludes with
two Epiphonemas, the one in the Affirmative, and t'other in
the Negative, wherein he giveth us to underſtand, that precept availeth but little, if it be not inforc'd by practical
Precedent; and it muſt be confeſs'd, that unworthy Magi-
ſtrates are but at beſt but ſo many Burleſques on their
Offices; far be it from me to reflect on the juſt and wiſe Body
of Aldermen of this City, and farther yet be it from me to
reflect on the right worſhipful *Cenſor* of *T. C.*

Ver 42. Faction he loves, &c. I wou'd not have the
Reader infer from this, that he interferes with the State
arcana. No, far be it from him to be ſuſpected for a *Poli-
tician,* it only relates to his Conduct in the common Wealth of
Learning, where the Superficial and Turbulent, are (*cæte-
ris paribus,*) as dangerous as in the Body Politick like
Faction

Faction he loves, tho' for its Tool defign'd
For this he'd ftand, the Teft of all Mank---
He hunts Reproach, lays Snares for Redicu---

45 And takes uncommon Pains to play the Fo---
    Eafy alike if Zeal or Party's bad,
    Or if he pafs for Popular or Mad.

ANNOTATIONS.

Moles, which tho' blind, are ever undermining, and *Sn*---
which touch nothing without leaving a Portion of their Sli---
on't.   *Spond.*---

Ver. 43. For this he'd ftand the Teft, *&c.* The W---
Teft hath, with good Reafon, given occafion to various Co---
jectures; fome imagine it ought to have been *Peft*, and t--
the Line fhou'd run thus

    In this he is the Peft of all Mankind.
Alii vero fic. In this he is the jeft of all Mankind,
Reader, thou haft variety, chufe which thou wilt.   *S*---

Ver. 45. And takes uncommon Pains, *&c.* The Courte---
Reader may perhaps accufe the Poet of running here i---
the improbable; but the following Story, may, I thin---
fuffice, to vindicate him from that Imputation.
   The Cenfor, whilft paying his Devoirs to a certain No-
bleman accidentally drop'd his *Handkerchief*, and ftooping t--
take it up, in it's ftead, he *innocently* feizes his Patron's *Slipp--*
and crams it into his Breaft, and tho' immediately told ---
his Miftake, cou'd fcarce be convinc'd, that the *Slipper* w---
not really the *Handkerchief.*
   Ver. 46. Eafy alike, &c. From this Infenfibility ---
Temper in our H E R O, it appears that he efpoufes the S---
Sect of Philofophers, to which the *Roman* Cenfor was fo i---
violably attach'd, tho' others affirm his Principles are *Epi--*
rean from his daily Experiments of the *Air Pump*, and h--
contending for a *Vacuum.*   And laftly, others are for maki--
out that he is a *Cartefian,* and that he *folidly* believes that ---
be a *Plenum,* which all others take for a *Vacuum. Scal.* ---

Witnefs that glorious Night, when flufh'd
(with Wine,
His folly fpurr'd him to a brave Defign,
WhenMifers dreaming, brood o'er hoardedPelf,
And ev'ry *Hog* lay fnoring, but *himfelf.*

ANNOTATIONS.

Ver. 48. When flufh'd with Wine. As we have already
in other refpects compar'd him to *Cato*, the Parallel will
hold good in this.

> *Arratur & prifci Catonis*
> *Sæpe meri caluiffe virtus.*

Ver. 49. His folly, &c. This whole Epifode is Matter of
Fact, and no poetical Fiction, as hath erroneoufly been held
by fome. From the Tenour of which, a very ufeful Mo-
ral may be drawn, viz. That all Magiftrates invefted with
any civil Power, fhould be well guarded, when they are dif-
charging the rigour of their Office. The circumfpect Mr.
Hawkins was fo well convinc'd of the truth of this Aphorifm,
that he never went upon any publick Enterprize without
his Train'd-band.

Ver 50. When Mifers dreaming, &c. The Antients as
well as Moderns have been very copious in their Defcripti-
ons of Night: Probably our Author had the following one
of *Virgil* in view.

> *Nox erat & terras animalia feffa per omnes*
> *Alituum PECUDUMQ; genus fopor altus habebat.*

As Night and Chaos are reprefented by the Poets to have
been the Progenitors of Dullnefs and Stupidity, certainly
ourAuthor cou'd not have pointed out a fairerScene of Action for his H E R O, than that vacant fpace of Time, when
the more thoughtful Part of Mortals fufpend their purfuits,
and recruit their Spirits for the Bufinefs of the Day——
feffius

Ver 52. Back'd by one Vaffal. *Virgil*
——————————*Horrentibus umbris*
——————*Ipfe uno graditur comitatus Achate.*

B   Back'd

Back'd by one Vaſſal, thro' the mazy Glo�

He boldly ſtagger'd to a Scholar's Room,

Thrice knock'd with pond'rous Feet ⸗

                    (Mutton F⸗

55 And thrice the bolted Door his rage reſiſt⸗

At length he tries the Proweſs of his Pate,

And open flies the barricado'd Gate;

A N N O T A T I O N S.

Ver. 54. Thrice knock'd, &c. So *Lucan.*
——— *Bis terq; manu, quaſſantia tectum,*
Limina commovit———

Ver. 56. At length he tries, &c. I can't well juſtifie ⸗
Author in this, for he ſeems to attribute a degree of R⸗
ſon and Reflection to the Cenſor; how much better had ⸗
deſcrib'd him according to *Horace.*

                    Iracundus, Inexora⸗
        Difficilis, Querulus, &c.

Ver. 57. And open flies, &c. Our Author in this hath
ſhewn himſelf well vers'd in the Beauties of the Claſſick
For it is obſervable that all Epic Writers, when the
ſtudy'd to exalt the Characters of their Heroes, deſcrib⸗
them breaking Gates and burſting open Doors: Thus *Ho⸗*
(*Iliad* 12.) magnifies *Hector* for breaking the Gate of t⸗
Grecian Wall with the Fragment of a Rock, *Milton* aggran⸗
dizes the Courage of *Satan*, by deſcribing him breaking o⸗
pen Hell-Gates, and the Author of *Hudibraſs*, to exalt the
Character of *Magnano*, repreſents him indeed like our H⸗
ʀ o, coming off with the worſt in his Encounter, but ſeem⸗
to think him ſufficiently extoll'd in the other part of the
Deſcription.

        ———The brave *Magnano* came,
Magnano great in Martial Fame,
But when with *Orſin* he wag'd Fight,
'Tis Sung he got but little by't;

                              Fo⸗

For what is Oak or Iron, but a Sham,
Againſt the Force of ſuch a batt'ring Ram ?
The Cenſor enters——and about he flings
The injur'd Glaſſes, and the Chamber rings:
See *Locke* and *Clarke* in floods of Liquor ſwim,
He ſeiz'd the Scholar, and the Scholar him ;
Off fly their Wigs; they give alternate Cuffs,
65 The *Scholar Labours*, and the *Cenſor Puſs :*

ANNOTATIONS.

Yet Doors were feeble to reſiſt
The Fury of his armed Fiſt.
Ver. 65. The Cenſor puffs. So *Virgil.*
Vaſtos quatit æger anhelitus artus.

Though much it irketh me to accuſe our Author of *Pla-
ſiariſm;* yet Reader, perceiveſt thou not, that the following
Deſcription is purloin'd from a Paſſage in the fifth *Æneid*
of *Virgil,* where *Dares* and *Entellus* are contending at Whirl-
bats? Albeit, we muſt allow the Application to be meet e-
nough.

> *Ille, pedum melior motu, fretuſq; juventa :*
> *Hic membris & mole valens; ſed tarda trahenti*
> *Genua labant*————
> *Multa viri nequidquam inter ſe vulnera jactant,*
> *Multa cavo lateri ingeminant & pectore vaſtos*
> *Dant Sonitus, erratq; aures & tempora circum*
> *Crebra manus: duro crepitant ſub vulnere malæ.*

> *Stat gravis Entellus,* &c.
> *Oſtendit dextram inſurgens*————*& alto*
> *Extulit : ille ictum venientem a vertice velox*
> *Prævidit, celerique elapſus corpore ceſſit.*
> *Entellus vires in ventum effudit, & ultro*
> *Ipſe gravis, graviterq; ad terram pondere vaſto*
> *Concidit*————   Dunceſe.
                                            This

This on Activity and youth relies,
In Martial Spirit Greater, less in Size:
Not so the Censor ; the dull heavy Hulk
Chiefly depends on his enormous Bulk ;
70 But as he moves his Body in a heat,
His Joints relax beneath th'unweildy weight.
Bloodless they yet contend with many Bumps,
Their hollow Sides repeat the heavy Thumps;
And now their Nails indent heroic Scars,
75 They tug and lengthen one another's Ears:
With formidable Hands they lay around ⎤
Repeated Wounds, at each repeated Wound ⎮
Their Heads are dizzy'd, and their Cheeks ⎬
(resound. ⎦
Yet lo! unmov'd the Mighty Censor stands,
80 Shakes off the Foe, and weighs his potent hands,
The feebler Foe, as when with fatal Knocks,
The Butcher's bent, to kill the stately Ox,
The Censor views in Majesty of Fat,
And tries, with insult vain, this way and that.
85 Aloft his weighty Hand the Censor lifts,
And bravely charges—but the Scholar shifts;
The yielding Air receiv'd the Censor's Strength,
And down he fell—a huge unweildy Length!
Then, oh! what Scenes of Gallantry & Blood,
90 What Noble Theme for Poets had ensu'd,
Had

Had not pacific Dullneſs, all unſeen,
Ruſh'd in a Freſhman's Habitude between,
Anxious to ſave her genuine Offspring's Life,
And put a Period to the doubtful Strife?

95 Him ſtraight the Goddeſs to his Room con-
And in a downy Bed ſupinely laid ;   vey'd,
Then gently round his conſecrated Head,
A miſty Cloud of drowſy vapours ſhed.

To ſooth his Dolours with Nutation bland,
100 Thrice o'er his temples ſhook her Magic wand
Thrice ſweetly hum'd, to Lullaby his pain,
Pambaicks ſoft --- *aſleep creating* Strain !
And thrice her parent Breath with his com-
                              (mix'd
And his dim Eyes in leaden ſlumber fix'd.

ANNOTATIONS.

Ver. 91. Had not pacific Dullneſs — the Interpoſition of
Deities is frequently us'd by *Homer* and other Epic Wri-
ters: from many Inſtances take the following out of the 21ſt
Illiad, where *Apollo* reſcues his Favourite *Agenor* from the
Violence of *Pelides.*

———Ὀυ᷉ε τ᷉εαϲεν Ἀπόλλων Κυϐος ἀρέϲϑαι
Ἀλλα μίν ἐξήρπαξε, κάλυϩε δ᷉αρ ἤερι πολλῆ

Ver. 101. Thrice o'er his Temples. The Goddeſs is here
introduc'd with all ſuitable Pomp and Solemnity, who at the
ſame time ſhe diſplays her Divinity, ſhews all the tender
care and concern of a Parent : to mitigate his late misfortune
ſhe breaths her influence on him ; ſhe lulls him aſleep. The
Goddeſs of Wiſdom herſelf cou'd do no more to her favourite
Penelope in her afflictions,
                              ———ὁι ὑπνον,
Ἧϑυν ἐπι Βλεϕάϱοιϲιϐάλε γλυϰϙ᷉αϲ πς Ἀϑηνη

105. But

105 But let the Censor's folly be his guide,
      Since this is all that can support his Pri[...]
      In every Scrape his Politicks must run,
      And where his Schemes do nothing--nothi[ng]

                                          (do[ne;]
      When daring faults call hasty venge'nce dow[n]
110 Presumptuous sins, too big for half o'Crow[n,]
      Then gentle R—s stupidly complains,
      Whose Conscience so much overweighs h[is]

                                          (Brain[s];
      But Gr—— sighs to see a Crime so larg[e,]
      For none but paultry Sinners are his Charg[e]
115 Yet grins and leers at least, to shew his Ze[al,]
      Impertinence succeeds, tho' Power may fail[;]
      He shall tell Tales, work Infamy more warm[,]
      Invent, inlarge, *think Nonsense*—then inform[.]

                                                  [E]

A N N O T A T I O N S.

Certain it is, that nothing can give greater Ornaments [to]
Poetry than this Figure, when well wrought and aptly apply'd——*Nec deus intersit, nisi dignus vindice nodus*——*inci-*
derit—— It must be a Matter of the last Importance, that demands the Presence of a Deity. So that with the same poetical Justice, wherewith the *God* of *Wit* preserv'd his *Votary,*
the *Goddess* of *Dullness* preserv'd her's.

                                          Gronovius

Ver. 103. Pambaicks soft. A Peculiar and inoffensive
kind of things so nominated from their soft and simple mean-
ing Author Namby Pamby. By the Critick dignified with
                                                  th[e]

If by the Looks the inmoſt Soul we trace,
125 Who cannot read his Dulneſs in his *Face?*
Well does *Grimace* his Sentiments befit,
His *Smiles* are *Commentators* on his Wit.
Sardonic *Smiles* diſtort his hideous *Jaws,*
Senſeleſs he jeſts, and laughs without a Cauſe.
                                        125. In

ANNOTATIONS.

the Titles of the Infantine, the Finical, the See-Saw, *&c:*
and which to uſe his own eaſy Dialect.
        Readers abſolutely keep
        Half awake——— or half aſleep.
                                        Dydimus.

* * * * * * * * * * * * * *
* * * * * *Hiatus in* M. S. * * * * *
* * * * * * *valde deflendus* * * * * *
* * * * * * * * * * * * * *

As to this lamentable Chaſm in the M. S. Commentators
are ſtrangely divided; ſome tell us we have loſt above thirty
or forty Lines, for which little or no account can be given;
others are of opinion the Poem reach'd no farther, and that,
what lines follow are but a ſpurious Supplement, a practice
too notorious among ſome Scholiaſts! For my part I ſhall not
pretend to be deciſive, but this I can affirm, that I have
delivered it to the World, as I found it in a M. S. of the
Grubſtreet Vatican, which is reckoned the moſt ancient, now
extant.   *Faber.*

Ver. 111. Then gentle R——s ſtupidly. I have ſeen an
old M. S. wherein for *ſtupidly* is written *heavily,* and it is
more than probable the former hath been foiſted in either
thro' the inadvertence or conceit of the Tranſcriber; becauſe
Heavy Complaints, hath been an old Mode of Speech, not
but that both may be equally applicable to the Perſon.

Ver. 118. Think Nonſenſe. A Vulgar Author here wou'd
have ſaid, ſpeak Nonſenſe (as I have ſeen it in one of the
                                        ſurreptiti-

125 In vain *Democritus* he wou'd appear
    With not one sign of Wisdom--but the Sn...
    But much I grieve your Errors to expose,
    To pawn Advice in Verse for Faults in Prose
    Can you renounce those Follies all despise,
130 Will future Ages say, *you once were Wise?*
    Sooner shall scribling * *Coffey* sue for Grace,
    Or dull † *Arbuckle*'s weekly Labours cease.

ANNOTATIONS.

surreptitious Editions of this Poem) but better knew our
Poet to penetrate into the Medullar causes of things, for me
thinks there is a wide difference between one that thinks an
one that only speaks Nonsense ; a wise Man *per lapsum lingu*
may throw out Nonsense ; but to think Nonsense is a pecu
liar gift, a talent not to be acquir'd by Art, and as I may say,
implanted on the minds of some of the favourites of Nature
herself, who are therefore called Naturals.

Ver. 121. Well does *Grimace*, &c. The doctrine of Phi
siognomy is what hath been always maintained, whence the
Latin *Adage, Vultus est index animi*, is daily quoted, and cer
tain it is, that the Countenance of a *Felon* at the Bar has of
ten been the strongest Evidence against him. 'Tis from this
received Opinion that *Dryden* in his Fable of *Cymon* and I
phigenia has introduced the former Witnessing——*his Wonder
with an Idiot Laugh.* And we find that *Homer* to express
Impudence, has used the Epithet Κυνῶπις. How far these
Remarks may be applicable to the *Censor's* Circumstances, is
best known to those, that have had Eyes, to see, and Ears,
to hear him.

Ver. 123. *Sardonic Smiles.* Hear Servius upon this. *In
Sardinia nascitur quædam herba, quæ Sardoa dicitur : hæc com
mesa ora hominum rictus dolore contrahit, & quasi ridentes interi
mit : unde vulgo* Σαρδίνι☉ γέλως

                                                Sooner

* Two notorious Scriblers, one as remarkable for bad Verse as
the other for bad Prose.

Sooner shall ——— outshine a Barber's Block,
— rise at six, and ——— think like *Locke*.
135 Yet with unhallow'd Feet in endless Round,
You boldly trespass on poetick Ground,
Profane the Flowers, and Pollute the Strain
Of *Homer*, *Horace*, and the *Mantuan Swain*;
Lost to Reproof, tho' *Pallas* shakes her Spear,
140 And * *Phœbus* often threats to pull thy Ear;
As when a sluggish *Ass*, whom Hunger leads
To Fields of bladed Corn, or verdant Meads,
Feeds on, nor values the collected Noise,
Of *Peasants*, *Mastives*, *Curs* and *Village-boys*:
145 They wave their Clubs, and plentifully pour
Fast on his groaning Sides, a wooden Show'r:
                                    Yet

ANNOTATIONS.

* So *Virgil* ——— *Mihi Cynthius aurem*
              Vellit ———
As when a sluggish *Ass*, &c. doubtless our Author had the
following *Simile* of *Homer*'s in view, where the passive Courage of *Ajax* is liken'd unto that of an *Ass*; yet verily, it is
much more happily apply'd to our Hero.

Ὡς δ' ὅτ' ὄνος παρ' ἄρουραν ἰὼν ἐβιήσατο παῖδας
Νωθὴς, ᾧ δὴ πολλὰ περὶ ῥόπαλ' ἀμφὶς ἐάγη,
Κείρει τ' εἰσελθὼν βαθὺ λήϊον· οἱ δέ τε παῖδες
Τύπτουσιν ῥοπάλοισι, βίη δέ τε νηπίη αὐτῶν,
Σπουδῇ τ' ἐξήλασαν, ἐπεί τ' ἐκορέσσατο φορβῆς.
                            Iliad II. *Leunclavius*.

C   No:

Yet *He*, tho' much he bears, and muc'
(bk
Mocks their united Rage, and *bears*, and *;*
But know, O thou of undiſcerning *He.:*,
250 With Front of *Braſs*, and Intellects of *L.*
Not all the Time you ſquander to exp|
Thro' dark *Meanders*, *Nature*'s Myſtic St:
Nor *Globe*, nor *Glaſs*, nor any *Inſtrument*
That * *Senex* forms, or *Helſham* can inven:

A N N O T A T I O N S.

Not all the time you ſquander, &c. *tu nihil invita*
facieſve Minervâ.—ſaith *Horace* ; and yet how frequent.,
we obſerve this Precept tranſgreſs'd, to the great Detr:
of Society, whoſe Intereſt terminates in a proper Applic:
of the Talents of its ſeveral Members? 'Tis from this
fringement upon Nature, that the Publick is often depriv'
good *Coblers*, jolly *Tinkers*, full-fed *Aldermen*, luſty *Dra;-*
and able *Butchers* ; is it not a matter of daily Experic:
that ſome by peruſing Books abuſe them, when they n:
have been better employ'd in binding them for the uſe:
others? This Miſapplication of Parts is well expreſs'd i.
Paſquinade ; which was fix'd to the *Cenſor*'s Door.
                                                   Lambi;;;

A Curſe on him, that ſent thee firſt to School,
He ſpoil'd a *Plow-man*, to improve a *Fool*.

———————*tellus inarata quieſcit.*————Virg.——
—————*Deſuntque manus poſcentibus arvis.*——Luc.——
                                                   S.:

* A celebrated Mathematical Inſtrument-maker in London.

155 Not all thy bufy Schemes, and fage Device
Of reading *Books*, and fuffocating *Mice*,
Can make thy Learning, or thy Senfe extend
Beyond thy old, *Id Velim*, in the end.
So have I feen upon a Sign difplay'd,
160 Aloft in Air, a *Horfe* with *Wings* array'd,
Which (as Sir *Toby* faid) appear'd to Prance
Progreffive ftill, but never cou'd advance,
And yet fome good we boaft fome learned few,
Such as *Old Athens* wou'd not blufh to view;
165 And ye uninfluenc'd Few, whofe candid Hearts
Difdain the practice of inglorious Arts;
Who thro' the Paths of Virtue follow Praife
And value Merit, in the worft of Days;

Who

ANNOTATIONS.

Suffocating Mice, &c. among the various Entertainments of the *Cenfor's*, the choaking *Mice* in an Air-Pump is no inconfiderable one.

So have I feen, &c. refembling this, is the *Simile* illuftrating the Character of *Sidrophel* in *Hudibras*, but with greater juftice, applicable to the *Cenfor*:

> He as a Dog that turns the Spit,
> Beftirs himfelf and plies his Feet
> To climb the Wheel, but all in vain,
> His own Weight drags him down again,
> And ftill is in the felf-fame Place,
> Where at his fetting out he was, &c.   *Hudibras.*

Gronovius

Who view with mournful, but indignant I

170 The Coxcomb triumph, and the *Blockhe...*
Who blufh to think, that *Alma* fhou'd adv...
A *Dolt* from *Eng—d*, or an *Ape* from *Fra...*
While old *Iernes*'s Progeny bewail,
Her Genius languifh in the lighter Scale.

175 Forgive my *Satyr*, and indulge my Spleen,
So may your Fame be fafe, your Laurels green,
Tho' bad the Numbers are, the *Satyr*'s juf,
You can't deny one Line, and yet -- I muf.

VARIÆ

Variæ Lectiones

excerptæ ex eruditissimis Commentariis
Ric Bentleii, Lud. Theobaldi,
Nec non Leonardi Welstedii.

14. 15. { Who teach unpolish'd Monsters to declaim,
{ And servile Hearts to tremble at a Theme.

I have seen this in an old Manuscript, written thus,

Who teach unfledged Monsters to declaim,
And servile Hearts to tremble at a Name.

Unfledged ! Barbarous ! Gothick ! improper ! being only peculiar to *Fowl !* I shou'd rather conclude, *Rude* was the original Epithet, but that a Monosyllable wou'd not answer the Measure of the Verse, but trembling at a *Name*, in the subsequent Line is entirely spurious and vernacular.

Bentleius.

Ver. 25. And fickle as the Beast, *&c.* I have read it in the *Grub-street* Manuscripts thus, Thoughtfully dull, and safely insincere : But this we thought proper not to preserve, it seeming admitted more for its verity, than the beauty of the Versification.

Welstedius.

Ver. 29. For *Imbu'd Lege, Indu'd* or *Endu'd.*　　*Theobaldus.*

Ver. 31. To curb the Sallies, *&c.* I have seen Crub for Curb in a certain Copy, but this is an Error too obvious to be overseen by any Reader of tolerable Understanding.

Bent.

Ver. 44. ———— lays Snares for *Redicule*, &c. Redicule ! Kakography ! an Error of the last Concoction ! this must have been a blunder of the Editors.　Blot out that (*e*) boldly, and supply it with (*i*)

Theobs.

Ver. 53. He boldly stagger'd, *&c.* in an antient Edition is
written

written swagger'd, which appears to be more Con[...]
dent to the *Censor's* Person, were he not in Liquor.

Welf[...]

Ver. 99. 100. } To sooth his Dolors with Nutation bl[...],
} Thrice o'er his Temples shook her M[...]

(W[...]

I shall only offer in this Place, a conjectural Emendat[...],
which seems not unnatural.

To sooth his Sorrows with Lethargick Nod,
Thrice o'er his Temples shook her Magick Rod.

Theobal[...]

Ver. 132.——dull *Arbuckle's* weekly *Labours* cease, &c.

All the Copies amazingly disagree in the different Lection[...]
of this Line; in some it is weekly *Tribunes*, in others weekly *Nonsense*, in others weekly *Journals*; but methinks the
Word *Labours*, implys all the Degrees of bad Writing, [...]
which this Author daily distinguishes himself.

MARTINI

A MODEST

DEFENCE

OF

Mr. *G——n.*

BEING AN

ANSWER

TO THE

CENSORIAD.

——*Defensoribus istis*
Tempus eget——　　　　Virg. Æn.

DUBLIN:

Printed by GEORGE FAULKNER, (lately remov'd from *Skinner-Row*,) in *Essex-street*, opposite to the *Bridge*, MDCCXXX.　　　D

A MODEST
DEFENCE
OF
Mr. G——n, &c.

O What a sad Age of Corruption we live in,
When pennyless Poets so lewdly are given!
Behold with what Spirit of Malice they drive at
All Stations promiscuous, both publick and private!
'Twou'd make a Man crazy, to see at what rate here
They plague us with Libels, Lampooning and Satire;
If a Person of Business, of Credit, and Worth,
Be *bulky*, and *tipsy*, and *dull*, and *so forth*;
He cannot pass by, but he suddenly meets
His Talents, bespater'd in *dirty half-Sheets*.

Ye double-chin'd Aldermen, evermore witty,
And *You*, that with *white-Rod* afrighten the City,
Are ye not well paid to remove the *Town-dirt*?
Then why will ye fuffer fuch Dabblers to flirt?

Let other Men think what they will of the Times,
I cannot think well of their damnable Rhymes,
I fay, fuch a Clan of Poetical Toads
Are worfe than your Fellows, that rob on the Roads,
To them if you tamely furrender your felf,
Your Perfon they fpare, tho' they plunder your Pelf,
And this you may chance to retrieve by the Bounty
Of Chriftians, or fwearing a Tax on the County:
But once you lye under an evil Afperfion,
You never can hope for a *Fame* in *Reverfion*.

In his Heart and his Pencil of Poifon what Store he had
Who wrote fuch a Song as the wicked *Cenforiad*?
A Song where each Line and each *Note* raife a Laugh on
The *poor, inoffenfive, good-natur'd Hugh Gr——n!*
In right of whofe Honour my Pen I fhall brandifh,
While Brains in my Noddle or Ink in my Standifh.

Yo

You dull Poetaster, what Reason had you,
To Scribble, and be so severe upon *Hugh*?
To fall upon *Hugo*, a Person so *harmless*,
Was drawing your Weapons on one, that was *armless*:

Had he libel'd the State; had he once in a Journal,
Or other such scandalous Paper diurnal,
But publish'd his Labours, it had been less matter,
You might have some Privilege then to bespatter:
But since we have very good Reason to guess,
A Sheet of his never yet burthen'd the Press;
Since he has offended not one of his betters
In scurvy Invectives, or Letters on Letters;
Nor written * a Sonnet, nor grated the Ears
Of *Phœbus* with any impertinent Pray'rs;
You might have been better employ'd, you must own,
And let him, as he has let others, alone.

'Twas nothing but Malice, that prompted thee first,
But what have you done now in doing your worst?

---

* Our Author seems to be very grossly mistaken; for it is reported he had no small Hand in the Songs of the *Beggar's Wedding*.

Thy

Thy Satyr on *Gr——n* has loſt all it's Edge,
He cares not a Farthing for what you alledge.
The *Moon*, in her Glory, reflects on the Water,
While *Maſtives* are raiſing ſuch *Hubbubs* ſtill at her;
Like them you may Bark on, and hurt him as ſoon
For *Hugo's* as ſafe, as the Man in the Moon.

In vain you arraign him for wanting of Knowledge
Is he not a Fellow—of Tr-n--y C——ge?
In Manners you ſhould not have ſo much reflected,
A Man in his Station ſhou'd not be ſuſpected.

Your Muſe has related (for which I cou'd whip her
That he for an Handkerchief took up a Slipper;
To take up a Slipper, a wonderful Wonder!
And pray where's the Harm in ſo ſimple a Blunder?
Contemplative Men are loſt in ſtrange Mazes,
While their mind in the Field of Philoſophy grazes,
Aſcending aloft, they ſhake off their dull Fetters,
And leave common Senſe to Men of low Letters.
To *Hugo* you cannot impute that a Shame,
Which, rightly conſider'd, enhances his Fame;

His

His Thoughts were employ'd in a loftier Sphere,
In *squaring a Circle*, or *building in Air*
Great *Newton*, whom Envy can never befoul,
Was *Phœnix* of Science; capacious his Soul,
Like *Pompey*'s transported to Regions of Day,
Disdain'd to be ty'd to a Mansion of Clay,
Yet smoaking his Pipe once, however improper,
He us'd his Friend's Finger, instead of a Stopper.
But hold, quoth a Critic, however commodious
The Parallel, yet the Comparison's odious :
Is this, quoth another, the way you confute one ?
Consider, that this was the Blunder of *Newton*——
And this was the Blunder of *Gr*————*n* —what then ?
A Blunder's a Blunder, and both were but Men.

You talk of his Tipling : A Glass of good Wine
Cou'd never offend him————so sound a Divine !
Full Bumpers of *Claret* give Speech to our Tongues,
Enliven our *Spirits*, and strengthen our Lungs :
Old *Cato* the *Censor*, and great *Aristotle*
Were Lovers of Learning, yet Friends to the Bottle.
That *Hugo* is beaten by one he engages
At Boxing, you tell us in two or three Pages.

So

So poor Mr. *Gr*———*n* was drubb'd--and what then, S
A Drubbing has oft been the Fate of great Men, Si
And was it his Fault, if his Foe was the ftronger,
Was nimbler, and younger, and held out the longer?
He fought while he cou'd, and behav'd himſelf galla
And who cou'd do more, were he ever ſo valiant?

Tho' *Fortune is fickle*, *the Honour's the ſame*,
To *give or receive in the Battle a Maim*,
Some in the Engagement are beaten, *and ſome beat*,
Then as equal the Toil, *ſo the Glory of Combat*.
'*Tis he*, *that won't fight*, *that deſerves to be branded*,
Not he, *who*, *tho' ſure of a Drubbing*, *wou d ſtand it*,
And thus having finiſh'd the Task of Defendant,
I put, *without Name*, *a bold Daſh at the End on't*.—

VARIOUS

VARIOUS
REMARKS
ON THE MODEST
DEFENCE.

DUBLIN:

Printed by GEORGE FAULKNER, (lately remov'd from
Skinner-Row,) in *Essex-street,* opposite to the *Bridge,*
MDCCXXX.   E

To the well-minded READER,
Health, Wealth, Increaſe of profound Sapience, and long length
of Days, wiſheth *A. B.*

Kind, and Courteous R ᴇᴀᴅᴇʀ,

IT may not be altogether Supervacaneous and un-
ſeemly, to animadvert, that the following pithy
and profitable Illuſtrations in the *Latin* Tongue,
were communicated unto me by my Laborious and
Learned Friend, *Skirtsſleiskius*, Profeſſor of Divinity at *Leyden*, and Adept in the occult Sciences:
In very truth he certifieth unto me, that he found them
in a *Moth*-eaten Fragment of a very aged MS. repoſited
in the Literatory of the famous *Heinſius*. As to the Father of ſuch well-favoured Offsprings, the Literati are
in great doubt and Heſitation: Howbeit my Friend
conjectureth them to have been written in the time of
Pope *Leo* the IXth. by the Analyſis of certain Capital
Letters in a Chronogrammatick Poem, written in Praiſe
of his Holineſs, by one *Rhythmo-Romanus*, an eminent
Monk in thoſe Days of Poetry, which was Bound in a
Piece of black Sheep-Skin, together with theſe our *Latin*
                                                    Notes.

Notes. My Friend did also favour me with a Fragm——
of *The Modest Defence*, in *Latin Hexameter* Rhyme, b———
Translation of the first Distichon of the Poem, Bo———
in the said Sheep-Skin: The Lines run thus,

O quali Lævo *damnati vivimus* ævo,
Cum turpes Vates *audent ostendere* Nates!

.Desunt cætera

This strengthens my Opinion, in co inciding with m[y]
Friend; howbeit *Polyglottus* (in *Tomo Vigesimo opus——*
rum) seemeth to gainsay it: Verily I am of Belief, th[at]
the said Numerical *Rythmo-Romanus* wrote the Notes, a[nd]
Translated the whole Poem.

And now full Sorry I am, that *Time* the Destroyer and
Devourer both of *Censors* and *Censoriads*, hath been s[o]
invidious to Posterity, as to leave us so little of th[e]
Notes and Versification: However, studious *Lector*, content thy self with these few Golden Remains, rescu[ed]
from the preying Teeth of greedy *Moths*, and the
squint-ey'd Malevolence of former Ages, and if, perad-
venture, hereafter I may lay mine Hands on more o[f]
them, by delving and scrutanizing into the Ruins of
Antiquity, you may expect them in another Edition:
In the mean while, rest you in Peace and Tranquillity;
for so prayeth your Friend in Verity,

The EDITOR.

P. S. Just as I had put an end unto my Preface, I receiv'd a Collection of Animadversions in the Vulgar
Tongue, which in Friendly wise I shall link unto the
Latin ones, (and certes they are cunningly and crafti-
ly enough compiled) principally for the Glee and Im-
provement of my Fair Readers, of modest Deportment.

N. B. I would have render'd the *Latin* Notes into
English, but that I would not deprive the Beaus of an
opportunity of shewing their Learning to the Ladies.

I N-

INCERTI AUTHORIS.

(*Quotquot extant*) *Animadversiones.*

O what a sad Age, &c.) *Optimum sane exordium; ex-clamatio simul indignantis et irascentis; qui quidem mos apud cæmos olim Poëtas, in Satiris componendis, imo et oratores ∊∿∍; plurimum valuit: Sic enim Juvenalis in ipso operis li-∿∿ contra sui Scriptores sæculi invehitur.*

Semper ego Auditor tantum? *&c.*

Et alibi.

Ecce iterum Crispinus !

Sic et Cicero *in Catilinam.* Quousq; *tandem abutère pa-tientiâ nostrâ? &c.*

Ye double chin'd Aldermen, *&c.) Pingues sc. in-ferio. Metonimia externi objecti ad internum; Mate-rialitatis ad immaterialitatem. Nec injuriâ quidem, quo-niam Aldermanni plerumq; sunt obesi tam mente, quam cute.*

And you that with White Rod, &c.) *Periphrasis, per quam describitur Prætor Urbanus, Angl.* Lord Mayor, *cujus Authoritatis insignia, sunt Aurata Catena & alba virgulta: Hæc etenim tantum populo terroris immittit, quantum illa ge-stanti honoris affert.*

You never can hope, &c.) *Non prorsus huic absimile Illud horatianum.*

——*Nec amissos colores*
Lana refert Medicata fuco.

Cætera desiderantur.

A Continuation of Notes, by way of Supplement to the former.

But once you lye under, &c.) This Observation may hold in a general Sense, but certainly not in the Case before us ; and *Crubins* stedfastly cleaveth unto mine Opinion, who affirmeth, that the Word hath determin'd this Line only to such Persons as have (as one may say) accidental-ly given occasion to *Lampoons,* and not to such, as have

or

or ought to have been the Subject of many, duri͟ ͟
whole Tenor of their Lives.

F͟ ͟

Drawing your Weapons, &c.) This is fufficiently ͟
ftrated by a Paffage in the *Cenforiad*, Page 4. L͟ ͟
and here give me Leave to offer a curfory Emendati͟ ͟
the preceding Line, viz. *Too bulky grown, to pafs un͟ ͟
by*,) 'tis only here (if with Modefty I may fpeak it) ͟
the former *Commentators* have fhewn their blind ͟ ͟
Marvellous it is to me, that Men of fuch fharp-fi͟ ͟
Sagacity, and profound Penetration, fhou'd not ͟ ͟
known, that fo learned an Author as *Martin* could n͟ ͟
have written a Word fo inapplicable to the prefent P.͟
pofe as *unnotic'd*; certainly *unheeded* was the Orig͟ ͟
Epithet, however it hath been fupplanted by the oth͟
the former feemeth to imply little more than that a P͟ ͟
fon is *nct known*; but the latter giveth us to underft͟ ͟,
that a Man is thoroughly known, and with this Aggra͟ ͟
tion, that he is for that Reafon defpifed.

L͟d͟ ͟

On one that was armlefs, &c.) The Word *armlefs* is t͟
ken in it's Predicamental or full Extent, being no ͟ ͟
limited by the Subject. Howbeit, it is altogether cr͟ ͟
and inhuman in a Chriftian Country, that a Perfon͟ ͟
fhou'd be libel'd, who would have been canonized for ͟
Saint in *Morocco*.

Albertus ͟ ͟

Since he has offended not one of his Betters,) Why did h͟ ͟
not fay the fame of him, in regard to his Inferiors?

R͟i͟ ͟

In fcurvy Invectives, &c.) Our Author feemeth here to
play the *Sophifter*, as if his being *Dormant or A-la-Mort*, i͟
th͟

Capacity of a Writer, argu'd him so, in that of an
———t and Speaker.

Rivius.

——*Or Letters on Letters*, &c.) of which Species were
those elaborate Pieces of Poesy, addrefs'd to D. D——y
——D. S——t, but for my part I see no just cause of Com-
—— against such innocent Compositions, which answer
S. *Jerom*'s Version of the Apocryphal Phrase, de-
——ced on the wicked, *Nascentes Moriuntur*, they no
—— begin to be, but draw nigh unto their end. So
Transitory, alas! is the Date of them, that, instead of
Monuments, that Triumph over Time and Fire, they
may, with all Propriety, be call'd Bills of Mortality.

Antonius Goveanus.

Thy Satyr on Gr—— *has lost all its edge,* &c.) not unlike
to this is the *Offendet Solido* of *Horace.*
——*As safe as the Man in the Moon,* &c.) Vide *Fonte-*
e's Plurality of Worlds.
Again you Arraign him, &c.) } our Author here uses
Is he not a Fellow, &c.) } that convincing Method of reasoning, which Mr. *Locke* calleth *Argumentum*
ad verecundiam : And (to give our *University* the greatest
Encomium) I might affirm upon the Word of an Author,
that since the Days of the learned *Usher*, it never had so
many Originals, so many unreading Judges, and so many unjudging Writers. But more of this in another
Treatise.

Great *Newton*, whom Envy can never besoul,
Was *Phœnix* of Science; capacious his Soul,
Like *Pompey*'s transported to Regions of Day,
Disdain'd to be ty'd to a Mansion of Clay.

These

These Lines bear a Semblance of the following in the beginning of the 9th Book of *Lucan*'s Pharsalia.

At non in Phariâ manes jacuere favillâ,
Nec cinis exiguus tantam compescuit umbram ;
Profiliit busto, semiustaq; membra relinquens,
Degeneremque rogum, sequitur convexa Tonantis.

The rest of the Poem, being so plain and conclusive needs no Gloss or Comment.

F I N I S.

THRENODIA:

OR, AN

ELEGY

On the unexpected and unlamented

DEATH

OF THE

CENSOR:

TOGETHER

With some Account of his Last *Will* and *Testament* : All faithfully collected from the Genuine MSS. in the *Grub-street* Vatican.

—————————pingui tentus omaso
Graffanius, animam exhalavit opimam. **Virg.**

Written Originally by *Martin Gulliver*, and now revis'd and publish'd by the Commentator on the *Censoriad*.

Printed in the Year 1730.

Right Marvailous (gentyl *Reader*) ll
been the Succefs of my Lucubrati
heretofore; yea verily, and moche
faunce hath mine Heart Y--- gathered,
grete confole hath it afoorded my mynde,
perceive, that in vayn mine Oyl hath not b
expended, but that haply my Labours h
liked thee well. Howbeit, me-feemeth, t
the oddnefs of the Subject Pricketh thee mo
nathlefs; if thou haft Joyance, and I Co
mendacioun thereby, I am content.. Wh
Obfervacioun remindeth me of an auncie
Statuary, hight *Crytias*, who gotten h
moche rychefs, and gode name, by welly-c
ving the lykenefs of an *Afs* ; and eke of C
tander Thebanus, who gotten hem grete A
myracioun, for the jocund, and peerlefs p
traicture of a *Sir-reveraunce*.

Certes, right felicitous fhull I. be deeme
yf in gode part thou accepteft this my poe
Studye, and defyrous minde, in reducynge i
to Light this *auncient* piece of *Poefy*, whycl
it were over Pyteous to have been in a
poynt Loft, maimed, falfyfyed or contemn
Reader, that thou mayft as moche delyte
the perufal thereof, as I in the Compylemen
wifheth,

       Thine with all Tendernefs.

              The Commentator.

THRENODIA:
OR, AN
ELEGY, &c.

EPITAPHIUM.

Eterna memoriæ Censoris, Trin. Coll. Dub. *Ditatum.*

Mortuus hoc tandèm tumulo Graffane quiescis,
Ingenio Levior sit tibi terra tuo.   Men :

YE Writers of Satire, ye Whips of the Times,
  Ye dealers in Doggrel, ye taggers of Rimes,
  Ye scourges of Dullness, ye bold Pamphleteers
Who spare not the Vices of *Fellows,* or P—rs,
Ye fool-hating Authors of ev'ry degree,
Ye Hawkers of Scandal, come mourn with me ;
With me, O Lament, for the *Censor* deceast,
Who dy'd, as he's said to have liv'd, *Like a Beast* ;
O spread it to *Albion,* where it is said he
Is famous, as Dullness can make him, already :

                                    Thro'

Thro' the streets of *Eblana* let News-cryers roar,
That *Hugo*, the Blunderful *Hugo*'s no more.

By the *Wags* in the College, 'tis conftantly faid,
That magical Studies diforder'd his Head ;
They ground their Conjecture on this one Remark,
That whoe'er he convers'd with, was *left in the dark*.

The Action fuppos'd to have haft'ned his Fate,
Let *Ierne* attend, and the Mufe fhall relate.
He read of a * *Dervife* who nimbly cou'd Shoot
His Soul, with a Word, into each other Brute,
This Art, with impatience he labour'd to find,
It kill'd his Repofe, and diftracted his Mind,
Till at Laft with hard-plodding, and Study unfound,
This wonderful Secret was happily found :
But eager, an Art fo furprizing to try,
He fix'd on an *Afs* that by chance trotted by,
The Word was pronounc'd, the Soul inftantly fled,
And down dropt the Carcafs of *Gr—ff—n* as dead :
The *Soul* from its Lubberly Manfion releaft,
Grew pleas'd with a Dwelling fo much to *It's* Tafte.
Before, while imprifon'd, 'twas tortur'd in vain
To work on a ftupid infenfible Brain,
Condemn'd for whole Years over *Euclid* to pore,
And remain, O furprifing! as Wife as before,
Or plagu'd and benumb'd with inordinate Drinking,
Seem'd cram'd in a Carcafe to keep it from Stinking :
But now, in a thrice, of *It's* Punifhments eas'd,
Might Saunter, or Bray, or be Dull as *It pleas*'d ;

---

* *This Story is told in one of the* Perfian Tales, *and is
from thence quoted by the* Spectator.

...ay be contemn'd and abus'd, but not more
... It patiently suffer'd in *Gr—ff—n* before,
... Prudent for once, rather chose to reside
With innocent Dullness, than Folly and Pride.

  The Story sounds odd, so I shall not insist on't,
... leave the kind Readers to think what they list on't.
  Who dies by the Rope, without Last-speech, or
                                 (Poem,
O: some such kind Methods to make the Town know
                                   (him?

What high-pamper'd *Alderman* loaded with Liquor
And Vices, can peacefully go to *Old Nick*, or
A contrary Place, which they seldom arrive at,
For courting Intemp'rance in Publick and Private,
I say, what fat *Alderman* dies, but you meet
His *Elegy* instantly bawl'd thro' the Streets?
And shall the fam'd *Censor* unnotic'd lie Dead,
Tho' as Fat as a *Justice* in Paunch and in Head?
Shall He, and his Talents so soon be forgotten,
E'er his Carcase is grown, like his Principles, rotten?
The *Muse* shall forbid it, transmitting his Merits,
As the Curious, for Show, preserve Monsters in Spirits.

  Oh! what is become of thy Countenance sleek,
The *Leer*, and the *Folly* that dwelt on thy Cheek!
Thy *Quibbles*, thy *Puns*, thy *Invectives*, thy *Jesting*,
Those Arts, which the Genius of *Hugo* was best in;
Thy broad-spreading *Grin*, and the unstinging *Gibe*
So highly ador'd by the Fools of thy Tribe;
Thy *Blunders* which kept all the Board in a Roar.
All these are Extinct——, and their Parent no more.

                                        If

If *Wit* only serves to make other Folks laugh on,
Why—thus much was caus'd by the *Follies* of Gr
And, if this be the Case, who wou'd be at the Pain
To Torture with Learning a handful of Brains,
To Thrash at old Authors from Morning till Night,
To Labour for Years to be Wise and Polite;
Since he, with Assurance, Conceit, and Grimace,
With a *Sneer*, and an aukward Distortion of Face,
Tho' Thoughtless, and Brainless, and dull from his Birth,
Cou'd, as well as the *Witty*, excite us to Mirth.

When assaulted by Death, who's commission'd to Strike
Both the *Peer*, and the *Fool*, and the *Fellow* alike,
With a Sigh, and a Groan he was heard to Invoke
His best-belov'd *Goddess* of *Dullness*, and Spoke.

" O *Goddess*, thou Foe to the Learned and Wise,
" By whom I have grown to this Station and Size,
" O thou, who with Care o'er my Infancy hung,
" And form'd ev'ry Sentence that dropt from my Tongue,
" Whose Hand, with a Parent's Affection, hath spread
" O'er the Mind of thy Offspring thy Mantle of Lead,
" Hath stamp'd thy own Mark on whatever I Writ,
" And gave me immortal Aversions to Wit,
" As thy Influence always my Intellects blest,
" O Hear, and Comply with this single Request,
" Transform me when Dead, and bid far-flying *Fame*
" Then give me, (what, Living, I want,) a *good Name!*

He ceas'd; and one half of his whimsical Pray'r
Was heard; but the other dissolv'd into Air.

The

The Goddess, to grant what her fav'rite requested,
Corps of it's Ornaments quickly divested,
ce breath'd on his Face, and surrounded with Shade,
* Essex-Street nimbly the Body convey'd,
en mutter'd, and did what a fond Parent cou'd,
with easy Transition it chang'd into *Wood*,
ansform'd to a Station that suited him most,
alted, and stuck with his Head to a *Post*.
The Curious, are constantly crowding to view
The wooden Remains of the much-injur'd *Hugh*,
With a prominent Paunch, and a sad-featur'd Face,
Thro' which all his manifold Follies they trace,
And hope, his Successor, (as frequent the Case is,)
May Inherit his *Dullness* as well as his *Places*.

* *This is a Description of the* Wooden-man *in* Essex-
Street; *and the justness of the Comparison, will appear to*
every one who is acquainted both with the Censor, *and this*
its Wooden Representative.

Curteous Reader,

NOT having Room in this Paper for his last Will
and Testament, we must inform thee, that in a
few Days it will be added to a new Edition of
this Poem, when it will appear with several curious
Annotations, and Remarks; and thereunto will be annexed a more Correct Edition of the *Censoriad* also; to
which will be prefix'd the Life of Martin Gulliver
both in *Latin* and *English*.

FINIS.

THE

Laſt Will and Teſtament

OF THE

CENSOR:

AS

It hath been, with all Faithfulneſs,
collected from the Original MSS.

DUBLIN:

Printed, and Sold by GEORGE FAULKNER at the Pamphlet Shop in *Eſſex-ſtreet*, opoſite to the Bridge.

THE

Laſt Will and Teſtament

OF THE

CENSOR, &c.

IT being Cuſtomary to publiſh all the Works of a
Great *Genius*, as ſoon as he is depoſited in the Earth,
‡ even to his Laſt Will and Teſtament : It ſeemeth
not improper to us, who have Laboured ſo inceſſant-
ly to exalt the Character of the *Cenſor*, and make Poſterity
acquainted with him, (which in all Likelihood never
would have happened, if our Affection for him, and unwearied Induſtry in tranſmitting him, had not in a manner
ſnatch'd him from Obſcurity and Oblivion ,) I ſay, *kind
Reader*, it ſeemeth not improper to us, to gratify the
World

---

‡ *As may be ſeen before the Works of Mr.* Prior, *and ſeveral
other* Engliſh *Authors.*

World with a Curious and Impartial Account of his Behaviour in his laſt Moments.

As he was ever the moſt odd, inconſiſtent, Whimſical
kind of Fellow breathing ; he died not, without leaving
full Evidences of his continuing unaltered to the laſt.

It was his peculiar Opinion, that every Man had as
good a right to diſpoſe of his Good and Bad Qualities,
the Virtues and Vices of which he was poſſeſs'd, as of his
Goods and Chattels. The reaſon of this Opinion he would
frequently communicate to his moſt intimate Friends ;
namely, that, from good Principles he could demonſtrate,
that every one had a juſt right to diſpoſe of the Fruit of
his Labours as he thought proper : Now he was convinc'd
that both Learning, Dullneſs, Luxury, Intemperance, &c.
were altogether the Effects of great Labour and Pains,
for all theſe (except the firſt, which now-adays is but
in ſmall repute) he had experimented himſelf; and therefore reſolv'd, ſeveral Days before his Tranſmutation, to
bequeath whatever he could for the Benefit of his Friends,
and this his Native Country.

Where this valuable MSS. hath lain for ſo many Years
is ſtill a Secret ; we only can aſſure the World, that many Loads of learned Lumber were tumbled about, many
Libraries (thoſe Sepulchres of Learning, where Volumes
rot away in great Quietneſs and Silence,) have been
ſearched, vaſt Quantities of Duſt, Moths, Bookworms, &c.
have been diſplaced, in order to obtain this Piece of Antiquity, which, However imperfect, overpayeth us for the
Fatigue in finding it. We have carefully extracted all
that we here preſent to the World, from a Duſty Moth-
eaten, Worm-holed Copy in the moſt Antient, and ever-
renown'd Grubſtreet Vatican, and we hope it will meet
with kind Acceptance.

Curteous

Courteous Reader, take it as followeth.

I *Hugo* Gr--ff--n Fellow of the Society celebrated f[..] the Propagation of Infolence and Luxury, find[...] my felf extreamly Unfound both in Mind and Bo[..], do in the following Manner bequeath unto my de[..] furviving Friends the feveral Gifts hereafter m[..]tioned, charitably hoping that they will one Day h[..] the Opportunity of obliging others in the fame Manner.

Here the *Copyer* taketh Notice of his Groaning a[..] Grunting feveral Times, which was fuppos'd to proce[..] from his reflecting on the fmall Stock of *Learning, Wifd[..], Humility,* &c. which he had to divide among his Friend[..] tho' they were univerfally allowed to be in great Want c[..] them.

Imprimis. I Leave——my Death upon the wicked A[..] thors, Publifhers, and Commentators of t[..] fatal Poem, call'd the CENSORIAD, which was the fir[..] thing that ever made made me afham'd of my felf. Not-withftanding, I Accufe them not for publifhing Falfitie[..] but, for drawing my Picture fo exactly, that I was know[..] by every Reader, and made, if Poffible, more Ridiculo[..] than ever.

Item. I give to J—— R—— all the *Honefty* I ever w[..] Mafter of, which, if any, is not one whit the worfe for th[..] ufing, it proving but of very fmall Service to one in m[..] Station.

Item. I give my Dullnefs and Stupidity * Here the ancient Tranfcriber obferv'd, that he made a long Paufe, which was interpreted to b[..] occafioned by his doubting who was fitteft to be *Legatee* i[..] this Cafe; and being Confcious that one great Part of th[..] Heads of his Society were already overftock'd with i[..] But at length it fell to the Share of his Succeffor *D——'[..] and thus he proceeded. *Item*

Item. I give my *Brains*, if any such be discovered in me after my Decease, to the above-mentioned *J———* *———*, who is generally reputed ☞ to be very Defective in that Part.

Item. My whole Collection of *Blunders*, whether Premeditated, or Extemporaneous, I give to my good Friend Mr. *D———'s*, who is to Succeed me, not doubting but he will one Day afford future Poets as large a Field for *Panegyrick* as his Predecessor

Item. I request the said Mr. *D———'s* carefully to inspect my *Intellects* with his nicest *Microscopes*, and if it shall be his good fortune to spy the smallest Seeds of Sense or Understanding therein, let him reserve them for his own Use, as a Reward for the Enquiry.

Item. My Insolence, and Oppression of Inferiors, I give willingly to *J——— R———* aforesaid: nor that I suspect him of having any Scarcity thereof; but, least that by practising these so incessantly as he does, his own Stock, tho' very great, may be worn out, and then he may have occasion for mine. But with this Restriction, that after his Decease, it shall devolve to his Successor.

Item. I give to * * * * * * * * * * *
* * * * * * * * * * * * * *
* * * * * * * * * * *

Here the MSS was no longer Legible : *Time* and *Vermin* having made a Terrible, and never-enough-to be- lamented Chasm therein, leaving the World in great Uncertainty, how he dispos'd of the rest of his singular Qualities, and scarce-to be-paralell'd Absurdities. But *Reader*, Well it is that so much hath been recovered and produced into Light, and our Toils will sufficiently be rewarded, if it in any wise contributeth to thy Delight or Edification.

ANNO-

ANNOTATIONS
TO THE
THRENODIA.

EPITAPHIUM.

Ingenio Le-
vior, &c. } **G**REAT Variance amongſt Criticks and
Commentators hath this Line occaſion-
ed, ſome affirming that it alludes to the Great *Levity and*
Volatility of the *Cenſor's* Mind, and that the Senſe of the
Line is no more than a Prayer of the Poet's, *that the*
Earth may be lighter, if poſſible, *to him than his natural Diſ-*
poſition. Others again affirm, that it is only a wiſh excited by
Compaſſion and Tenderneſs for the *Cenſor,* the Poet affec-
tionately praying, *that the Earth may be lighter to him than*
his Wit, Underſtanding or Genius, &c. becauſe otherwiſe
he ſeems apprehenſive, that it muſt be an immenſe Weight
upon him. But Reader, we ſhall not undertake to decide
this Matter unto thee, both being equally true and ex-
preſſive.   *Heinſ.*

Ye writers of Satire.) Ever Cuſtomary hath it been a-
mong the Ancients, to begin their *Elegiacks* with Invoca-
tions, as well as our Author. So *Moſchus* Id. 3. on *Bion.*

Αἰλινὰ́ μοι ϛοναχῆτε νὰπαι κ᾽ Δώριον ὕδωρ,
Καὶ ποταμοικλαίοιτε τὸν ἱμερόεντα Βίωνα,
Νῦν ϛυτά́ μοι μύρεϑε, κ᾽ αλσεα νῦν γοϰοιϑε.   *M.I.*

Bold Pamphleteers, &c.   } It ſeemeth, ſaith wiſe *Chry-*
Who ſpare not the Vices, &c. } *ſagoras* in his excellent Book
of *Ethicks,* that Perſons in high Stations have ſome kind
of right to be vicious, becauſe, doubtleſs they can plead
Precedents in all their Predeceſſors : and therefore the E-
pithet *Bold* ſeemeth to be well applied ; becauſe correct-
ing Vice in a Great Man, is (in a very unpractis'd and
unapprov'd Manner) to prefer the Love of Virtue to the
Hope

...ge of Advancement. Yet Pamphleteers in this Age seem ...increase in Audaciousness, and, directly contrary to the Opinion of our Moralist, have dar'd to censure publickly even an E——sh D——n, only for committing a R—pe, ...o' his being in Drink, as he religiously alledges, ought, ...methinks, to be esteem'd a sufficient Apology, Especially ...r one in his Station.   *Heins.*

O Goddess, &c.) We may well suppose that this Speech to the Goddess of Dullness hath been translated into seve- ral Languages, since the Translation of it into Leonine Verse hath been still preserved.

> *O Dea prudentes, pariterque exosa scientes,*
> *Cui simul efflatum ventrem, cui debeo Statum;*
> *Et Quæ mihi nascenti ridebas ore faventi,*
> *Atq; pubescentis fingebas verba loquentis ;*
> *Quæ circum lumbum, circum præcordia plumbum*
> *Tarda Sacerdotis sternebas chara nepotis ;*
> *Nostra tuis illis Signasti scripta sigillis,*
> *Atq; sales vanos Monuisti odisse profanos !*
> *Ut, quam formasti, mentem gravitate beasti,*
> *Hoc Saltem flenti votum concede Clienti ;*
> *Damnatus Morti, quoniam Succumbere morti*
> *Cogor ; casuram libeat mutare figuram ;*
> *Nec dicar Stultus, vivus ceu, quando Sepultus.*

He ceas'd and one half, &c.) This seemeth to be an apt Imitation of *Homer.* II. 16. v. 249.

> Ὡς ἔφατ᾽ εὐχόμενος. τῶ δ᾽ ἔκλυε μητίετα Ζεύς·
> Τῶ δ᾽ ἕτερον μὲν ἔδωκε πατὴρ, ἕτερον δ᾽ ἀνένευσε.

And in the same Manner *Virgil.* Lib. 11. v. 794.

> *Audiit et Voti Phœbus succedere partem,*
> *Mente dedit; partem volucres dispersit in auras.*   Turneb.

And surrounded with Shade, &c.) *Homer* in like manner maketh *Venus* preserve her Fav'rite *Paris* as the Goddess of Dullness is describ'd protecting her own undoubted Offspring.

————————————————— *Tor*

————————————————— Τον δ' 'Εξήρπαξ',

Ρεια μάλ' ώςε Θεος. εὐθλυψε δ' άρ ήερι πολλῇ. H..

Two Notes by way of Supplement to the Modest D .
fence.

If a Person of Business, &c.) In an ancient MSS. ..
Line is read differently, which we here thought m::: ..
Transcribe.

If a Person of Credit, be Foggy, and Fat,
  And Stupid, and Tipfy, and Dull, and all That ;
But good Reader, both are applicable enough, and th::
haft Variety.   *F..*

Your Satire on Gr—ff—, &c.) There is alfo a varic..
Reading of this Diftichon, in the faid MSS, *viz.* ..
  Your Satire on *G—ff—n* is nothing at moft,
  But toiling to thrafh an infenfible *Poft.*

And this Reading, indeed, we have feveral Inducemen.
to adhere to, were it not that we have always been careful to avoid Interpolations of any Kind.

FINIS.

A N
I N D E X.

N. B. The firſt Figure ſtands for the *Page*, the ſecond for the Line. The Letter C. refers to the *Cenſoriad*, D. to the *Defence*, and *Thren.* to the *Elegy*.

Beggar's

	Cenſ.	Def.	Thre.

—Very much cultivated by *G--n*;
J—, *R—*, and many others
with great Succeſs. } **ibid.**

Ignorance. *Vid G———n.*

L.

L *Augh. Laughing-Stock. Vide*
Hugo }

Learning. The Conflict between it
and the *Cenſor*, in which it was
entirely vanquiſh'd, and expell'd
out of the Univerſity. } **34**

—In great Diſeſteem in this Age **ibid.**

—Thought to Unqualify a Man
at preſent for any kind of Preferment. } **ibid.**

M.

M *Artin Gulliver.* A very antient
and celebrated Author. *Vide*
Teſtim. & *vit.*

N.

N *Onſenſe.* A great Ingredient
in the Writings and Diſ-
courſes of the *Cenſor.* } **32**

O.

O ! A Word greatly in Uſe a-
mong all who hear or ſee the
Cenſor; to expreſs their Wonder
at his Parts and Perſon. } **11: 17**

P.—

	Cenf.	Def	Thre.

P.

Pambaicks. A gentle, Gig-jog, See-saw kind of Metre; fo diftinguifh'd from the Works of Genius, by their Infantine Author's true Name *Namby-Pamby*, tho' fome are perverfe enough to call him *Ph—ll—ps*. **13**

Pamphleteers. A very dangerous Sett of Men in all vicious, corrupted, ill-governed and unlearned Societies; being often firmly attach'd to Virtue and Probity. *Vid.* Notes to the *Thren.*

R.

R—s. Deem'd not improperly, very ftupid. **14 : 7**
—Heir to the *Cenfor* in *Brains* and *Honefty*, tho' he is generaly thought to have got nothing by his *Legacy*, and yet is allow'd to be in great want of them *Vid.* The Laft Will.

S.

STupid. Applied elegantly to the *Cenfor*. **14**
—As juftly apply'd to *J—R——* **ibid.**
—And to Dull *Arbuckle* **ibid.**
Senfelefs *Jefts* the *Cenfor*'s very peculiar Talent **15 : 6**
—Practis'd with great Felicity by feveral of the F——ws. **ibid.**
Slipper. Taken up inftead of a *Handkerchief* by the *Cenfor*: but generally believed to be done with no difhoneft Defign. **8 : 20**

	Cenſ.	Def.
Saunter. The *Cenſor's* Soul extreamly happy in the Body of the *Aſs,* becauſe it might saunter or bray, or be Dull, as it pleas'd.		

T.

	Cenſ.	Def.
TAle-telling. One of *Gr—n's* Perfections.	14 : 13	
Tipſy. Another of his good Qualities		3 : 8
Tyrannic. Another	7 : 8	
Tippling. Another		7 : 15
‡*Tool.* The *Cenſor,* a remarkable one	8 : 1	

V.

	Cenſ.	Def.
VAin. The *Cenſor* aukwardly ſo	6 : 2	
Velim Id. Gr—n's moſt uſual and Elegant Phraſe in Converſation; as much as to ſay, he would be underſtood if it was poſſible.	19 : 4	

W.

	Cenſ.	Def.
WIt. The *Cenſor's* mortal Averſion.		6 : 22
Witleſs. Vid. Arbuckle, G—n, J—R—, D—s, Aldermen, *&c.*		
Wooden. The *Cenſor's* Head of this Stuff.	22	
Wooden Man, The *Cenſor* with very little Alteration chang'd into one.		7 : 6
—*Worſhip, Gr—n* Elegantly call'd the Tail of it.	1	

‡ *Some are of Opinion that this Article in the* Index *is wrong plac'd, and that it ought to be read* Fool: *And if ſo, we refer the Reader to it in the* Alphabet.

F I N I S.

A
LETTER
FROM
MARTIN GULLIVER,
TO
GEORGE FAULKNER,
Printer.

————————Demetri, *teq*; Tigelli.
Difcipulorum inter jubeo plorare cathedras.   HOR.

Printed in the Year MDCCXXX.

A

LETTER, &c.

WHY, FAULKNER, shou'd you be sur-
priz'd,
You have been basely Scandaliz'd?
The injur'd Town already knows
The † Scoundrel Author of the *Prose*;
A *Villain*, whom the *Rope* supplies
With *Monthly-Sentenc'd* Sacrifice!
Who never yet proceeded further,
Than a *Last Speech* or *Bloody Murther*!
Whose *Press* is but the common *Stews*
Of *Grubstreet*-lays, and lying News,   Compos'd

---

† An infamous poor N——s-M-ng-r, who wrote Notes
to G. F——KN-R's Petition, and printed the same.

Compos'd of uncorrected *Scraps*,
To *Rob* the *Publick* of their *Raps*?
  Justice may keep your Hand in Awe,
Necessity will have no Law :
'Twas this that made him *Print* his *Trash*,
Defy the *Legislature's Lash*,
And risk the *Forfeiture* of *Ears*,
To pay his *Belly* it's *Arrears*.
For who wou'd spare a little *Leather*,
To keep both *Flesh* and *Bones* together,
Since it's allow'd in ev'ry Art
The Whole is nobler than a Part?
So *Beavers* bite, when closely prest,
Some *Members* off, to save the Rest.
  If Penury provok'd the Slave,
To publish Lies, and play the Knave,
Why shou'd it give you Discontentment?
The Rascal is below Resentment.
What Lordly Lyon, bent to feast,
Encounters with *the braying Beast*?
What *Mastiff* ever rais'd his Fur,
Mov'd by the Barking of a *Cur*?
Wou'd you avoid the servile Gibe
Of *Him*, and all his hungry Tribe?
Give up the Business, which you follow,
Forsake the Service of *Apollo*.

What

What Man of Genius ever rose
In any Art, without his Foes?
Can any future Poets hope,
To Copy after Sw——t or P———pe,
And not expect to meet with Medlies
Of *Blackmores, Dennises,* and *Smedlie*
In vain shall *Learning* intercede,
In vain shall *Wit* and *Virtue* plead;
For Envy is a Kind of Ferret,
That's ever hunting after Merit;
An Elf-Shot, that, to strike it dead,
Is level'd chiefly at the *Head!*
  Behold, above the common Herd,
A ‡ Man of Merit is prefer'd;
Whose Probity is unarraign'd,
Whose Worth intrinsic and unstain'd;
Whose Eloquence is of a Piece
With what was heard in antient *Greece:*
Cry Whoop! the City's in Alarms,
And all the Scriblers up in Arms;
While he indignant of their Lays,
Intent upon his Maker's Praise,
‘ *And proud his Orders to perform,*
‘ *Moves calmly on amidst the Storm.*

As

---

‡ Doctor D——L——NY.

As, fresh beneath the vernal Show'rs,
A Garden blooms with fragrant Flow'rs,
So well dispos'd in ev'ry Part,
That Nature seems to vie with Art ,
But often, round about the Edge,
Is choak'd within a Briar-hedge ;
So Men of Merit have a Pack
Of snarling Blockheads at their Back,
That thrust their Malice still between,
For fear their Talents shou'd be seen.

   'Tis said by some, the Gods provide
These Instruments, to check our Pride ;
To make us Meek, and let us know
Th' imperfect State of Things below ;
That Hope and Fame, and Joy's a Flash,
Which Pain and Disappointment dash.
Achilles, who cou'd boast his Line
(As *Homer* sings) of Birth divine,
Whose Breast defy'd the pointed Steel,
Was Vulnerable in the Heel.——
Let Men of Parts apply the Story
To *Fame*, as a *Memento Mori*.

   But you object, I give the Hint
To those, who *Write*, and you but *Print*;
You get Materials ready wrought,
And only dress the Poet's Thought:

'Tis

Agreed: but can you hope to thrive
By *Wit*, while Dunces are alive,
And yet avoid the puny Rage
Of all the Scriblers of the Age?
For as of old the Charioteer,
The warlike Coursers wont to Steer,
The Hero's Fortune often found,
And fell, and falling bit the Ground;
So Printers of the modern Date
Must hope to share the Author's Fate.

The only Shield you can oppose
Against the Darts of dirty Foes,
Is but to prove serenely Just,
Sincere and steady to your Trust;
Nor usher Nonsence into Town,
Tho' writ by one, that wore a G——
Despise the Menaces and Bolts
Of all the *Academic* Dolts;
I mean the *Cabalistic* Throng,
That give no Right, and take no Wrong;
Those Strangers to the Ways of Truth,
Who prey upon the Sins of Youth!
Those mock-Philosophers, who put
Their *Summum bonum* in the Gut!
With plodding supercilious Looks,
And shallow Insight into Books,

Exert

Exert their Tyranny on Slaves,
And favour none, but Fools or Knaves !
Who in their Bosoms nurture Malice,
Yet once a Month approach the *Chalice*!
In thy Integrity persist,
Nor reck thy vile Antagonist ;
But leave the wretched CACOFUGO,
To rail at Wit, and——print for HUGO.

F I N I S.

THE

Proctor's Banquet:

A

PINDARICK

ODE.

By MARTIN GULLIVER

DUBLIN:

Printed in the Year MDCCXXXI.

THE

PROCTOR'S Banquet

A

Pindarick ODE.

'TWAS at the PROCTOR's Feaſt from Folly
won
By FLECKNO's blund'ring Son,
Aloft in awful State
The peerleſs *Cenſor* ſate,
Enthron'd in ſolemn Majeſty of Fat;
His bounteous *Knights*, in pomp profound,
Were deck'd with Quadrate-Caps inſtead of round,
(So ſhou'd Deſert in Arts be crown'd.)
The amphibious FANNY by his ſide
Sate like a gay *Fingallian* Bride,
In flower of Youth and Beauty's Pride;

Happy,

Happy, happy, happy pair,
None but the Fat,
None but the Fat,
None but the Fat deferves the Fair.

CHORUS.

Happy, happy, happy Pair,
None but the Fat,
None but the Fat,
None but the Fat deferves the Fair.

II.

VENTOSO fate on high,
Amid the piping Quire;
And, while he play'd for fervile hire,
The thurling Sounds torment the Sky
And earthly Joys infpire.
The Song from JONATHAN began,
Ever peevifh, ever wan,
Who ALMA's Benefits refigns,
And in refigning much repines:
Such, VENUS, is thy mighty Power,
The fable Robes, the Doctor's pride,
The Mifers griping Soul bely'd
When on he rode to BOLTON's Bower;
Then round her flender Waift he curl'd,   (World
And ftamp'd an Image of himfelf, the *Cynick* of the
The

The liftning croud admire the fnarling found
A prefent *Bafilisk* they fhout around,
A prefent *Bafilisk* the vaulted Roofs rebound.

    With ravifh'd Ears
    The *Cenfor* hears,
    Affects to clap,
    But takes a Nap,
And tumbles o're the Chairs.

CHORUS.

With ravifh'd Ears, &c.

III.

The praife of L——y next the Pur-blind *Piper* fung,
    Of L——y ever gay, and ever young;
    The jolly Fellow reeling comes;
  Ring your Glaffes, crack your Thumbs;
    Flufh'd with a purple Grace,
    He fhews his honeft Face.
Now give the Bag-pipe breath, he comes, he comes,
    L——y ever gay, and young;
  Drinking Joys is ftill repeating;
  Bacchus bleffings are a Treafure,
  Drinking is the Fellows pleafure.
    Rich the Treafure;
    Sweet the Pleafure,
Sweet is drinking after eating.

                  CHO-

C H O R U S.

Bacchus *bleffings are a Treafure,* &c.

IV.

Rous'd with the Noife the *Cenfor* awoke,
  And o'er again his Blunders fpoke,
And thrice repeated all his *Puns,* and thrice his Jefts he
    broke.
  The *Piper* faw his Folly rife,
  His fpreading grin, and fwimming Eyes ;
  And while he Wit and Senfe defy'd,
  Chang'd his Note, and check'd his Pride.
      He chofe the ftrains of *Namby's* Mufe,
      Soft Slumbers to infufe ;
He fung how COFFEE, great and good,
  By too fevere a Fate,
Fallen, fallen, fallen, fallen,
  Fallen from his low Eftate,
            Lay floundring in the Mud.
Deferted at his utmoft Need
By thofe who did, and did not read ;
In a cold Jayl confin'd he lies,
With not a Friend to heed his Cries,
With downcaft Eyes, the joylefs *Cenfor* fate,
  Revolving in his clouded Soul
      The various turns of Bards below,
  And now and then a belch he ftole,
      And Sweat began to flow.

CHO-

[7]

C H O R U S.

Revolving in his clouded Soul, &c.

V

The artful *Piper* smil'd to see
That Love was in the next degree,
Twas but a kindred Tone to move,
For Pity melts the Soul to love.

Softly sweet in *P A M B I A N* measures
Soon he lull'd his Soul to Pleasures ;
Learning was but Toil and Trouble,
Wit he sung an empty bubble ;
Never let a jolly Fellow
Pose his Pate with sober thinking,
If the Wine is good and mellow,
Think ! O think it worth the drinking !
Lovely F A N N Y sits beside thee,
Take the good the Gods provide thee,
The *Knights* in wonder roar their loud applause,
So Love was Crown'd, but Piping won the Cause.
Hu go, unable to conceal his pain,
Gap'd on the Fair,
Who caus'd his Care,
And belch'd, and gap'd, belch'd, and gap'd,
Belch'd and gap'd, and belch'd again :
At length with Love and Wine at once opprest,
The drowzy *Censor* snor'd upon her Breast.

C H O R U S.

Hu go *unable to conceal his Pain,* &c.

VI. Now

VI

Now blows the lowd tongu'd Drone again,
A louder yet, and yet a louder strain;
Break his Bonds of Sleep asunder,
And rouze him like a ratling peal of Thunder.

    Hark! Hark! the grumbling sound
        Has rais'd up his head,
        As awak'd from the Dead,
    And amaz'd he stares around.
Revenge, revenge, the *Piper* cries
        See! ARBUCKLE arise
        See! the Crutch that he rears,
        How revengeful he stares,
    And the Fury that glows in his Eyes!
        Behold! JONATHAN stand
        With all the ghastly Band
Of Heroes, who in the *CENSORIAD* were slain,
        And unpitied remain
        In GULLIVER's strain.
        Give the vengeance due,
        To the wretched Crew.   (high!
See! the Candles they seize, how they wave them on
    How they point to the *PRINTER*'s abodes:
    And airy Garrets fraught with MARTIN's *ODES!*
    The *Knights* all applaud with a turbulent Rage,
And HUGH snatch'd a Candle with Zeal to engage
        FANNY led the way,
        To light him to his Prey,
    And like another *Sibyl* fir'd a sacred Page.

F I N I S